Cosmic Evolution

Seven Stanzas
From The Book of Dzyan
With Commentaries

(Excerpted from The Secret Doctrine)

Written By
H.P. Blavatsky

Revised and Edited By
Dennis Logan

[2021]

Copyright 2021 by Rolled Scroll Publishing
ISBN: 9781952900341

Contents

Cosmic Evolution

    Stanza I. 1

    Stanza II. 2

    Stanza III. 2

    Stanza IV. 4

    Stanza V. 5

    Stanza VI. 6

    Stanza VII. 8

Commentaries On The Seven Stanzas And Their Terms, According To Their Numeration, In Stanzas And Shlokas. 9

    Stanza I. 9

    Stanza II. 25

    Stanza III. 34

    Stanza IV. 57

    Stanza V. 75

    Stanza VI. 105

    A Digression. 121

    Stanza VI. —*Continued*. 167

    Stanza VII. 188

    Summing Up. 250

    Extracts From An Eastern Private Commentary, Hitherto Secret. 272

Cosmic Evolution.

Seven Stanzas From The "Book Of Dzyan," With Commentaries.

Nor Aught nor Nought existed; yon bright sky
Was not, nor heaven's broad roof outstretched above.
What covered all? What sheltered? What concealed?
    Was it the water's fathomless abyss?
There was no death—yet there was nought immortal,
    There was no confine betwixt day and night;
    The only One breathed breathless by Itself,
    Other than It there nothing since has been.
Darkness there was, and all at first was veiled
    In gloom profound—an ocean without light.
    The germ that still lay covered in the husk
Burst forth, one nature, from the fervent heat.

Who knows the secret? Who proclaimed it here?
Whence, whence this manifold creation sprang?
    The Gods themselves came later into being—
Who knows from whence this great creation sprang?
    That, whence all this great creation came,
    Whether Its will created or was mute,
The Most High Seer that is in highest heaven,
He knows it—or perchance even he knows not.

    Gazing into eternity
Ere the foundations of the earth were laid.

Thou wert. And when the subterranean flame
Shall burst its prison and devour the frame,
    Thou shalt be still as thou wert before
And know no change, when time shall be no more.
    O, endless thought, divine Eternity.

Rig Veda (COLEBROOKE).

Seven Stanzas From The "Book Of Dzyan"

Stanza I.

1. The Eternal Parent, wrapped in her Ever-Invisible Robes, had slumbered once again for Seven Eternities.

2. Time was not, for it lay asleep in the Infinite Bosom of Duration.

3. Universal Mind was not, for there were no Ah-hi to contain it.

4. The Seven Ways to Bliss were not. The Great Causes of Misery were not, for there was no one to produce and get ensnared by them.

5. Darkness alone filled the Boundless All, for Father, Mother and Son were once more one, and the Son had not yet awakened for the new Wheel and his Pilgrimage thereon.

6. The Seven Sublime Lords and the Seven Truths had ceased to be, and the Universe, the Son of Necessity, was immersed in Paranishpanna, to be outbreathed by that which is, and yet is not. Naught was.

7. The Causes of Existence had been done away with; the Visible that was, and the Invisible that is, rested in Eternal Non-Being—the One Being.

8. Alone, the One Form of Existence stretched boundless, infinite, causeless, in Dreamless Sleep; and Life pulsated unconscious in Universal Space, throughout that All-Presence, which is sensed by the Opened Eye of Dangma.

9. But where was Dangma when the Âlaya of the Universe was in Paramârtha, and the Great Wheel was Anupâdaka?

Stanza II.

1. ... Where were the Builders, the Luminous Sons of Manvantaric Dawn?... In the Unknown Darkness in their Ah-hi Paranishpanna. The Producers of Form from No-Form—the Root of the World—the Devamâtri and Svabhâvat, rested in the Bliss of Non-Being.

2. ... Where was Silence? Where the ears to sense it? No, there was neither Silence nor Sound; naught save Ceaseless Eternal Breath, which knows itself not.

3. The Hour had not yet struck; the Ray had not yet flashed into the Germ; the Mâtripadma had not yet swollen.

4. Her Heart had not yet opened for the One Ray to enter, thence to fall, as Three into Four, into the Lap of Mâyâ.

5. The Seven were not yet born from the Web of Light. Darkness alone was Father-Mother, Svabhâvat; and Svabhâvat was in Darkness.

6. These Two are the Germ, and the Germ is One. The Universe was still concealed in the Divine Thought and the Divine Bosom.

Stanza III.

1. ... The last Vibration of the Seventh Eternity thrills through Infinitude. The Mother swells, expanding from within without, like the Bud of the Lotus.

2. The Vibration sweeps along, touching with its swift Wing the whole Universe and the Germ that dwelleth in Darkness, the Darkness that breathes over the slumbering Waters of Life.

3. Darkness radiates Light, and Light drops one solitary Ray into the Waters, into the Mother-Deep. The Ray shoots through the Virgin Egg, the Ray causes the Eternal Egg to thrill, and drop the non-eternal Germ, which condenses into the World-Egg.

4. The Three fall into the Four. The Radiant Essence becomes Seven inside, Seven outside. The Luminous Egg, which in itself is Three, curdles and spreads in milk-white Curds throughout the Depths of Mother, the Root that grows in the Depths of the Ocean of Life.

5. The Root remains, the Light remains, the Curds remain, and still Oeaohoo is One.

6. The Root of Life was in every Drop of the Ocean of Immortality, and the Ocean was Radiant Light, which was Fire, and Heat, and Motion. Darkness vanished and was no more; it disappeared in its own Essence, the Body of Fire and Water, of Father and Mother.

7. Behold, O Lanoo, the Radiant Child of the Two, the unparalleled refulgent Glory—Bright Space, Son of Dark Space, who emerges from the Depths of the great Dark Waters. It is Oeaohoo, the Younger, the ——. He shines forth as the Sun, he is the Blazing Divine Dragon of Wisdom; the Eka is Chatur, and Chatur takes to itself Tri, and the Union produces the Sapta, in whom are the Seven, which become the Tridasha, the Hosts and the Multitudes. Behold him lifting the Veil, and unfurling it from East to West. He shuts out the Above, and leaves the Below to be seen as the Great Illusion. He marks the places for the Shining Ones, and turns the Upper into a shoreless Sea of Fire, and the One Manifested into the Great Waters.

8. Where was the Germ, and where was now Darkness? Where is the Spirit of the Flame that burns in thy Lamp, O Lanoo? The Germ is That, and That is Light, the White Brilliant Son of the Dark Hidden Father.

9. Light is Cold Flame, and Flame is Fire, and Fire produces Heat, which yields Water—the Water of Life in the Great Mother.

10. Father-Mother spin a Web, whose upper end is fastened to Spirit, the Light of the One Darkness, and the lower one to its shadowy end, Matter; and this Web is the Universe, spun out of the Two Substances made in One, which is Svabhâvat.

11. It expands when the Breath of Fire is upon it; it contracts when the Breath of the Mother touches it. Then the Sons dissociate and scatter, to return into their Mother's Bosom, at the end of the Great Day, and re-become one with her. When it is cooling, it becomes radiant. Its Sons expand and contract through their own Selves and Hearts; they embrace Infinitude.

12. Then Svabhâvat sends Fohat to harden the Atoms. Each is a part of the Web. Reflecting the "Self-Existent Lord," like a Mirror, each becomes in turn a World.

Stanza IV.

1. ... Listen, ye Sons of the Earth, to your Instructors—the Sons of the Fire. Learn, there is neither first nor last; for all is One Number, issued from No-Number.

2. Learn what we, who descend from the Primordial Seven, we, who are born from the Primordial Flame, have learnt from our Fathers....

3. From the Effulgency of Light—the Ray of the Ever-Darkness—sprang in Space the reäwakened Energies; the One from the Egg, the Six, and the Five. Then the Three, the One, the Four, the One, the Five—the Twice Seven, the Sum Total. And these are the Essences, the Flames, the Elements, the Builders, the Numbers, the Arûpa, the Rûpa, and the Force or Divine Man, the Sum Total. And from the Divine Man emanated

the Forms, the Sparks, the Sacred Animals, and the Messengers of the Sacred Fathers within the Holy Four.

4. This was the Army of the Voice, the Divine Mother of the Seven. The Sparks of the Seven are subject to, and the servants of, the First, the Second, the Third, the Fourth, the Fifth, the Sixth, and the Seventh of the Seven. These are called Spheres, Triangles, Cubes, Lines and Modellers; for thus stands the Eternal Nidâna—the Oi-Ha-Hou.

5. The Oi-Ha-Hou, which is Darkness, the Boundless, or the No-Number, Âdi-Nidâna Svabhâvat, the :

I. The Âdi-Sanat, the Number, for he is One.

II. The Voice of the Word, Svabhâvat, the Numbers, for he is One and Nine.

III. The "Formless Square."
And these Three, enclosed within the , are the Sacred Four; and the Ten are the Arûpa Universe. Then come the Sons, the Seven Fighters, the One, the Eighth left out, and his Breath which is the Light-Maker.

6. ... Then the Second Seven, who are the Lipika, produced by the Three. The Rejected Son is One. The "Son-Suns" are countless.

Stanza V.

1. The Primordial Seven, the First Seven Breaths of the Dragon of Wisdom, produce in their turn from their Holy Circumgyrating Breaths the Fiery Whirlwind.

2. They make of him the Messenger of their Will. The Dzyu becomes Fohat: the swift Son of the Divine Sons, whose Sons are the Lipika, runs circular errands. Fohat is the Steed, and the Thought is the Rider. He passes like lightning through the fiery

clouds; takes Three, and Five, and Seven Strides through the Seven Regions above, and the Seven below. He lifts his Voice, and calls the innumerable Sparks, and joins them together.

3. He is their guiding spirit and leader. When he commences work, he separates the Sparks of the Lower Kingdom, that float and thrill with joy in their radiant dwellings, and forms therewith the Germs of Wheels. He places them in the Six Directions of Space, and One in the middle—the Central Wheel.

4. Fohat traces spiral lines to unite the Sixth to the Seventh—the Crown. An Army of the Sons of Light stands at each angle; the Lipika, in the Middle Wheel. They say: "his is good." The first Divine World is ready; the First, the Second. Then the "Divine Arûpa" reflects itself in Chhâyâ Loka, the First Garment of Anupâdaka.

5. Fohat takes five strides, and builds a winged wheel at each corner of the square for the Four Holy Ones ... and their Armies.

6. The Lipika circumscribe the Triangle, the First One, the Cube, the Second One, and the Pentacle within the Egg. It is the Ring called "Pass Not" for those who descend and ascend; who during the Kalpa are progressing towards the Great Day "Be With Us."... Thus were formed the Arûpa and the Rûpa: from One Light, Seven Lights; from each of the Seven, seven times Seven Lights. The Wheels watch the Ring....

Stanza VI.

1. By the power of the Mother of Mercy and Knowledge, Kwan-Yin—the Triple of Kwan-Shai-Yin, residing in Kwan-Yin-Tien—Fohat, the Breath of their Progeny, the Son of the Sons, having called forth, from the lower Abyss, the Illusive Form of Sien-Tchan and the Seven Elements.

2. The Swift and the Radiant One produces the seven Laya Centres, against which none will prevail to the Great Day "Be

With Us"; and seats the Universe on these Eternal Foundations, surrounding Sien-Tchan with the Elementary Germs.

3. Of the Seven—first One manifested, Six concealed; Two manifested, Five concealed; Three manifested, Four concealed; Four produced, Three hidden; Four and One Tsan revealed, Two and One-Half concealed; Six to be manifested, One laid aside. Lastly, Seven Small Wheels revolving: one giving birth to the other.

4. He builds them in the likeness of older Wheels, placing them on the Imperishable Centres.

How does Fohat build them? He collects the Fiery-Dust. He makes Balls of Fire, runs through them, and round them, infusing life thereïnto, then sets them into motion; some one way, some the other way. They are cold, he makes them hot. They are dry, he makes them moist. They shine, he fans and cools them. Thus acts Fohat from one Twilight to the other, during Seven Eternities.

5. At the Fourth, the Sons are told to create their Images. One-Third refuses. Two obey.

The Curse is pronounced. They will be born in the Fourth, suffer and cause suffering. This is the First War.

6. The Older Wheels rotated downward and upward.... The Mother's Spawn filled the whole. There were Battles fought between the Creators and the Destroyers, and Battles fought for Space; the Seed appearing and reäppearing continuously.

7. Make thy calculations, O Lanoo, if thou wouldst learn the correct age of thy Small Wheel. Its Fourth Spoke is our Mother. Reach the Fourth Fruit of the Fourth Path of Knowledge that leads to Nirvana, and thou shalt comprehend, for thou shalt see....

Stanza VII.

1. Behold the beginning of sentient formless Life.

First, the Divine, the One from the Mother-Spirit; then, the Spiritual; the Three from the One, the Four from the One, and the Five, from which the Three, the Five and the Seven. These are the Three-fold and the Four-fold downward; the Mind-born Sons of the First Lord, the Shining Seven. It is they who are thou, I, he, O Lanoo; they who watch over thee and thy mother, Bhûmî.

2. The One Ray multiplies the smaller Rays. Life precedes Form, and Life survives the last atom. Through the countless Rays the Life-Ray, the One, like a Thread through many Beads.

3. When the One becomes Two, the Threefold appears, and the Three are One; and it is our Thread, O Lanoo, the Heart of the Man-Plant called Saptaparna.

4. It is the Root that never dies; the Three-tongued Flame of the Four Wicks. The Wicks are the Sparks, that draw from the Three-tongued Flame shot out by the Seven—their Flame—the Beams and Sparks of one Moon reflected in the running Waves of all the Rivers of Earth.

5. The Spark hangs from the Flame by the finest thread of Fohat. It journeys through the Seven Worlds of Mâyâ. It stops in the First, and is a Metal and a Stone; it passes into the Second, and behold—a Plant; the Plant whirls through seven changes and becomes a Sacred Animal. From the combined attributes of these, Manu, the Thinker, is formed. Who forms him? The Seven Lives and the One Life. Who completes him? The Fivefold Lha. And who perfects the last Body? Fish, Sin, and Soma....

6. From the First-born the Thread between the Silent Watcher and his Shadow becomes more strong and radiant with every Change. The morning Sunlight has changed into noon-day glory....

7. "This is thy present Wheel," said the Flame to the Spark. "Thou art myself, my image and my shadow. I have clothed myself in thee, and thou art my Vâhan to the Day 'Be With Us,' when thou shalt re-become myself and others, thyself and me." Then the Builders, having donned their first Clothing, descend on radiant Earth and reign over Men—who are themselves....

Commentaries On The Seven Stanzas And Their Terms, According To Their Numeration, In Stanzas And Shlokas.

Stanza I.

1. THE ETERNAL PARENT, WRAPPED IN HER EVER-INVISIBLE ROBES, HAD SLUMBERED ONCE AGAIN FOR SEVEN ETERNITIES.

The "Parent," Space, is the eternal, ever-present Cause of all—the incomprehensible DEITY, whose "Invisible Robes" are the mystic Root of all Matter, and of the Universe. Space is the *one eternal thing* that we can most easily imagine, immovable in its abstraction and uninfluenced by either the presence or absence in it of an objective Universe. It is without dimension, in every sense, and self-existent. Spirit is the first differentiation from "THAT," the Causeless Cause of both Spirit and Matter. As taught in the Esoteric Catechism, it is neither "limitless void," nor "conditioned fulness," but both. It was and ever will be.

Thus, the "Robes" stand for the noumenon of undifferentiated Cosmic Matter. It is not matter as we know it, but the spiritual essence of matter, and is coëternal and even one with Space in its abstract sense. Root-Nature is also the source of the subtile invisible properties in visible matter. It is the Soul, so to say, of the One Infinite Spirit. The Hindûs call it Mûlaprakriti, and say that it is the primordial Substance, which is the basis of the Upâdhi or Vehicle of every phenomenon, whether physical, psychic or mental. It is the source from which Âkâsha radiates.

By the "Seven Eternities," æons or periods are meant. The word Eternity, as understood in Christian theology, has no meaning to the Asiatic ear, except in its application to the One Existence; nor is the term "sempiternity," the eternal only in futurity, anything better than a misnomer. Such words do not and cannot exist in philosophical metaphysics, and were unknown till the advent of ecclesiastical Christianity. The Seven Eternities mean the seven periods, or a period answering in its duration to the seven periods, of a Manvantara, extending throughout a Mahâkalpa or "Great Age" (100 Years of Brahmâ), making a total of 311,040,000,000,000 of years; each Year of Brahmâ being composed of 360 Days, and of the same number of Nights of Brahmâ (reckoning by the Chandrâyana or lunar year); and a Day of Brahmâ consisting of 4,320,000,000 of mortal years. These Eternities belong to the most secret calculations, in which, in order to arrive at the true total, every figure must be 7x, x varying according to the nature of the cycle in the subjective or real world; and every figure relating to, or representing, the different cycles—from the greatest to the smallest—in the objective or unreal world, must necessarily be multiples of seven. The key to this cannot be given, for herein lies the mystery of esoteric calculations, and for the purposes of ordinary calculation it has no sense. "The number seven," says the *Kabalah*, "is the great number of the Divine Mysteries"; number ten is that of all human knowledge (the Pythagorean Decad); 1,000 is the number ten to the third power, and therefore the number 7,000 is also symbolical. In the Secret Doctrine the figure 4 is the male symbol only on the highest plane of abstraction; on the plane of matter the 3 is the masculine and the 4 the feminine—the upright and the horizontal in the fourth stage of symbolism, when the symbols become the glyphs of the generative powers on the physical plane.

2. Time was not, for it lay asleep in the Infinite Bosom of Duration.

"Time" is only an illusion produced by the succession of our states of consciousness as we travel through Eternal Duration, and it does not exist where no consciousness exists in which the illusion can be produced, but "lies asleep." The Present is only a mathematical line which divides that part of Eternal Duration which we call the Future, from that part which we call the Past. Nothing on earth has real duration, for nothing remains without change—or the same—for the billionth part of a second; and the sensation we have of the actuality of the division of Time known as the Present, comes from the blurring of the momentary glimpse, or succession of glimpses, of things that our senses give us, as those things pass from the region of ideals, which we call the Future, to the region of memories that we name the Past. In the same way we experience a sensation of duration in the case of the instantaneous electric spark, by reason of the blurred and continuing impression on the retina. The real person or thing does not consist solely of what is seen at any particular moment, but is composed of the sum of all its various and changing conditions from its appearance in material form to its disappearance from earth. It is these "sum-totals" that exist from eternity in the Future, and pass by degrees through matter, to exist for eternity in the Past. No one would say that a bar of metal dropped into the sea came into existence as it left the air, and ceased to exist as it entered the water, and that the bar itself consisted only of that cross-section thereof which at any given moment coincided with the mathematical plane that separates, and, at the same time, joins, the atmosphere and the ocean. Even so of persons and things, which, dropping out of the "to be" into the "has been," out of the Future into the Past— present momentarily to our senses a cross-section, as it were, of their total selves, as they pass through Time and Space (as Matter) on their way from one eternity to another: and these two eternities constitute that Duration in which alone anything has true existence, were our senses but able to cognize it.

3. Universal Mind was not, for there were No Ah-hi to contain it.

"Mind" is a name given to the sum of the States of Consciousness, grouped under Thought, Will and Feeling. During deep sleep ideation ceases on the physical plane, and memory is in abeyance; thus for the time-being "Mind is not," because the organ, through which the Ego manifests ideation and memory on the material plane, has temporarily ceased to function. A noumenon can become a phenomenon on any plane of existence only by manifesting on that plane through an appropriate basis or vehicle; and during the long Night of rest called Pralaya, when all the Existences are dissolved, the "Universal Mind" remains as a permanent possibility of mental action, or as that abstract absolute Thought, of which Mind is the concrete relative manifestation. The Ah-hi (Dhyân Chohans) are the collective hosts of spiritual Beings—the Angelic Hosts of Christianity, the Elohim and "Messengers" of the Jews—who are the Vehicle for the manifestation of the Divine or Universal Thought and Will. They are the Intelligent Forces that give to, and enact in, Nature her "Laws," while they themselves act according to Laws imposed upon them in a similar manner by still higher Powers; but they are not the "personifications" of the Powers of Nature, as erroneously thought. This Hierarchy of spiritual Beings, through which the Universal Mind comes into action, is like an army—a host, truly—by means of which the fighting power of a nation manifests itself, and which is composed of army-corps, divisions, brigades, regiments, and so forth, each with its separate individuality or life, and its limited freedom of action and limited responsibilities; each contained in a larger individuality, to which its own interests are subservient, and each containing lesser individualities in itself.

4. The Seven Ways to Bliss were not (*a*). The Great Causes of Misery were not, for there was no one to produce and get ensnared by them (*b*).

(*a*) There are "Seven Paths" or "Ways" to the "Bliss" of Non-Existence, which is absolute Being, Existence and Consciousness. They were not, because the Universe, so far, was empty, and existed only in the Divine Thought.

(*b*) For it is ... the Twelve Nidânas, or Causes of Being. Each is the effect of its antecedent cause, and a cause, in its turn, to its successor; the sum total of the Nidânas being based on the Four Truths, a doctrine especially characteristic of the Hînayâna System. They belong to the theory of the stream of catenated law which produces merit and demerit, and finally brings Karma into full sway. It is a system based upon the great truth that reïncarnation is to be dreaded, as existence in this world entails upon man only suffering, misery and pain; death itself being unable to deliver man from it, since death is merely the door through which he passes to another life on earth after a little rest on its threshold—Devachan. The Hînayâna System, or School of the Little Vehicle, is of very ancient growth; while the Mahâyâna, or School of the Great Vehicle, is of a later period, having originated after the death of Buddha. Yet the tenets of the latter are as old as the hills that have contained such schools from time immemorial, and the Hînayâna and Mahâyâna Schools both teach the same doctrine in reality. Yâna, or Vehicle, is a mystic expression, both "Vehicles" inculcating that man may escape the sufferings of rebirth and even the false bliss of Devachan, by obtaining Wisdom and Knowledge, which alone can dispel the Fruits of Illusion and Ignorance.

Mâyâ, or Illusion, is an element which enters into all finite things, for everything that exists has only a relative, not an absolute, reality, since the appearance which the hidden noumenon assumes for any observer depends upon his power of cognition. To the untrained eye of the savage, a painting is at first an unmeaning confusion of streaks and daubs of colour, while an educated eye sees instantly a face or a landscape. Nothing is permanent except the one hidden absolute Existence which contains in itself the noumena of all realities. The Existences belonging to every plane of being, up to the highest Dhyân Chohans, are, comparatively, like the shadows cast by a magic lantern on a colourless screen. Nevertheless all things are relatively real, for the cognizer is also a reflection, and the things cognized are therefore as real to him as himself. Whatever reality things possess, must be looked for in them before or after they have passed like a flash through the material world; for we cannot cognize any such existence directly, so long as we have sense-instruments which bring only material existence into the field of our consciousness. Whatever plane our consciousness may be acting in, both we and the things belonging to that plane are, for the time being, our only realities. But as we rise in the scale of development, we perceive that in the stages through which we have passed, we mistook shadows for realities, and that the upward progress of the Ego is a series of progressive awakenings, each advance bringing with it the idea that now, at last, we have reached "reality"; but only when we shall have reached absolute Consciousness, and blended our own with it, shall we be free from the delusions produced by Mâyâ.

5. DARKNESS ALONE FILLED THE BOUNDLESS ALL (*a*), FOR FATHER, MOTHER AND SON WERE ONCE MORE ONE, AND THE SON HAD NOT YET AWAKENED FOR THE NEW WHEEL AND HIS PILGRIMAGE THEREON (*b*).

(*a*) "*Darkness is Father-Mother: Light their Son,*" says an old Eastern proverb. Light is inconceivable except as coming from some source which is the cause of it: and as, in the case of Primordial Light, that source is unknown, though so strongly demanded by reason and logic, therefore it is
called "Darkness" by us, from an intellectual point of view. As to borrowed or secondary light, whatever its source, it can be only of a temporary mâyâvic character. Darkness, then, is the Eternal Matrix in which the Sources of Light appear and disappear. Nothing is added to darkness to make of it light, or to light to make it darkness, on this our plane. They are interchangeable; and, scientifically, light is but a mode of darkness and *vice versâ*. Yet both are phenomena of the same noumenon—which is absolute darkness to the scientific mind, and but a gray twilight to the perception of the average Mystic,

though to that of the spiritual eye of the Initiate it is absolute light. How far we discern the light that shines in darkness depends upon our powers of vision. What is light to us is darkness to certain insects, and the eye of the clairvoyant sees illumination where the normal eye perceives only blackness. When the whole Universe was plunged in sleep—had returned to its one primordial element—there was neither centre of luminosity, nor eye to perceive light, and darkness necessarily filled the "Boundless All."

(*b*) The "Father" and "Mother" are the male and female principles in Root-Nature, the opposite poles that manifest in all things on every plane of Kosmos—or Spirit and Substance, in a less allegorical aspect, the resultant of which is the Universe, or the "Son." They are "once more one," when in the Night of Brahmâ, during Pralaya, all in the objective Universe has returned to its one primal and eternal cause, to reäppear at the following Dawn—as it does periodically. Kârana—Eternal Cause—was alone. To put it more plainly: Kârana is alone during the Nights of Brahmâ. The previous objective Universe has dissolved into its one primal and eternal Cause, and is, so to say, held in solution in Space, to differentiate again and crystallize out anew at the following Manvataric Dawn, which is the commencement of a new Day or new activity of Brahmâ—the symbol of a Universe. In esoteric parlance, Brahmâ is Father-Mother-Son, or Spirit, Soul and Body at once; each personage being symbolical of an attribute, and each attribute or quality being a graduated efflux of Divine Breath in its cyclic differentiation, involutionary and evolutionary. In the cosmico-physical sense, it is the Universe, the Planetary Chain and the Earth; in the purely spiritual, the Unknown Deity, Planetary Spirit, and Man—the son of the two, the creature of Spirit and Matter, and a manifestation of them in his periodical appearances on Earth during the "Wheels," or the Manvantaras.

6. THE SEVEN SUBLIME LORDS AND THE SEVEN TRUTHS HAD CEASED TO BE, (*a*) AND THE UNIVERSE, THE SON OF NECESSITY, WAS IMMERSED IN PARANISHPANNA, (*b*) TO BE OUTBREATHED BY THAT WHICH IS, AND YET IS NOT. NAUGHT WAS (*c*).

(a) The "Seven Sublime Lords" are the Seven Creative Spirits, the Dhyân Chohans, who correspond to the Hebrew Elohim. It is the same Hierarchy of Archangels to which St. Michael, St. Gabriel, and others belong, in Christian Theogony. Only while St. Michael, for instance, is allowed in dogmatic Latin Theology to watch over all the promontories and gulfs, in the Esoteric System the Dhyânis watch successively over one of the Rounds and the great Root-Races of our Planetary Chain. They are, moreover, said to send their Bodhisattvas, the human correspondents of the Dhyâni-Buddhas during every Round and Race. Out of the "Seven Truths" and Revelations, or rather revealed secrets, four only have been handed to us, as we are still in the Fourth Round, and the world also has had only four Buddhas, so far. This is a very complicated question, and will receive more ample treatment later on.

So far "there are only Four Truths, and Four *Vedas*"—say the Buddhists and Hindûs. For a similar reason Irenæus insisted on the necessity of Four Gospels. But as every new Root-Race at the head of a Round must have its revelation and revealers, the next Round will bring the Fifth, the following the Sixth, and so on.

(b) "Paranishpanna" is the Absolute Perfection to which all Existences attain at the close of a great period of activity, or Mahâmanvantara, and in which they rest during the succeeding period of repose. In Tibetan it is called "Yong-Grub." Up to the day of the Yogâchârya School the true nature of Paranirvâna was taught publicly, but since then it has become entirely esoteric; hence so many contradictory interpretations of it. It is only a true Idealist who can understand it. Everything has to be viewed as ideal, with the exception of Paranirvâna, by him who would comprehend that state, and acquire a knowledge of how Non-Ego, Voidness, and Darkness are Three in One, and alone self-existent and perfect. It is absolute, however, only in a relative sense, for it must give room to still further absolute perfection, according to a higher standard of excellence in the following period of activity—just as a perfect flower must cease to be a perfect flower and die, in order to grow into a perfect fruit, if such a mode of expression may be permitted.

The Secret Doctrine teaches the progressive development of everything, worlds as well as atoms; and this stupendous development has neither conceivable beginning nor imaginable end. Our "Universe" is only one of an infinite number of Universes, all of them "Sons of Necessity," because links in the great cosmic chain of Universes, each one standing in the relation of an effect as regards its predecessor, and of a cause as regards its successor.

The appearance and disappearance of the Universe are pictured as an outbreathing and inbreathing of the "Great Breath," which is eternal, and which, being Motion, is one of the three symbols of the Absolute—Abstract Space and Duration being the other two. When the Great Breath is projected, it is called the Divine Breath, and is regarded as the breathing of the Unknowable Deity—the One Existence—which breathes out a thought, as it were, which becomes the Kosmos. So also is it that when the Divine Breath is inspired, the Universe disappears into the bosom of the Great Mother, who then sleeps "wrapped in her Ever-Invisible Robes."

(c) By "that which is, and yet is not" is meant the Great Breath itself, which we can only speak of as Absolute Existence, but cannot picture to our imagination as any form of Existence that we can distinguish from Non-Existence. The three periods—the Present, the Past and the Future—are in Esoteric Philosophy a compound time; for the three are a composite number only in relation to the phenomenal plane, but in the realm of noumena have no abstract validity. As said in the Scriptures: "The Past Time is the Present Time, as also the Future, which, though it has not come into existence, still is," according to a precept in the Prasanga Madhyamika teaching, whose dogmas have been known ever since it broke away from the purely esoteric schools. Our ideas, in short, on duration and time are all derived from our sensations according to the laws of association. Inextricably bound up with the relativity of human knowledge, they nevertheless can have no existence except in the experience of the individual Ego, and perish when its evolutionary march dispels the Mâyâ of phenomenal existence. What is time, for instance, but the panoramic succession of our states of consciousness? In the words of a Master, "I feel irritated at having to use these three clumsy words—Past, Present, and Future—miserable concepts of the objective phases of the subjective whole, they are about as ill-adapted for the purpose as an axe for fine carving." One has to acquire Paramârtha lest one should become too easy a prey to Samvriti—is a philosophical axiom.

7. THE CAUSES OF EXISTENCE HAD BEEN DONE AWAY WITH; (*a*) THE VISIBLE THAT WAS, AND THE INVISIBLE THAT IS, RESTED IN ETERNAL NON-BEING—THE ONE BEING (*b*).

(a) "The Causes of Existence" mean not only the physical causes known to Science, but the metaphysical causes, the chief of which is the desire to exist, an outcome of Nidâna and Mâyâ. This desire for a sentient life shows itself in everything, from an atom to a sun, and is a reflection of the Divine Thought propelled into objective existence, into a law that the Universe should exist. According to Esoteric teaching, the real cause of that supposed desire, and of all existence, remains for ever hidden, and its first emanations are the most complete abstractions mind can conceive. These abstractions must of necessity be postulated as the cause of the material Universe which presents itself to the senses and intellect, and must underlie the secondary and subordinate powers of Nature, which have been anthropomorphized and worshipped as "God" and "gods" by the common herd of every age. It is impossible to conceive anything without a cause; the attempt to do so makes the mind a blank. This is virtually the condition to which the mind must come at last when we try to trace back the chain of causes and effects, but both Science and Religion jump to this condition of blankness much more quickly than is necessary, for they ignore the metaphysical abstractions which are the only conceivable causes of physical concretions. These abstractions become more and more concrete as they approach our plane of existence, until finally they phenomenalize in the form of the material Universe, by a process of conversion of metaphysics into physics, analogous to that by which steam can be condensed into water, and water frozen into ice.

(b) The idea of "Eternal Non-Being," which is the "One Being," will appear a paradox to anyone who does not remember that we limit our ideas of Being to our present consciousness of Existence; making it a specific, instead of a generic term. An unborn infant, could it think in our acceptation of that term, would necessarily in a similar manner limit its conception of Being to the intra-uterine life which alone it knows; and were it to endeavour to express to its consciousness the idea of life after birth (death to it), it would, in the absence of data to go upon, and of faculties to comprehend such data, probably express that life as "Non-Being which is Real Being." In our case the One Being is the noumenon of all the noumena which we know must underlie phenomena, and give them whatever shadow of reality they possess, but which we have not the senses or the intellect to cognize at present. The impalpable atoms of gold scattered through the substance of a ton of auriferous quartz may be imperceptible to the naked eye of the miner, yet he knows that they are not only present there, but that they alone give his quartz any appreciable value; and this relation of the gold to the quartz may faintly shadow forth that of the noumenon to the phenomenon. Only the miner knows what the gold will look like when extracted from the quartz, whereas the common mortal can form no conception of the reality of things separated from the Mâyâ which veils them, and in which they are hidden. Alone the Initiate, rich with the lore acquired by numberless generations of his predecessors, directs the "Eye of Dangma" toward the essence of things on which no Mâyâ can have any influence. It is here that the teachings of Esoteric Philosophy in relation to the Nidânas and the Four Truths become of the greatest importance; but they are secret.

8. ALONE, THE ONE FORM OF EXISTENCE (A) STRETCHED BOUNDLESS, INFINITE, CAUSELESS, IN DREAMLESS SLEEP (B); AND LIFE PULSATED UNCONSCIOUS IN UNIVERSAL SPACE, THROUGHOUT THAT ALL-PRESENCE, WHICH IS SENSED BY THE OPENED EYE OF DANGMA.

(a) The tendency of modern thought is to recur to the archaic idea of a homogeneous basis for apparently widely different things—heterogeneity developed from homogeneity. Biologists are now searching for their homogeneous protoplasm and Chemists for their protyle, while Science is looking for the force of which electricity, magnetism, heat, and so forth, are the differentiations. The Secret Doctrine carries this idea into the region of metaphysics, and postulates a "One Form of Existence" as the basis and source of all things. But perhaps the phrase, the "One Form of Existence," is not altogether correct. The Sanskrit word is Prabhavâpyaya, "the place whence is the origination, and into which is the resolution of all things," as a commentator says. It is not the "Mother of the World," as translated by Wilson; for Jagad Yoni, as shown by Fitzedward Hall, is scarcely so much the "Mother of the World," or the "Womb of the World," as the "Material Cause of the World." The Purânic commentators explain it by Kârana, "Cause," but Esoteric Philosophy, by the *ideal spirit of that cause.* In its secondary stage, it is the Svabhâvat of the Buddhist philosopher, the Eternal Cause and Effect, omnipresent yet abstract, the self-existent plastic Essence and the Root of all things, viewed in the same dual light as the Vedântin views his Parabrahman and Mûlaprakriti, the one under two aspects. It seems indeed extraordinary to find great scholars speculating on the possibility of the Vedânta, and the Uttara Mîmânsâ especially, having been "evoked by the teachings of the Buddhists"; whereas, on the contrary, it is Buddhism, the teaching of Gautama Buddha, that was "evoked" and entirely upreared on the tenets of the Secret Doctrine, of which a partial sketch is here attempted, and on which, also, the *Upanishads* are made to rest. According to the teachings of Shrî Shankarâchârya our contention is undeniable.
(b) "Dreamless Sleep" is one of the seven states of consciousness known in Oriental Esotericism. In each of these states a different portion of the mind comes into action; or as a Vedântin would express it, the individual is conscious in a different plane of his being. The term "Dreamless Sleep," in this case, is applied allegorically to the Universe to express a condition somewhat analogous to that state of consciousness in man, which, not

being remembered in a waking state, seems a blank, just as the sleep of the mesmerized subject seems to him an unconscious blank when he returns to his normal condition, although he has been talking and acting as a conscious individual would.

9. BUT WHERE WAS DANGMA WHEN THE ÂLAYA OF THE UNIVERSE WAS IN PARAMÂRTHA (a), AND THE GREAT WHEEL WAS ANUPÂDAKA (b)?

(a) Here we have before us the subject of centuries of scholastic disputations. The two terms "Âlaya," and "Paramârtha," have been the causes of dividing schools and splitting the truth into more different aspects than any other mystic words. Âlaya is the Soul of the World or Anima Mundi—the Over-Soul of Emerson—which according to esoteric teaching changes its nature periodically. Âlaya, though eternal and changeless in its inner essence on the planes which are unreachable by either men or cosmic gods (Dhyâni-Buddhas), changes during the active life-period with respect to the lower planes, ours included. During that time not only the Dhyâni-Buddhas are one with Âlaya in Soul and Essence, but even the man strong in Yoga (Mystic Meditation) "is able to merge his soul with it," as Aryâsanga, of the Yogâchârya school, says. This is not Nirvâna, but a condition next to it. Hence the disagreement. Thus, while the Yogâchâryas of the Mahâyâna School say that Âlaya (Nyingpo and Tsang in Tibetan) is the personification of the Voidness, and yet Âlaya is the basis of every visible and invisible thing, and that, though it is eternal and immutable in its essence, it reflects itself in every object of the Universe "like the moon in clear tranquil water"; other schools dispute the statement. The same for Paramârtha. The Yogâchâryas interpret the term as that which is also dependent upon other things (*paratantra*); and the Madhyamikas say that Paramârtha is limited to Paranishpanna or Absolute Perfection; *i.e.*, in the exposition of these "Two Truths" of the Four, the former believe and maintain that, on this plane, at any rate, there exists only Samvritisatya or relative truth; and the latter teach the existence of Paramârthasatya, Absolute Truth. "No Arhat, O mendicants, can reach absolute knowledge before he becomes one with

Paranirvâna. Parikalpita and Paratantra are his two great enemies." Parikalpita (in Tibetan Kun-tag) is error, made by those unable to realize the emptiness and illusionary nature of all; who believe something to exist which does not—*e.g.*, the Non-Ego. And Paratantra is that, whatever it is, which exists only through a dependent or causal connection, and which has to disappear as soon as the cause from which it proceeds is removed—*e.g.*, the flame of a wick. Destroy or extinguish it, and light disappears.

Esoteric Philosophy teaches that everything lives and is conscious, but not that all life and consciousness are similar to those of human or even animal beings. Life we look upon as the One Form of Existence, manifesting in what is called Matter; or what, incorrectly separating them, we name Spirit, Soul and Matter in man. Matter is the Vehicle for the manifestation of Soul on this plane of existence, and Soul is the Vehicle on a higher plane for the manifestation of Spirit, and these three are a Trinity synthesized by Life, which pervades them all. The idea of Universal Life is one of those ancient conceptions which are returning to the human mind in this century, as a consequence of its liberation from anthropomorphic Theology. Science, it is true, contents itself with tracing or postulating the signs of Universal Life, but has not yet been bold enough to even whisper "Anima Mundi"! The idea of "crystalline life," now familiar to Science, would have been scouted half a century ago. Botanists are now searching for the nerves of plants; not that they suppose that plants can feel or think as animals do, but because they believe that some structure, bearing the same relation functionally to plant life that nerves bear to animal life, is necessary to explain vegetable growth and nutrition. It seems hardly possible that Science, by the mere use of terms such as "force" and "energy," can disguise from itself much longer the fact that things that have life are living things, whether they be atoms or planets.

But what is the belief of the inner Esoteric Schools, the reader may ask. What are the doctrines taught on this subject by the Esoteric "Buddhists"? With them, we answer, Âlaya has a double and even a threefold meaning. In the Yogâchârya system of the contemplative Mahâyâna School, Âlaya is both the Universal Soul, Anima Mundi, and the Self of a progressed Adept. "He who is strong in the Yoga can introduce at will his Âlaya by means of meditation into the true nature of Existence." "The Âlaya has an absolute eternal existence," says Aryâsanga, the rival of Nâgârjuna. In one sense it is Pradhâna, which is explained in *Vishnu Purâna* as, "that which is the unevolved cause, is emphatically called, by the most eminent sages, Pradhâna, original base, which is subtile Prakriti, *viz.*, that which is eternal, and which at once is and is not, or is mere process." "The indiscrete cause which is uniform, and both cause and effect, and which those who are acquainted with first principles, call Pradhâna and Prakriti, is the incognizable Brahma who was before all," *i.e.*, Brahma does not put forth evolution itself or create, but only exhibits various aspects of itself, one of which is Prakriti, an aspect of Pradhâna. "Prakriti," however, is an incorrect word, and Âlaya would explain it better; for Prakriti is not the "uncognizable Brahma." It is a mistake of those who know nothing of the universality of the Occult doctrines from the very cradle of the human races, and especially so of those scholars who reject the very idea of a "primordial revelation," to teach that the Anima Mundi, the One Life or Universal Soul, was made known only by Anaxagoras, or during his age. This philosopher brought the teaching forward simply to oppose the too materialistic conceptions of Democritus on cosmogony, based on the exoteric theory of *blindly* driven atoms. Anaxagoras of Clazomenæ, however, was not its inventor, but only its propagator, as was also Plato. That which he called Mundane Intelligence, Nous (Νοῦς), the principle that according to his views is absolutely separated and free from matter and acts with design, was called Motion, the One Life, or Jîvâtmâ, in India, ages before the year 500 B.C. Only the Âryan philosophers never endowed this principle, which with them is infinite, with the finite "attribute of thinking."

This leads naturally to the "Supreme Spirit" of Hegel and the German Transcendentalists—a contrast that it may be useful to point out. The schools of Schelling and Fichte have diverged

widely from the primitive archaic conception of an Absolute Principle, and have mirrored an aspect only of the basic idea of the Vedânta. Even the "Absoluter Geist" shadowed forth by von Hartmann in his pessimistic philosophy of
the "Unconscious," while it is, perhaps, the closest approximation made by European speculation to the Hindû Advaitin doctrines, yet similarly falls far short of the reality.

According to Hegel, the "Unconscious" would never have undertaken the vast and laborious task of evolving the Universe, except in the hope of attaining clear Self-Consciousness. In this connection it is to be borne in mind that in designating Spirit, a term which the European Pantheists use as equivalent to Parabrahman, as Unconscious, they do not attach to the expression the connotation it usually bears. It is employed in the absence of a better term to symbolize a profound mystery.

The "Absolute Consciousness behind phenomena," they tell us, which is only termed unconsciousness in the absence of any element of personality, transcends human conception. Man, unable to form a single concept except in terms of empirical phenomena, is powerless from the very constitution of his being to raise the veil that shrouds the majesty of the Absolute. Only the liberated Spirit is able to faintly realize the nature of the source whence it sprung and whither it must eventually return. As the highest Dhyân Chohan, however, can but bow in ignorance before the awful mystery of Absolute Being; and since, even in that culmination of conscious existence—"the merging of the individual in the universal consciousness," to use a phrase of Fichte's—the Finite cannot conceive the Infinite, nor can it apply to it its own standard of mental experiences, how can it be said that the Unconscious and the Absolute can have even an instinctive impulse or hope of attaining clear Self-Consciousness? A Vedântin, moreover, would never admit this Hegelian idea; and the Occultist would say that it applies perfectly to the awakened Mahat, the Universal Mind already projected into the phenomenal world as the first aspect of the changeless Absolute, but never to the latter. "Spirit and Matter, or Purusha and Prakriti, are but the two primeval aspects of the One and Secondless," we are taught.

The matter-moving Nous, the animating Soul, immanent in every atom, manifested in man, latent in the stone, has different degrees of power; and this Pantheistic idea of a general Spirit-Soul pervading all Nature is the oldest of all the philosophical notions. Nor was the Archæus a discovery either of Paracelsus or of his pupil Van Helmont; for this same Archæus is "Father-Æther," the manifested basis and source of the innumerable phenomena of life—localized. The whole series of the numberless speculations of this kind are but variations on the same theme, the key-note of which was struck in this "primeval revelation."

(b) The term "Anupâdaka," parentless, or without progenitors, is a mystical designation having several meanings in our philosophy. By this name Celestial Beings, the Dhyân Chohans or Dhyâni-Buddhas, are generally meant. These correspond mystically to the human Buddhas and Bodhisattvas, known as the Mânushi (Human) Buddhas, which latter are also designated Anupâdaka, once that their whole personality is merged in their compound Sixth and Seventh Principles, or Âtmâ-Buddhi, and they have become the "Diamond-Souled" (Vajrasattvas), or full Mahâtmâs. The "Concealed Lord" (Sangbai Dag-po), "the one merged with the Absolute," can have no parents since he is Self-Existent, and one with the Universal Spirit (Svayambhû), the Svabhâvat in its highest aspect. The mystery of the Hierarchy of the Anupâdaka is great, its apex being the universal Spirit-Soul, and the lower rung the Mânushi-Buddha: and even every soul-endowed man also is an Anupâdaka in a latent state. Hence—when speaking of the Universe in its formless, eternal, or absolute condition, before it was fashioned by the Builders—the expression, "the great Wheel was Anupâdaka."

Stanza II.

1. ... WHERE WERE THE BUILDERS, THE LUMINOUS SONS OF MANVANTARIC DAWN?... (*a*) IN THE UNKNOWN DARKNESS IN THEIR AH-HI PARANISHPANNA. THE PRODUCERS OF FORM FROM NO-FORM—THE ROOT OF THE WORLD—THE DEVÂMATRI AND SVABHÂVAT, RESTED IN THE BLISS OF NON-BEING (*b*).

(a) The "Builders," the "Sons of Manvantaric Dawn," are the real creators of the Universe; and in this doctrine, which deals only with our Planetary System, they, as the architects of the latter, are also called the "Watchers" of the Seven Spheres, which exoterically are the seven planets, and esoterically the seven earths or spheres (Globes) of our Chain also. The opening sentence of Stanza I, when mentioning "Seven Eternities," applies both to the Mahâkalpa or "the (Great) Age of Brahmâ," as well as to the Solar Pralaya and subsequent resurrection of our Planetary System on a higher plane. There are many kinds of Pralaya (dissolution of a thing visible), as will be shown elsewhere.

(b) "Paranishpanna," remember, is the *summum bonum*, the Absolute, hence the same as Paranirvâna. Besides being the final state, it is that condition of subjectivity which has no relation to anything but the One Absolute Truth (Paramârthasatya) on its own plane. It is that state which leads one to appreciate correctly the full meaning of Non-Being, which, as explained, is Absolute Being. Sooner or later, all that now *seemingly* exists, will be in reality and actually in the state of Paranishpanna. But there is a great difference between *conscious* and *unconscious* Being. The condition of Paranishpanna, without Paramârtha, the Self-analysing Consciousness (Svasamvedâna), is no bliss, but simply extinction for Seven Eternities. Thus, an iron ball placed under the scorching rays of the sun will get heated through, but will not feel or appreciate the warmth, while a man will. It is only *"with a mind clear and undarkened by Personality, and an assimilation of the merit of manifold Existences devoted to Being in its collectivity ,"* that one gets rid of personal existence, merging into, becoming one with, the Absolute, and continuing in full possession of Paramârtha.

2. ... Where was Silence? Where the ears To Sense It? No, there was neither Silence nor Sound (*a*); naught save Ceaseless Eternal Breath, which knows itself not (*b*).

(a) The idea that things can cease to *exist* and still *be*, is a fundamental one in Eastern psychology. Under this apparent contradiction in terms, there rests a fact of Nature, to realize which in the mind, rather than to argue about words, is the important thing. A familiar instance of a similar paradox is afforded by chemical combination. The question whether hydrogen and oxygen cease to exist, when they combine to form water, is still a moot one; some arguing that since they are found again when the water is decomposed, they must be there all the while; others contending that as they actually turn into something totally different, they must cease to exist as themselves for the time being; but neither side is able to form the faintest conception of the real condition of a thing, which has become something else and yet has not ceased to be itself. Existence as water for oxygen and hydrogen may be said to be a state of Non-Being, which is more real Being than their existence as gases; and it may faintly symbolize the condition of the Universe when it goes to sleep, or ceases to be, during the Nights of Brahmâ—to awaken or reäppear again, when the dawn of the new Manvantara recalls it to what we call existence.

(b) The "Breath" of the One Existence is only used in application to the spiritual aspect of Cosmogony by Archaic Esotericism; in other cases, it is replaced by its equivalent on the material plane—Motion. The One Eternal Element, or element-containing Vehicle, is Space, dimensionless in every sense; coëxistent with which are Endless Duration, Primordial (hence Indestructible) Matter, and Motion—Absolute "Perpetual Motion," which is the "Breath" of the One Element. This Breath, as seen, can never cease, not even during the Pralayic Eternities.

But the Breath of the One Existence does not, all the same, apply to the One Causeless Cause or the All-Be-ness, in contradistinction to All-Being, which is Brahmâ, or the Universe. Brahmâ, the four-faced god, who, after lifting the Earth out of the waters, "accomplished the creation," is held to be only the Instrumental, and not, as clearly implied, the Ideal Cause. No Orientalist, so far, seems to have thoroughly comprehended the real sense of the verses in the *Purânas*, that treat of "creation."

Therein Brahmâ is the cause of the potencies that are to be generated subsequently for the work of "creation." For instance, in the *Vishnu Purâna*, the translation, "and from him proceed the potencies to be created, after they have become the real cause," would perhaps be more correctly rendered, "and from IT proceed the potencies that *will create* as they *become* the real cause ." Save that One Causeless Ideal Cause there is no other to which the Universe can be referred. "Worthiest of ascetics, through its potency—*i.e.*, through the potency of that cause—every created thing comes by its inherent or proper nature." If, "in the Vedânta and Nyâya, *nimitta* is the efficient cause, as contrasted with *upâdana*, the material cause, in the Sânkhya, *pradhâna* implies the functions of both"; in the Esoteric Philosophy, which reconciles all these systems, and the nearest exponent of which is the Vedânta as expounded by the Advaita Vedântists, none but the *upâdâna* can be speculated upon. That which is, in the minds of the Vaishnavas (the Visishthadvaitas), as the ideal in contradistinction to the real—or Parabrahman and Îshvara—can find no room in published speculations, since that ideal even is a misnomer, when applied to that of which no human reason, even that of an Adept, can conceive.

To know itself or oneself, necessitates consciousness and perception to be cognized—both limited faculties in relation to any subject except Parabrahman. Hence the "Eternal Breath which knows itself not." Infinity cannot comprehend Finiteness. The Boundless can have no relation to the Bounded and the Conditioned. In the Occult teachings, the Unknown and the Unknowable Mover, or the Self-Existing, is the Absolute Divine Essence. And thus being Absolute Consciousness, and Absolute

Motion—to the limited senses of those who describe this indescribable—it is unconsciousness and immovableness. Concrete consciousness cannot be predicated of abstract consciousness, any more than the quality wet can be predicated of water—wetness being its own attribute and the cause of the wet quality in other things. Consciousness implies limitations and qualifications; something to be conscious of, and someone to be conscious of it. But Absolute Consciousness contains the cognizer, the thing cognized and the cognition, all three in itself and all three *one*. No man is conscious of more than that portion of his knowledge which happens to be recalled to his mind at any particular time, yet such is the poverty of language that we have no term to distinguish the knowledge not actively thought of, from knowledge we are unable to recall to memory. To forget is synonymous with not to remember. How much greater must be the difficulty of finding terms to describe, and to distinguish between, abstract metaphysical facts or differences! It must not be forgotten, also, that we give names to things according to the appearances they assume for ourselves. We call Absolute Consciousness "unconsciousness," because it seems to us that it must necessarily be so, just as we call the
Absolute, "Darkness," because to our finite understanding it appears quite impenetrable; yet we recognize fully that our perception of such things does not do them justice. We involuntarily distinguish in our minds, for instance, between unconscious Absolute Consciousness, and unconsciousness, by secretly endowing the former with some indefinite quality that corresponds, on a higher plane than our thoughts can reach, with what we know as consciousness in ourselves. But this is not any kind of consciousness that we can manage to distinguish from what appears to us as unconsciousness.

3. THE HOUR HAD NOT YET STRUCK; THE RAY HAD NOT YET FLASHED INTO THE GERM (*a*); THE MÂTRIPADMA HAD NOT YET SWOLLEN (*b*).
(*a*) The "Ray" of the "Ever Darkness" becomes, as it is emitted, a Ray of effulgent Light or Life, and flashes into the "Germ"—the Point in the Mundane Egg, represented by Matter in its abstract sense. But the term "Point" must not be understood as applying to any particular point in Space, for a germ exists in the centre

of every atom, and these collectively form the "Germ;" or rather, as no atom can be made visible to our physical eye, the collectivity of these (if the term can be applied to something which is boundless and infinite) forms the noumenon of eternal and indestructible Matter.

(*b*) One of the symbolical figures for the Dual Creative Power in Nature (matter and force on the material plane) is "Padma," the water-lily of India. The Lotus is the product of heat (fire) and water (vapour or ether); fire standing in every philosophical and religious system, even in Christianity, as a representation of the Spirit of Deity, the active, male, generative principle; and ether, or the soul of matter, the light of the fire, for the passive female principle, from which everything in this Universe emanated. Hence, ether or water is the Mother, and fire is the Father. Sir William Jones—and before him archaic botany—showed that the seeds of the Lotus contain—even before they germinate—perfectly formed leaves, with the miniature shape of what one day, as perfect plants, they will become: nature thus giving us a specimen of the preformation of its production ... the seeds of all phanerogamous plants bearing proper flowers containing an embryo plantlet ready formed. This explains the sentence, "The Mâtri-Padma had not yet swollen"—the form being usually sacrificed to the inner or root idea in archaic symbology.

The Lotus, or Padma, is, moreover, a very ancient and favourite symbol for the Cosmos itself, and also for man. The popular reasons given are, firstly, the fact just mentioned, that the Lotus-seed contains within itself a perfect miniature of the future plant, which typifies the fact that the spiritual prototypes of all things exist in the immaterial world, before these things become materialized on earth. Secondly, the fact that the Lotus-plant grows up through the water, having its root in the Ilus, or mud, and spreading its flower in the air above. The Lotus thus typifies the life of man and also that of the Cosmos; for the Secret Doctrine teaches that the elements of both are the same, and that both are developing in the same direction. The root of the Lotus sunk in the mud represents material life, the stalk passing up through the water typifies existence in the astral world, and the flower floating on the water and opening to the sky is emblematical of spiritual being.

4. HER HEART HAD NOT YET OPENED FOR THE ONE RAY TO ENTER, THENCE TO FALL, AS THREE INTO FOUR, INTO THE LAP OF MÂYÂ.

The Primordial Substance had not yet passed out of its precosmic latency into differentiated objectivity, or even become the (to man, so far) invisible Protyle of Science. But, as the "Hour strikes" and it becomes receptive of the Fohatic impress of the Divine Thought—the Logos, or the male aspect of the Anima Mundi, Alaya—its "Heart" opens. It differentiates, and the Three (Father, Mother, Son) are transformed into Four. Herein lies the origin of the double mystery of the Trinity and the Immaculate Conception. The first and fundamental dogma of Occultism is Universal Unity (or Homogeneity) under three aspects. This leads to a possible conception of Deity, which as an absolute Unity must remain forever incomprehensible to finite intellects.

If thou wouldest believe in the Power which acts within the root of a plant, or imagine the root concealed under the soul, thou hast to think of its stalk or trunk, and of its leaves and flowers. Thou canst not imagine that Power independently of these objects. Life can be known only by the Tree of Life....

The idea of Absolute Unity would be broken entirely in our conception, had we not something concrete before our eyes to contain that Unity. And the Deity being absolute, must be omnipresent; hence not an atom but contains It within itself. The roots, the trunk, and its many branches, are three distinct objects, yet they are one tree. Say the Kabalists: "The Deity is one, because It is infinite. It is triple, because It is ever manifesting." This manifestation is triple in its aspects, for it requires, as Aristotle has it, three principles for every natural body to become objective: privation, form, and matter. Privation meant in the mind of the great philosopher that which the Occultists call the prototypes impressed in the Astral Light—the lowest plane and world of Anima Mundi. The union of these three principles depends upon a fourth—the Life which radiates from the summits of the Unreachable, to become a universally diffused Essence on the manifested planes of Existence. And this Quaternary (Father, Mother, Son, as a Unity, and a Quaternary—as a living manifestation) has been the means of leading to the very archaic idea of Immaculate Conception, now finally crystallized into a dogma of the Christian Church, which has carnalized this metaphysical idea beyond any common sense. For one has but to read the *Kabalah* and study its numerical methods of interpretation to find the origin of the dogma. It is purely astronomical, mathematical, and preëminently metaphysical: the Male Element in Nature (personified by the male deities and Logoi—Virâj, or Brahmâ, Horus, or Osiris, etc., etc.) is born through, not from, an immaculate source, personified by the "Mother," for—the Abstract Deity being sexless, and not even a Being but Be-ness, or Life itself—that Male having a "Mother" cannot have a "Father." Let us render this in the mathematical language of the author of *The Source of Measures*. Speaking of the "Measure of a Man" and his numerical (Kabalistic) value, he writes that in *Genesis*, iv. 1—

It is called the "Man even Jehovah" Measure, and this is obtained in this way, viz.: 113 x 5 = 565, and the value 565 can be placed under the form of expression 56.5 x 10 = 565. Here the Man-number 113 becomes a factor of 56.5 x 10, and the (Kabalistic) reading of this last numbered expression is Jod, He, Vau, He, or Jehovah.... The expansion of 565 into 56·5 x 10 is purposed to show the emanation of the male (Jod) from the female (Eva) principle; or, so to speak, the birth of a male element from an immaculate source, in other words, an immaculate conception.

Thus is repeated on earth the mystery enacted, according to the Seers, on the divine plane. The Son of the Immaculate Celestial Virgin (or the Undifferentiated Cosmic Protyle, Matter in its infinitude) is born again on earth as the Son of the terrestrial Eve, our mother Earth, and becomes Humanity as a total—past, present, and future—for Jehovah, or Jod-Hé-Vau-Hé, is androgyne, or both male and female. Above, the Son is the whole Kosmos; below, he is Mankind. The Triad or Triangle becomes

Tetraktys, the sacred Pythagorean number, the perfect Square, and a six-faced Cube on earth. The Macroprosopus (the Great Face) is now Microprosopus (the Lesser Face); or, as the Kabbalists have it, the Ancient of Days, descending on Adam Kadmon whom he uses as his vehicle to manifest through, gets transformed into Tetragrammaton. It is now in the "Lap of Mâyâ," the Great Illusion, and between itself and the Reality has the Astral Light, the Great Deceiver of man's limited senses, unless Knowledge through Paramârthasatya comes to the rescue.

5. THE SEVEN WERE NOT YET BORN FROM THE WEB OF LIGHT, DARKNESS ALONE WAS FATHER-MOTHER, SVABHÂVAT; AND SVABHÂVAT WAS IN DARKNESS.

The Secret Doctrine, in the Stanzas here given, occupies itself chiefly, if not entirely, with our Solar System, and especially with our Planetary Chain. The "Seven Sons," therefore, are the creators of the latter. This teaching will be explained more fully hereafter.

Svabhâvat, the "Plastic Essence" that fills the Universe, is the root of all things. Svabhâvat is, so to say, the Buddhistic concrete aspect of the abstraction called in Hindû philosophy Mûlaprakriti. It is the body of the Soul, and that which Ether would be to Âkâsha, the latter being the informing principle of the former. Chinese mystics have made of it the synonym of "Being." In the Chinese translation of the *Ekashloka-Shâstra* of Nâgârjuna (the Lung-shu of China), called the *Yih-shu-lu-kia-lun*, it is said that the
term "Being," or "Subhâva," (Yeu in Chinese) means "the Substance giving substance to itself"; it is also explained by him as meaning "without action and with action," "the nature which has no nature of its own." Subhâva, from which Svabhâvat, is composed of two words: *su* fair, handsome, good; *sva*, self, and *bhâva*, being or states of being.

6. THESE TWO ARE THE GERM, AND THE GERM IS ONE. THE UNIVERSE WAS STILL CONCEALED IN THE DIVINE THOUGHT AND THE DIVINE BOSOM.

The "Divine Thought" does not imply the idea of a Divine Thinker. The Universe, not only past, present and future—a human and finite idea expressed by finite thought—but in its totality, the Sat (an untranslateable term), Absolute Being, with the Past and Future crystallized in an eternal Present, is that Thought itself reflected in a secondary or manifested cause. Brahman (neuter), as the Mysterium Magnum of Paracelsus, is an absolute mystery to the human mind. Brahmâ, the male-female, the aspect and anthropomorphic reflection of Brahman, is conceivable to the perceptions of blind faith, though rejected by human intellect when it attains its majority.

Hence the statement that during the prologue, so to say, of the drama of creation, or the beginning of cosmic evolution, the Universe, or the Son, lies still concealed "in the Divine Thought," which had not yet penetrated into the "Divine Bosom." This idea, note well, is at the root, and forms the origin, of all the allegories about the "Sons of God" born of immaculate virgins.

Stanza III.

1. ... THE LAST VIBRATION OF THE SEVENTH ETERNITY THRILLS THROUGH INFINITUDE (*a*). THE MOTHER SWELLS, EXPANDING FROM WITHIN WITHOUT, LIKE THE BUD OF THE LOTUS (*b*).

(*a*) The seemingly paradoxical use of the term, "Seventh Eternity," thus dividing the indivisible, is sanctified in Esoteric Philosophy. The latter divides boundless Duration into unconditionally eternal and universal Time (Kâla); and conditioned Time (Khandakâla). One is the abstraction or noumenon of infinite Time, the other its phenomenon appearing periodically, as the effect of Mahat—the Universal Intelligence, limited by manvantaric duration. With some schools, Mahat is the first-born of Pradhâna (undifferentiated Substance, or the periodical aspect of Mûlaprakriti, the Root of Nature), which (Pradhâna) is called Mâyâ, Illusion. In this respect, I believe, Esoteric teaching differs from the Vedântin doctrines of both the Advaita and the Visishthadvaita schools. For it says that, while Mûlaprakriti, the noumenon, is self-existing and without any origin—is, in short, parentless, Anupâdaka, as one with Brahman—Prakriti, its phenomenon, is periodical and no better than a phantasm of the former; so Mahat, the first-born of Jñâna (or Gnôsis), Knowledge, Wisdom or the Logos—is a phantasm reflected from the Absolute Nirguna (Parabrahman), the One Reality, "devoid of attributes and qualities"; while with some Vedântins Mahat is a manifestation of Prakriti, or Matter.

(*b*) Therefore, the "last Vibration of the Seventh Eternity" was "fore-ordained"—by no God in particular, but occurred in virtue of the eternal and changeless Law which causes the great periods of Activity and Rest, called so graphically, and at the same time so poetically, the Days and Nights of Brahmâ. The expansion "from within without" of the Mother, called elsewhere the "Waters of Space," "Universal Matrix," etc., does not allude to an expansion from a small centre or focus, but means the development of limitless subjectivity into as limitless objectivity, without reference to size or limitation or area. *"The ever invisible and immaterial Substance present in eternity, threw its periodical Shadow from its own plane into the Lap of Mâyâ."* It implies that this expansion, not being an increase in size—for infinite extension admits of no enlargement—was a change of condition. It expanded "like the Bud of the Lotus"; for the Lotus plant exists not only as a miniature embryo in its seed (a physical characteristic), but its prototype is present in an ideal form in the Astral Light from "Dawn" to "Night" during the manvantaric period, like everything else, as a matter of fact, in this objective Universe; from man to mite, from giant trees to the tiniest blades of grass.

All this, teaches the Hidden Science, is but the temporary reflection, the shadow of the eternal ideal prototype in Divine Thought; the word "Eternity," note well again, standing here only in the sense of "Æon," as lasting throughout the seemingly interminable, but still limited cycle of activity, called by us Manvantara. For what is the real esoteric meaning of Manvantara, or rather a Manu-antara? It means, literally, "between two Manus," of whom there are fourteen in every Day of Brahmâ, such a Day consisting of 1,000 aggregates of four Ages, 1,000 "Great Ages" or Mahâyugas. Let us now analyse the word or name Manu. Orientalists in their dictionaries tell us that the term "Manu" is from the root *man*, "to think"; hence "the thinking man." But, esoterically, every Manu, as an anthropomorphized patron of his special cycle (or Round), is but the personified idea of the "Thought Divine" (as the Hermetic Pymander); each of the Manus, therefore, being the special god, the creator and fashioner of all that appears during his own respective cycle of being or Manvantara. Fohat runs the Manus' (or Dhyân Chohans') errands, and causes the ideal prototypes to expand from within without—that is, to cross gradually, on a descending scale, all the planes, from the noumenal to the lowest phenomenal, to bloom finally on the last into full objectivity—the acme of Illusion, or the grossest matter.

2. THE VIBRATION SWEEPS ALONG, TOUCHING WITH ITS SWIFT WING THE WHOLE UNIVERSE AND THE GERM THAT DWELLETH IN DARKNESS, THE DARKNESS THAT BREATHES OVER THE SLUMBERING WATERS OF LIFE.

The Pythagorean Monas is also said to dwell in solitude and "Darkness" like the "Germ." The idea of the Breath of Darkness moving over "the slumbering Waters of Life," which is Primordial Matter with the latent Spirit in it, recalls the first chapter of *Genesis*. Its original is the Brâhmanical Nârâyana (the Mover on the Waters), who is the personification of the Eternal Breath of the unconscious All (or Parabrahaman) of the Eastern Occultists. The Waters of Life, or Chaos—the female principle in symbolism—are the vacuum (to our mental sight), in which lie the latent Spirit and Matter. This it was that made Democritus assert, after his instructor Leucippus, that the primordial principles of all were atoms and a vacuum, in the sense of space, but not of empty space, for "Nature abhors a vacuum," according to the Peripatetics and every ancient philosopher.

In all Cosmogonies "Water" plays the same important part. It is the base and source of material existence. Scientists, mistaking the word for the thing, understand by it the definite chemical combination of oxygen and hydrogen, thus giving a specific meaning to a term used by Occultists in a generic sense, and which is employed in Cosmogony with a metaphysical and mystical meaning. Ice is not water, neither is steam, although all three have precisely the same chemical composition.

3. DARKNESS RADIATES LIGHT, AND LIGHT DROPS ONE SOLITARY RAY INTO THE WATERS, INTO THE MOTHER-DEEP. THE RAY SHOOTS THROUGH THE VIRGIN EGG, THE RAY CAUSES THE ETERNAL EGG TO THRILL, AND DROP THE NON-ETERNAL GERM, WHICH CONDENSES INTO THE WORLD-EGG.

The "solitary Ray" dropping into the "Mother-Deep" may be taken to mean Divine Thought, or Intelligence, impregnating Chaos. This, however, occurs on the plane of metaphysical abstraction, or rather the plane whereon that which we call a metaphysical abstraction, is a reality. The "Virgin-Egg," being in one sense the abstract of all ova, or the power of becoming developed through fecundation, is eternal and for ever the same. And just as the fecundation of an egg takes place before it is dropped; so the non-eternal periodical Germ, which later becomes in symbolism the Mundane Egg, contains in itself, when it emerges from the said symbol, "the promise and potency" of all the Universe. Though the idea *per se* is, of course, an abstraction, a symbolical mode of expression, it is a true symbol, for it suggests the idea of infinity as an endless circle. It brings before the mind's eye the picture of Kosmos emerging from and in boundless Space, a Universe as shoreless in magnitude, if not as endless in its objective manifestation. The symbol of an egg also expresses the fact taught in Occultism that the primordial form of everything manifested, from atom to globe, from man to angel, is spheroidal, the sphere being with all nations the emblem of eternity and infinity—a serpent swallowing its tail. To realize the meaning, however, the sphere must be thought of as seen from its centre. The field of vision, or of thought, is like a sphere whose radii proceed from one's self in every direction, and extend out into space, opening up boundless vistas all around. It is the symbolical circle of Pascal and the Kabalists, "whose centre is everywhere and circumference nowhere"—a conception which enters into the compound idea of this emblem.

The "World-Egg" is, perhaps, one of the most universally adopted symbols, highly suggestive as it is, equally in the spiritual, physiological, and cosmological sense. Therefore, it is found in every world-theogony, where it is largely associated with the serpent symbol, the latter being everywhere, in philosophy as in religious symbolism, an emblem of eternity, infinitude, regeneration, and rejuvenation, as well as of wisdom. The mystery of apparent self-generation and evolution through its own creative power, repeating in miniature, in the egg, the process of cosmic evolution—both due to heat and moisture under the efflux of the unseen creative spirit—fully justified the selection of this graphic symbol. The "Virgin-Egg" is the microcosmic symbol of the macrocosmic prototype, the "Virgin Mother"—Chaos or the Primeval Deep. The male creator (under whatever name) springs forth from the virgin female, the Immaculate Root fructified by the Ray. Who, if versed in astronomy and natural sciences, can fail to see its suggestiveness? Kosmos, as receptive Nature, is an egg fructified—yet left immaculate; for once regarded as boundless, it could have no other representation than a spheroid. The Golden Egg was surrounded by seven natural Elements, "four ready , three secret." This may be found stated in *Vishnu Purâna*, where elements are translated "envelopes," and a *secret* one is added—Ahamkâra. The original text has no Ahamkâra; it mentions seven Elements without specifying the last three.

4. The Three fall into the Four. The Radiant Essence becomes Seven inside, Seven outside (*a*). The Luminous Egg, which in itself is Three, curdles and spreads in milk-white Curds throughout the Depths of Mother, the Root that grows in the Depths of the Ocean of Life (*b*).

The use of geometrical figures and the frequent allusions to figures in all ancient scriptures, as in the *Purânas*, the Egyptian *Book of the Dead* and even the *Bible*—must be explained. In the *Book of Dzyan*, as in the *Kabalah*, there are two kinds of numerals to be studied—the Figures, often simple blinds, and the Sacred Numbers, the values of which are all known to the Occultists through Initiation. The former are but conventional glyphs; the latter, the basic symbols of all. That is to say, the one are purely physical, the other purely metaphysical, the two standing in relation to each other as Matter stands to Spirit—the extreme poles of the One Substance.

As Balzac, the unconscious Occultist of French literature, says somewhere, the Number is to Mind the same as it is to Matter, "an incomprehensible agent." Perhaps so to the profane, never to the initiated mind. Number is, as the great writer thought, an Entity, and, at the same time, a Breath emanating from what he called God and what we call the ALL, the Breath which alone could organize the physical Cosmos, "where naught obtains its form but through the Deity, which is an effect of Number." It is instructive to quote Balzac's words upon this subject:

The smallest as the most immense creations, are they not to be distinguished from each other by their quantities, their qualities, their dimensions, their forces and attributes, all begotten by Number? The infinitude of Numbers is a fact proven to our mind, but of which no proof can be physically given. The mathematician will tell us that the infinitude of Numbers exists but is not to be demonstrated. God is a Number endowed with motion, which is felt but not demonstrated. *As Unity, it begins the Numbers, with which it has nothing in common....* The existence of Numbers depends on Unity, which without a single

Number, begets them all.... What! unable either to measure the first abstraction yielded to you by the Deity, or to get hold of it, you still hope to subject to your measurements the mystery of the Secret Sciences which emanate from that Deity? .... And what would you feel, were I to plunge you into the abysses of Motion, the Force which organizes the Numbers? What would you think, were I to add that *Motion* and *Number* are begotten by the Word, the Supreme Reason of the Seers and Prophets, who, in days of old, sensed the mighty Breath of God, a witness to which is the Apocalypse?

(*b*) "The Radiant Essence curdles and spreads throughout the Depths" of Space. From an astronomical point of view this is easy of explanation: it is the Milky Way, the World-Stuff, or Primordial Matter in its first form. It is more difficult, however, to explain it in a few words, or even lines, from the standpoint of Occult Science and Symbolism, as it is the most complicated of glyphs. Herein are enshrined more than a dozen symbols. To begin with, it contains the whole pantheon of mysterious objects, every one of them having some definite Occult meaning, extracted from the Hindû allegorical "Churning of the Ocean" by the Gods. Besides Amrita, the water of life or immortality, Surabhi, the "cow of plenty," called "the fountain of milk and curds," was extracted from this "sea of milk." Hence the universal adoration of the cow and bull, one the productive, the other the generative power in Nature: symbols connected with both the solar and the cosmic deities. The specific properties, for Occult purposes, of the "fourteen precious things," being explained only at the Fourth Initiation, cannot be given here; but the following may be remarked. In the *Shatapatha Brâhmana* it is stated that the Churning of the Ocean of Milk took place in the Satya Yuga, the first Age which immediately followed the "Deluge." As, however, neither the *Rig Veda* nor *Manu*—both preceding Vaivasvata's "Deluge," that of the bulk of the Fourth Race—mention this Deluge, it is evident that it is neither the Great Deluge, nor that which carried away Atlantis, nor even the Deluge of Noah, which is here meant. This "Churning" relates to a period before the earth's formation, and is in direct connection with another universal legend, the various and contradictory versions of which culminated in the Christian dogma of the "War in Heaven," and the "Fall of the Angels." The *Brâhmanas*, reproached by the Orientalists with their versions on the same subjects often clashing with each other, *are preëminently occult works*, hence used purposely as blinds. They are allowed to survive for public use and property only because they were and are absolutely unintelligible to the masses. Otherwise they would have disappeared from circulation as long ago as the days of Akbar.

5. THE ROOT REMAINS, THE LIGHT REMAINS, THE CURDS REMAIN, AND STILL OEAOHOO IS ONE.

"Oeaohoo" is rendered "Father-Mother of the Gods" in the Commentaries, or the "Six in One," or *the Septenary Root from which all proceeds*. All depends upon the accent given to these seven vowels, which may be pronounced as one, three, or even seven syllables, by adding an *e* after the final *o*. This mystic name is given out, because without a thorough mastery of the triple pronunciation it remains for ever ineffectual.

"Is One" refers to the Non-Separateness of all that lives and has its being, whether in an active or passive state. In one sense, Oeaohoo is the Rootless Root of All; hence, one with Parabrahman: in another sense it is a name for the manifested One Life, the eternal living Unity. The "Root" means, as already explained, Pure Knowledge (Sattva), eternal (*nitya*) unconditioned Reality, or Sat (Satya), whether we call it Parabrahman or Mûlaprakriti, for these are but the two symbols of the One. The "Light" is the same Omnipresent Spiritual Ray, which has entered and now fecundated the Divine Egg, and calls cosmic matter to begin its long series of differentiations.
The "Curds" are the first differentiation, and probably also refer to that cosmic matter which is supposed to be the origin of the Milky Way—the matter we know. This "matter," which, according to the revelation received from the primeval Dhyâni-Buddhas, is, during the periodical Sleep of the Universe, of the ultimate tenuity conceivable to the eye of the perfect Bodhisattva—this matter, radiant and cool, becomes, at the first reawakening of cosmic motion, scattered through Space; appearing, when seen from the Earth, in clusters and lumps,

like curds in thin milk. These are the seeds of the future worlds, the "star-stuff."

6. THE ROOT OF LIFE WAS IN EVERY DROP OF THE OCEAN OF IMMORTALITY, AND THE OCEAN WAS RADIANT LIGHT, WHICH WAS FIRE, AND HEAT, AND MOTION. DARKNESS VANISHED AND WAS NO MORE; IT DISAPPEARED IN ITS OWN ESSENCE, THE BODY OF FIRE AND WATER, OF FATHER AND MOTHER.

The Essence of Darkness being Absolute Light, Darkness is taken as the appropriate allegorical representation of the condition of the Universe during Pralaya, or the term of Absolute Rest, or Non-Being, as it appears to our finite minds. The "Fire, and Heat, and Motion," here spoken of, are, of course, not the fire, heat, and motion of Physical Science, but the underlying abstractions, the noumena, or the soul, of the essence of these material manifestations—the "things in themselves," which, as Modern Science confesses, entirely elude the instruments of the laboratory, and which even the mind cannot grasp, although it can equally as little avoid the conclusion that these underlying essences of things must exist. "Fire and Water, or Father and Mother," may be taken here to mean the divine Ray and Chaos. "Chaos, from this union with Spirit obtaining sense, shone with pleasure, and thus was produced the Protogonos ," says a fragment of Hermas. Damascius calls it Dis, the "disposer of all things."
According to the Rosicrucian tenets, as handled and explained by the profane for once correctly, if only partially, "Light and Darkness are identical in themselves, being only divisible in the human mind"; and according to Robert Fludd, "Darkness adopted illumination in order to make itself visible." According to the tenets of Eastern Occultism, Darkness is the one true actuality, the basis and the root of Light, without which the latter could never manifest itself, nor even exist. Light is Matter, and Darkness pure Spirit. Darkness, in its radical, metaphysical basis, is subjective and absolute Light; while the latter in all its seeming effulgence and glory, is merely a mass of shadows, as it can never be eternal, and is simply an Illusion, or Mâyâ.

Even in the mind-baffling and science-harassing *Genesis*, light is created out of darkness—"and darkness was upon the face of the deep"—and not *vice versâ*. "In him was life; and the life was the *light* of men." A day may come when the eyes of men will be opened; and then they may comprehend better than they do now the verse in the Gospel of John that says, "And the light shineth in darkness; and the darkness comprehendeth it not." They will see then that the word "darkness" does not apply to man's spiritual eyesight, but indeed to Darkness, the Absolute, that comprehendeth not (cannot cognize) transient Light, however transcendent to human eyes. *Demon est Deus inversus*. The Devil is now called "darkness" by the Church, whereas in the *Bible*, in the *Book of Job*, he is called the "Son of God," the bright star of the early morning, Lucifer. There is a whole philosophy of dogmatic craft in the reason why the first Archangel, who sprang from the depths of Chaos, was called Lux (Lucifer), the luminous "Son of the Morning," or Manvantaric Dawn. He has been transformed by the Church into Lucifer or Satan, because he is higher and older than Jehovah, and had to be sacrificed to the new dogma.

7. BEHOLD, O LANOO, THE RADIANT CHILD OF THE TWO, THE UNPARALLELED REFULGENT GLORY—BRIGHT SPACE, SON OF DARK SPACE, WHO EMERGES FROM THE DEPTHS OF THE GREAT DARK WATERS. IT IS OEAOHOO, THE YOUNGER, THE —— (*a*). HE SHINES FORTH AS THE SUN, HE IS THE BLAZING DIVINE DRAGON OF WISDOM; THE EKA IS CHATUR, AND CHATUR TAKES TO ITSELF TRI, AND THE UNION PRODUCES THE SAPTA, IN WHOM ARE THE SEVEN, WHICH BECOME THE TRIDASHA, THE HOSTS AND THE MULTITUDES (*b*). BEHOLD HIM LIFTING THE VEIL, AND UNFURLING IT FROM EAST TO WEST. HE SHUTS OUT THE ABOVE, AND LEAVES THE BELOW TO BE SEEN AS THE GREAT ILLUSION. HE MARKS THE PLACES FOR THE SHINING ONES, AND TURNS THE UPPER INTO A SHORELESS SEA OF FIRE (*c*), AND THE ONE MANIFESTED INTO THE GREAT WATERS.

(*a*) "Bright Space, Son of Dark Space," corresponds to the Ray dropped at the first thrill of the new Dawn into the great Cosmic

Depths, from which it reëmerges differentiated as "Oeaohoo, the Younger" (the "New Life"), to be to the end of the Life-Cycle the Germ of all things. He is "the Incorporeal Man who contains in himself the Divine Idea," the generator of Light and Life, to use an expression of Philo Judæus. He is called the "Blazing Dragon of Wisdom," because, firstly, he is that which the Greek philosophers called the Logos, the Verbum of the Thought Divine; and secondly, because in Esoteric Philosophy this first manifestation, being the synthesis or the aggregate of Universal Wisdom, Oeaohoo, the "Son of the Sun," contains in himself the Seven Creative Hosts (Sephiroth), and is thus the essence of manifested Wisdom. *He who bathes in the Light of Oeaohoo will never be deceived by the Veil of Mâyâ.*

"Kwan-Shai-Yin" is identical with, and an equivalent of the Sanskrit Avalokiteshvara, and as such is an androgynous deity, like the Tetragrammaton and all the Logoi of antiquity. It is only by some sects in China that he is anthropomorphized, and represented with female attributes; under his female aspect becoming Kwan-Yin, the Goddess of Mercy, called the "Divine Voice." The latter is the patron deity of Tibet and of the island of Puto in China, where both deities have a number of monasteries.

The higher gods of antiquity are all "Sons of the Mother" before they become "Sons of the Father." The Logoi, like Jupiter or Zeus, son of Cronus-Saturn, "Infinite Time" (Kâla), in their origin were represented as male-female. Zeus is said to be the "beautiful virgin," and Venus is made bearded. Apollo was originally bisexual, so is Brahmâ-Vâch in *Manu* and the *Purânas*. Osiris is interchangeable with Isis, and Horus is of both sexes. Finally in St. John's vision in *Revelation*, the Logos, who is now connected with Jesus, is hermaphrodite, for he is described as having female breasts. So also is Tetragrammaton, or Jehovah. But there are two Avalokiteshvaras in Esotericism; the First and the Second Logos.

No religious symbol can escape profanation and even derision in our days of politics and science. In Southern India the writer has seen a converted native making pûjâ with offerings before a statue of Jesus clad in woman's clothes and with a ring in its nose. On asking the meaning of this masquerade, we were answered that it was Jesu-Maria blended in one, and that it was done by the permission of the Padre, as the zealous convert had no money to purchase two statues, or "idols" as they, very properly, were called by a witness, another but a non-converted Hindû. Blasphemous this will appear to a dogmatic Christian, but the Theosophist and the Occultist must award the palm of logic to the converted Hindû. The esoteric Christos in the Gnôsis is, of course, sexless, but in exoteric Theology he is male and female.

(b) The "Dragon of Wisdom" is the One, the "Eka" or Saka. It is curious that Jehovah's name in Hebrew should also be One, Achad. "His name is Achad," say the Rabbins. The Philologists ought to decide which of the two is derived from the other, linguistically and symbolically; surely, not the Sanskrit.
The "One" and the "Dragon" are expressions used by the ancients in connection with their respective Logoi. Jehovah—esoterically Elohim—is also the Serpent or Dragon that tempted Eve; and the Dragon is an old glyph for the Astral Light (Primordial Principle), "which is the Wisdom of Chaos." Archaic philosophy, recognizing neither Good nor Evil as a fundamental or independent power, but starting from the
Absolute ALL (Universal Perfection eternally), traces both through the course of natural evolution to pure Light condensing gradually into form, and hence becoming Matter or Evil. It was left with the early and ignorant Christian Fathers to degrade the philosophical and highly scientific idea of this emblem into the absurd superstition called the "Devil." They took this from the later Zoroastrians, who saw Devils or Evil in the Hindû Devas, and the word Evil has become by a double transmutation D'Evil (Diabolos, Diable, Diavolo, Teufel). But the Pagans have always shown a philosophical discrimination in their symbols. The primitive symbol of the serpent symbolized divine Wisdom and Perfection, and has always stood for psychical Regeneration and Immortality. Hence, Hermes calling the serpent the most spiritual of all beings; Moses, initiated into the Wisdom of Hermes, following suit in *Genesis*; the Gnostic Serpent with the

seven vowels over its head, being the emblem of the Seven Hierarchies of the Septenary or Planetary Creators. Hence, also, the Hindû serpent Shesha or Ananta, the Infinite, a name of Vishnu, and his first Vâhana, or Vehicle, on the Primordial Waters. Like the Logoi and the Hierarchies of Powers, however, these serpents have to be distinguished one from the other. Shesha or Ananta, the "Couch of Vishnu," is an allegorical abstraction, symbolizing infinite Time in Space, which contains the Germ and throws off periodically the efflorescence of this Germ, the Manifested Universe; whereas, the Gnostic Ophis contains the same triple symbolism in its seven vowels as the one, three and seven-syllabled Oeaohoo of the archaic doctrine; *i.e.*, the First Unmanifested Logos, the Second Manifested, the Triangle concreting into the Quaternary or Tetragrammaton, and the Rays of the latter on the material plane.

Yet they all made a difference between the good and the bad Serpent (the Astral Light of the Kabalists)—between the former, the embodiment of divine Wisdom in the region of the Spiritual, and the latter, Evil, on the plane of Matter. For the Astral Light, or the Ether, of the ancient Pagans—the name Astral Light is quite modern—is Spirit-Matter. Beginning with the pure spiritual plane, it becomes grosser as it descends, until it becomes Mâyâ, or the tempting and deceitful Serpent on our plane.

Jesus accepted the serpent as a synonym of Wisdom, and this formed part of his teaching: "Be ye wise as serpents," he says. *"In the beginning, before Mother became Father-Mother, the Fiery Dragon moved in the Infinitudes alone."* The *Aitareya Brahmana* calls the Earth Sarparâjni, the "Serpent Queen," and the "Mother of all that moves." Before our globe became egg-shaped (and the Universe also), "a long trail of cosmic dust moved and writhed like a serpent in Space." The "Spirit of God moving on Chaos" was symbolized by every nation in the shape of a fiery serpent breathing fire and light upon the primordial waters, until it had incubated cosmic matter and made it assume the annular shape of a serpent with its tail in its mouth—which symbolizes not only eternity and infinitude, but also the globular shape of all the bodies formed within the Universe from that fiery mist. The Universe, as also the Earth and Man, serpent-like, periodically cast off their old skins, to assume new ones after a time of rest. The serpent is surely not a less graceful or a more unpoetical image than the caterpillar and chrysalis from which springs the butterfly, the Greek emblem of Psyche, the human soul! The Dragon was also the symbol of the Logos with the Egyptians, as with the Gnostics. In the *Book of Hermes*, Pymander, the oldest and the most spiritual of the Logoi of the Western Continent, appears to Hermes in the shape of a Fiery Dragon of "Light, Fire, and Flame." Pymander, the "Thought Divine" personified, says:

The Light is I, I am the Nous , I am thy God, and I am far older than the human principle which escapes from the shadow . I am the germ of thought, the resplendent Word, the Son of God. All that thus sees and hears in thee is the Verbum of the Master; it is the Thought which is God, the Father. The celestial Ocean, the Æther, ... is the Breath of the Father, the life-giving principle, the Mother, the Holy Spirit, ... for these are not separated, and their union is Life.

Here we find the unmistakable echo of the archaic Secret Doctrine, as now expounded. Only the latter does not place at the head of the Evolution of Life the "Father," who comes third and is the "Son of the Mother," but the "Eternal and Ceaseless Breath of the ALL." Mahat (Understanding, Universal Mind, Thought, etc.), before it manifests itself as Brahmâ or Shiva, appears as Vishnu, says the *Sânkhya Sâra*. Hence it has several aspects, just as the Logos has. Mahat is called the Lord, in the *Primary* Creation, and is, in this sense, Universal Cognition or Thought Divine; but, "that Mahat which was first produced is (afterwards) called *Ego-ism*, when it is born as (the feeling itself) 'I,' that is said to be the *Secondary* Creation." And the translator (an able and learned Brâhman, not a European Orientalist) explains in a foot-note, "*i.e.*, when Mahat develops into the feeling of Self-Consciousness—I—then it assumes the name of Egoism," which, translated into our Esoteric phraseology, means—when Mahat is transformed into the human Manas (or even that of the finite gods), and becomes *Aham*-ship. Why it is called the Mahat of the *Secondary* Creation (or the *Ninth*, the Kaumâra in *Vishnu Purâna*), will be explained hereafter.

(c) The "Sea of Fire" is, then, the Super-Astral (*i.e.*, Noumenal) Light, the first radiation from the Root Mûlaprakriti, Undifferentiated Cosmic Substance, which becomes Astral Matter. It is also called the "Fiery Serpent," as above described. If the student bears in mind that there is but One Universal Element, which is infinite, unborn, and undying and that all the rest—as in the world of phenomena—are but so many various differentiated aspects and transformations (correlations, they are now called) of that One, from macrocosmical down to microcosmical effects, from super-human down to human and sub-human beings, the totality, in short, of objective existence—then the first and chief difficulty will disappear and Occult Cosmology may be mastered. Thus in the Egyptian also as in the Indian Theogony there was a *Concealed* Deity, the ONE, and a creative, androgynous god; Shoo being the god of creation, and Osiris in his original primary form, the god "whose name is unknown."

All the Kabalists and Occultists, Eastern and Western, recognize (*a*) the identity of "Father-Mother" with Primordial Æther, or Âkâsha (Astral Light); and (*b*) its homogeneity before the evolution of the "Son," cosmically Fohat, for it is Cosmic Electricity. "*Fohat hardens and scatters the Seven Brothers*"; which means that the Primordial Electric Entity—for the Eastern Occultists insist that Electricity is an Entity—electrifies into life, and separates primordial stuff or pregenetic matter into atoms, themselves the source of all life and consciousness. "There exists a universal *agent unique* of all forms and of life, that is called Od, Ob, and Aour, active and passive, positive and negative, like day and night: it is the first light in Creation" (Éliphas Lévi)—the "first light" of the primordial Elohim, the Adam, "male and female," or (scientifically) Electricity and Life.

The ancients represented it by a serpent, for "*Fohat hisses as he glides hither and thither*," in zigzags. The Kabalah figures it with the Hebrew letter Teth, ט, whose symbol is the serpent which played such a prominent part in the Mysteries. Its universal value is nine, for it is the ninth letter of the alphabet, and the ninth door of the fifty portals, or gateways, that lead to the concealed mysteries of being. It is the magical agent *par excellence*, and designates in Hermetic philosophy "Life infused into Primordial Matter," the essence that composes all things, and the spirit that determines their form. But there are two secret Hermetical operations, one spiritual, the other material, correlative and for ever united. As Hermes says:

Thou shalt separate the earth from the fire, the subtile from the solid ... that which ascends from earth to heaven and descends again from heaven to earth. It is the strong force of every force, for it conquers every subtile thing and penetrates into every solid. Thus was the world formed.

It was not Zeno, the founder of the Stoics, alone, who taught that the Universe evolves, and its primary substance is transformed from the state of fire into that of air, then into that of water, etc. Heraclitus of Ephesus maintained that the one principle that underlies all phenomena in Nature is fire. The intelligence that moves the Universe is fire, and fire is intelligence. And while Anaximenes said the same of air, and Thales of Miletus (600 years B.C.) of water, the Esoteric Doctrine reconciles all these philosophers, by showing that though each was right, the system of none was complete.

8. WHERE WAS THE GERM, AND WHERE WAS NOW DARKNESS? WHERE IS THE SPIRIT OF THE FLAME THAT BURNS IN THY LAMP, O LANOO? THE GERM IS THAT, AND THAT IS LIGHT, THE WHITE BRILLIANT SON OF THE DARK HIDDEN FATHER..

The answer to the first question, suggested by the second, which is the reply of the teacher to the pupil, contains in a single phrase one of the most essential truths of Occult Philosophy. It indicates the existence of things imperceptible to our physical senses which are of far greater importance, more real and more permanent, than those that appeal to these senses themselves. Before the Lanoo can hope to understand the transcendentally metaphysical problem contained in the first question, he must be able to answer the second; while the very answer he gives to the second will furnish him with the clue to the correct reply to the first.

In the Sanskrit Commentary on this Stanza, the terms used for the concealed and the unrevealed Principle are many. In the earliest MSS. of Indian literature this Unrevealed Abstract Deity has no name. It is generally called "That" (Tad, in Sanskrit), and means all that is, was, and will be, or that can be so received by the human mind.
Among such appellations given—of course, only in Esoteric Philosophy—as the "Unfathomable
Darkness," the "Whirlwind," etc., it is also called the "It of the Kâlahansa," the "Kâla-ham-sa," and even the "Kâli
Hamsa" (Black Swan). Here the m and the n are convertible, and both sound like the nasal French an or am. As in the Hebrew so also in the Sanskrit many a mysterious sacred name conveys to the profane ear no more than some ordinary, and often vulgar word, because it is concealed anagrammatically or otherwise. This word Hansa, or Hamsa, is just such a case. Hamsa is equal to "A-ham-sa"—three words meaning "I am He"; while divided in still another way it will read "So-ham," "He I." In this single word is contained, for him who understands the language of wisdom, the universal mystery, the doctrine of the identity of man's essence with god-essence. Hence the glyph of, and the allegory about, Kâlahansa (or Hamsa), and the name given to Brahman (neuter), later on to the male Brahmâ, of Hamsa-vâhana, "he who uses the Hamsa as his vehicle." The same word may be read "Kâlaham-sa," or "I am I, in the eternity of time," answering to the Biblical, or rather Zoroastrian, "I am that I am." The same doctrine is found in the *Kabalah*, as witness the following extract from an unpublished MS. by Mr. S. Liddell McGregor Mathers, the learned Kabalist:

The three pronouns, אני, אתה, הוא, Hua, Ateh, Ani—He, Thou, I—are used to symbolize the ideas of Macroposopus and Microprosopus in the Hebrew Qabalah. Hua, "He," is applied to the hidden and concealed Macroprosopus; Ateh, "Thou," to Microprosopus; and Ani, "I," to the latter when He is represented as speaking. (See *Lesser Holy Assembly*, 204 *et seq.*) It is to be noted that each of these names consists of three letters, of which the letter Aleph א, A, forms the conclusion of the first word Hua, and the commencement of Atah and Ani, as if it were the connecting link between them. But א is the symbol of the Unity and consequently of the unvarying Idea of the Divine operating through all these. But behind the א in the name Hua are the letters ו and ה, the symbols of the numbers Six and Five, the Male and the Female, the Hexagram and the Pentagram. And the numbers of these three words, Hua, Ateh, Ani, are 12, 406, and 61, which are resumed in the key numbers of 3, 10, and 7, by the Qabalah of the Nine Chambers which is a form of the exegetical rule of Temura.

It is useless to attempt to explain the mystery in full. Materialists and the men of Modern Science will never understand it, since, in order to obtain clear perception of it, one has first of all to admit the postulate of a universally diffused, omnipresent, eternal Deity in Nature; secondly, to have fathomed the mystery of electricity in its true essence; and thirdly, to credit man with being the septenary symbol, on the terrestrial plane, of the One Great Unit, the Logos, which is Itself the seven-vowelled sign, the Breath crystallized into the Word. He who believes in all this, has also to believe in the multiple combination of the seven planets of Occultism and of the *Kabalah*, with the twelve zodiacal signs; and attribute, as we do, to each planet and to each constellation an influence which, in the words of Mr. Ely Star (a French astrologer), "is proper to it, beneficent or maleficent, and this, after the planetary spirit which rules it, who, in his turn, is capable of influencing men and things which are found in harmony with him and with which he has any affinity." For these reasons, and since few believe in the foregoing, all that can now be given is that in both cases the symbol of Hansa (whether I, He, Goose or Swan) is an important symbol, representing, among other things, Divine Wisdom, Wisdom in Darkness beyond the reach of men. For all exoteric purposes, Hansa, as every Hindû knows, is a fabulous bird which, when (in the allegory) given milk mixed with water for its food, separated the two, drinking the milk and leaving the water; thus showing inherent wisdom—milk standing symbolically for spirit, and water for matter.

That this allegory is very ancient and dates from the very earliest archaic period, is shown by the mention, in the *Bhâgavata Purâna*, of a certain caste named Hamsa or Hansa, which was the "one caste" *par excellence*; when far back in the mists of a forgotten past there was among the Hindûs only "One Veda, One Deity, One Caste." There is also a range in the Himâlayas, described in the old books as being situated north of Mount Meru, called Hamsa, and connected with episodes pertaining to the history of religious mysteries and initiations. As to Kâlahansa being the supposed Vehicle of Brahmâ-Prajâpati, in the exoteric texts and translations of the Orientalists, it is quite a mistake. Brahman, the neuter, is called by them Kâla-hansa, and Brahmâ, the male, Hansa-vâhana, because, forsooth, "his vehicle is a swan or goose." This is a purely exoteric gloss. Esoterically and logically, if Brahman, the infinite, is all that is described by the Orientalists, and, agreeably with the Vedântic texts, is an abstract deity, in no way characterized by the ascription of any human attributes, and at the same time it is maintained that he or it is called Kâlahansa—then how can it ever become the Vâhan of Brahmâ, the manifested finite god? It is quite the reverse. The "Swan or Goose" (Hansa) is the symbol of the male or temporary deity, Brahmâ, the emanation of the primordial Ray, which is made to serve as a Vâhan or Vehicle for the Divine Ray, which otherwise could not manifest itself in the Universe, being, antiphrastically, itself an emanation of Darkness—for our human intellect, at any rate. It is Brahmâ, then, who is Kâlahansa, and the Ray, Hansa-vâhana.

As to the strange symbol thus chosen, it is equally suggestive; the true mystic significance being the idea of a Universal Matrix, figured by the Primordial Waters of the Deep, or the opening for the reception, and subsequently for the issuing, of that One Ray (the Logos) which contains in itself the other Seven Procreative Rays or Powers (the Logoi or Builders). Hence the choice by the Rosecroix of the aquatic fowl—whether swan or pelican—with seven young ones, for a symbol, modified and adapted to the religion of every country. Ain Suph is called the "Fiery Soul of the Pelican" in the *Book of Numbers*. Appearing with every Manvantara as Nârâyana, or Svâyambhuva, the Self-Existent, and penetrating into the

Mundane Egg, it emerges from it at the end of the divine incubation as Brahmâ, or Prajâpati, the progenitor of the future Universe, into which he expands. He is Purusha (Spirit), but he is also Prakriti (Matter). Therefore it is only after separating itself into two halves—Brahmâ-Vâch (the female) and Brahmâ-Virâj (the male)—that the Prajâpati becomes the male Brahmâ.

9. LIGHT IS COLD FLAME, AND FLAME IS FIRE, AND FIRE PRODUCES HEAT, WHICH YIELDS WATER—THE WATER OF LIFE IN THE GREAT MOTHER.

It must be remembered that the
words "Light," "Flame" and "Fire," have been adopted by the translators from the vocabulary of the old "Fire Philosophers," in order to render more clearly the meaning of the archaic terms and symbols employed in the original. Otherwise they would have remained entirely unintelligible to a European reader. To a student of the Occult, however, the above terms will be sufficiently clear.

All these—
"Light," "Flame," "Cold," "Fire," "Heat," "Water," and "Water of Life"—are, on our plane, the progeny, or, as a modern Physicist would say, the correlations of Electricity. Mighty word, and a still mightier symbol! Sacred generator of a no less sacred progeny; of Fire—the creator, the preserver and the destroyer; of Light—the essence of our divine ancestors; of Flame—the soul of things. Electricity, the One Life at the upper rung of Being, and Astral Fluid, the Athanor of the Alchemists, at the lower; God and Devil, Good and Evil.

Now, why is Light called "Cold Flame"? In the order of Cosmic Evolution (as taught by the Occultist), the energy that actuates matter, after its first formation into atoms, is generated on our plane by Cosmic Heat; and before that period Cosmos, in the sense of dissociated matter, was not. The first Primordial Matter, eternal and coëval with Space, *"which has neither a beginning nor an end, neither hot nor cold, but is of its own special nature,"* says the Commentary. Heat and cold are relative qualities and pertain to the realms of the manifested worlds, which all proceed from the manifested Hyle, which, in its absolutely latent aspect, is referred to as the "Cold Virgin," and when awakened to life, as the "Mother." The ancient Western cosmogonic myths state that at first there was only cold mist (the Father) and the prolific slime (the Mother, Ilus or Hyle), from which crept forth the Mundane Snake (Matter). Primordial Matter, then, before it emerges from the plane of the never-manifesting, and awakens to the thrill of action under the impulse of Fohat, is but "a cool radiance, colourless, formless, tasteless, and devoid of every quality and aspect." Even such are her First-born, the "Four Sons," who "are One, and become Seven,"—the Entities, by whose qualifications and names the ancient Eastern Occultists called the four of the seven primal "Centres of Force," or Atoms, that develop later into the great Cosmic "Elements," now divided into the seventy or so sub-elements, known to Science. The four "Primal Natures" of the first Dhyân Chohans are the so-called (for want of better terms) Âkâshic, Ethereal, Watery and Fiery. They answer, in the terminology of practical Occultism, to the scientific definitions of gases, which—to convey a clear idea to both Occultists and laymen—may be defined as parahydrogenic, paraoxygenic, oxyhydrogenic, and ozonic, or perhaps nitrozonic; the latter forces, or gases (in Occultism, supersensuous, yet atomic substances), being the most effective and active when energizing on the plane of more grossly differentiated matter. These elements are both electro-positive and electro-negative. These and many more are probably the missing links of Chemistry. They are known by other names in Alchemy and to Occultists who practise phenomenal powers. It is by combining and recombining, or dissociating, the "Elements" in a certain way, by means of Astral Fire, that the greatest phenomena are produced.

10. FATHER-MOTHER SPIN A WEB, WHOSE UPPER END IS FASTENED TO SPIRIT, THE LIGHT OF THE ONE DARKNESS, AND THE LOWER ONE TO ITS SHADOWY END, MATTER; AND THIS WEB IS THE UNIVERSE SPUN OUT OF THE TWO SUBSTANCES MADE IN ONE, WHICH IS SVABHÂVAT.

In the *Mândukya Upanishad* it is written, "As a spider throws out and retracts its web, as herbs spring up in the ground ... so is the Universe derived from the undecaying one," Brahmâ, for the "Germ of unknown Darkness," is the material from which all evolves and develops, "as the web from the spider, as foam from the water," etc. This is only graphic and true, if the term Brahmâ, the "Creator," is derived from the root *brih*, to increase or expand. Brahmâ "expands," and becomes the Universe woven out of his own substance.

The same idea has been beautifully expressed by Goethe, who says:

Thus at the roaring loom of Time I ply,
And weave for God the garment thou see'st Him by.

11. IT EXPANDS WHEN THE BREATH OF FIRE IS UPON IT; IT CONTRACTS WHEN THE BREATH OF THE MOTHER TOUCHES IT. THEN THE SONS DISSOCIATE AND SCATTER, TO RETURN INTO THEIR MOTHER'S BOSOM, AT THE END OF THE GREAT DAY, AND RE-BECOME ONE WITH HER. WHEN IT IS COOLING, IT BECOMES RADIANT. ITS SONS EXPAND AND CONTRACT THROUGH THEIR OWN SELVES AND HEARTS; THEY EMBRACE INFINITUDE.

The expanding of the Universe, under the "Breath of Fire," is very suggestive in the light of the fire-mist period, of which Modern Science speaks so much, and knows in reality so little.

Great heat breaks up the compound elements and resolves the heavenly bodies into their Primeval One Element, explains the Commentary.

"Once disintegrated into its primal constituent, by getting within the attraction and reach of a focus, or centre of heat, of which many are carried about to and fro in space, a body, whether alive or dead, will be vapourized, and held in the 'Bosom of the Mother,' until Fohat, gathering a few of the clusters of Cosmic Matter, will, by giving it an impulse, set it in motion anew, develop the required heat, and then leave it to follow its own new growth."

The expanding and contracting of the "Web" *i.e.*, the world-stuff, or atoms—express here the pulsatory movement; for it is the regular contraction and expansion of the infinite and shoreless Ocean, of that which we may call the noumenon of Matter, emanated by Svabhâvat, which causes the universal vibration of atoms. But it is also suggestive of something else. It shows that the ancients were acquainted with that which is now the puzzle of many Scientists and especially of Astronomers—the cause of the first ignition of matter, or world-stuff, the paradox of the heat produced by refrigerative contraction, and other such cosmic riddles—for it points unmistakably to a knowledge by the ancients of such phenomena. *"There is heat internal and heat external in every atom,"* say the MSS. Commentaries, to which the writer has had access, *"the Breath of the Father , and the Breath of the Mother "*; and they give explanations which show that the modern theory of the extinction of the solar fires, by loss of heat through radiation, is erroneous. The assumption is false even on the Scientists' own admission. For, as Professor Newcomb points out, "by losing heat a gaseous body contracts, and the heat generated by the contraction exceeds that which it had to lose in order to produce the contraction." This paradox, that a body gets hotter, as the shrinking produced by its getting colder is greater, has led to long disputes. The surplus of heat, it is argued, is lost by radiation, and to assume that the temperature is not lowered *pari passu* with a decrease of volume under a constant pressure, is to set at naught the law of Charles. Contraction develops heat, it is true; but contraction (from cooling) is incapable of developing the whole amount of heat at any time existing in the mass, or even of maintaining a body at a constant temperature, etc. Professor Winchell tries to reconcile the paradox—only a seeming one in fact, as J. Homer Lane proved—by suggesting "something besides heat." "May it not be," he asks, "simply a repulsion among the molecules, which varies according to some law of the distance"? But even this will be found irreconcilable, unless this "something besides heat" is ticketed "Causeless Heat," the "Breath of Fire," the all-creative Force *plus* Absolute Intelligence, which Physical Science is not likely to accept.

However it may be, the reading of this Stanza, notwithstanding its archaic phraseology, shows it to be more scientific than even Modern Science.

12. THEN SVABHÂVAT SENDS FOHAT TO HARDEN THE ATOMS. EACH IS A PART OF THE WEB. REFLECTING THE "SELF-EXISTENT LORD," LIKE A MIRROR, EACH BECOMES IN TURN A WORLD.

Fohat hardens the Atoms; *i.e.*, by infusing energy into them, he scatters the "Atoms," or Primordial Matter. *"He scatters himself while scattering Matter into Atoms."*

It is through Fohat that the ideas of the Universal Mind are impressed upon Matter. Some faint idea of the nature of Fohat may be gathered from the appellation "Cosmic Electricity," sometimes applied to it; but, in this case, to the commonly known properties of electricity, must be added others, including intelligence. It is of interest to note that Modern Science has come to the conclusion, that all cerebration and brain-activity are attended by electrical phenomena.

Stanza IV.

1. ... LISTEN, YE SONS OF THE EARTH, TO YOUR INSTRUCTORS—THE SONS OF THE FIRE (*a*). LEARN THERE IS NEITHER FIRST NOR LAST; FOR ALL IS ONE NUMBER, ISSUED FROM NO-NUMBER (*b*).

(*a*) The terms, the "Sons of the Fire," the "Sons of the Fire-Mist," and the like, require explanation. They are connected with a great primordial and universal mystery, and it is not easy to make it clear. There is a passage in the *Bhagavadgîtâ*, wherein Krishna, speaking symbolically and esoterically, says:

I will state the times ... at which devotees departing do so never to return, or to return. The fire, the flame, the day, the bright fortnight, the six months of the northern solstice, departing ... in these, those who know the Brahman go to the Brahman. Smoke, night, the dark fortnight, the six months of the southern solstice, (dying) in these, the devotee goes to the lunar light and returns. These two paths, bright and dark, are said to be eternal in this world. By the one (a man) goes never to return, by the other he comes back.

Now these terms "fire," "flame," "day," the "bright fortnight," etc., "smoke," "night," and so on, leading only to the end of the Lunar Path, are incomprehensible without a knowledge of Esotericism. These are all *names of various deities* which preside over the cosmo-psychic Powers. We often speak of the Hierarchy of "Flames," of the "Sons of Fire," etc. Shankarâchârya, the greatest of the Esoteric Masters of India, says that Fire means a deity which presides over Time (Kâla). The able translator of the *Bhagavadgîtâ*, Kâshinâth Trimbak Telang, M.A., of Bombay, confesses he has "no clear notion of the meaning of these verses." It seems quite clear, on the contrary, to him who knows the Occult doctrine. With these verses the mystic sense of the solar and lunar symbols are connected. The Pitris are Lunar Deities and our Ancestors, because they *created the physical man*. The Agnishvatta, the Kumâras (the Seven Mystic Sages), are Solar Deities, though they are Pitris also; and these are the "Fashioners of the *Inner* Man." They are "The Sons of Fire," because they are the first Beings, called "Minds," in the Secret Doctrine, evolved from Primordial Fire. "The Lord ... is a consuming fire." "The Lord shall be revealed ... with his mighty angels in flaming fire." The Holy Ghost descended on the Apostles as "cloven tongues like as of fire"; Vishnu will return on Kalkî, the White Horse, as the last Avatâra, amid fire and flames; and Sosiosh will also descend on a White Horse in a "tornado of fire." "And I saw heaven opened, and behold a white horse; and he that sat upon him ... and his name is called the Word of God," amid flaming Fire. Fire is Æther in its purest form, and hence is not regarded as matter, but is the unity of Æther—the second, manifested deity—in its universality. But there are two "Fires," and a distinction is made between them in the Occult teachings. The first, or the
purely *formless* and *invisible* Fire, concealed in the *Central Spiritual Sun*, is spoken of as Triple (metaphysically); while the Fire of the Manifested Cosmos is Septenary, throughout both the Universe and our Solar System. *"The fire of knowledge burns up all action on the plane of illusion,"* says the

Commentary. *"Therefore, those who have acquired it and are emancipated, are called 'Fires'."* Speaking of the *seven* senses, symbolized as Hotris, or Priests, Nârada says in *Anugitâ*: "Thus these seven are the causes of emancipation"; and the translator adds: "It is from these seven from which the Self is to be emancipated. 'I' must mean the Self, not the Brâhmana who speaks."

(*b*) The expression, "all is One Number, issued from No-Number," relates again to that universal and philosophical tenet just explained in the commentary on Shloka 4 of Stanza III. That which is absolute, is of course No-Number; but in its later significance it has an application both in Space and in Time. It means that not only every increment of time is part of a larger increment, up to the most indefinitely prolonged duration conceivable by the human intellect, but also that no manifested thing can be thought of except as part of a whole: the total aggregate being the One Manifested Universe that issues from the Unmanifested or Absolute—called Non-Being, or "No-Number," to distinguish it from Being, or the "One Number."

2. LEARN WHAT WE, WHO DESCEND FROM THE PRIMORDIAL SEVEN, WE, WHO ARE BORN FROM THE PRIMORDIAL FLAME, HAVE LEARNT FROM OUR FATHERS....

This is explained in Book II, and the term, "Primordial Flame," corroborates what is said in the first paragraph of the preceding commentary on Stanza IV.

The distinction between the "Primordial" and the subsequent Seven Builders is that the former are the Ray and direct emanation of the first "Sacred Four," the Tetraktys, that is, the eternally Self-Existent One—eternal in *essence* note well, not in manifestation, and distinct from the Universal One. Latent, during Pralaya, and active, during Manvantara, the "Primordial" proceed from "Father-Mother" (Spirit-Hyle, or Ilus); whereas the other Manifested Quaternary and the Seven proceed from the Mother alone. It is the latter who is the immaculate Virgin-Mother, who is overshadowed, not impregnated, by the Universal Mystery—when she emerges from her state of Laya, or undifferentiated condition. In reality, they are, of course, all one; but their aspects on the various planes of Being are different.

The first Primordial are the highest Beings on the Scale of Existence. They are the Archangels of Christianity, those who refuse to create or rather to multiply—as did Michael in the latter system, and as did the eldest "Mind-born Sons" of Brahmâ (Vedhâs).

3. FROM THE EFFULGENCY OF LIGHT—THE RAY OF THE EVER-DARKNESS—SPRANG IN SPACE THE REÄWAKENED ENERGIES; THE ONE FROM THE EGG, THE SIX, AND THE FIVE (*a*). THEN THE THREE, THE ONE, THE FOUR, THE ONE, THE FIVE—THE TWICE SEVEN, THE SUM TOTAL (*b*). AND THESE ARE THE ESSENCES, THE FLAMES, THE ELEMENTS, THE BUILDERS, THE NUMBERS (*c*), THE ARÛPA, THE RÛPA, AND THE FORCE, OR DIVINE MAN—THE SUM TOTAL. AND FROM THE DIVINE MAN EMANATED THE FORMS, THE SPARKS, THE SACRED ANIMALS (*d*), AND THE MESSENGERS OF THE SACRED FATHERS WITHIN THE HOLY FOUR.

(a) This relates to the Sacred Science of the Numerals; so sacred, indeed, and so important in the study of Occultism that the subject can hardly be skimmed, even in such a large work as the present. It is on the Hierarchies and the correct numbers of these Beings—invisible (to us) except upon very rare occasions—that the mystery of the whole Universe is built. The Kumâras, for instance, are called the "Four"—though in reality seven in number—because Sanaka, Sananda, Sanâtana and Sanatkumâra are the chief Vaidhâtra (their patronymic name), who sprang from the "four-fold mystery." To make the whole clearer, we have to turn for our illustrations to tenets more familiar to some of our readers, namely the Brâhmanical.

According to *Manu*, Hiranyagarbha is Brahmâ, the first *male*, formed by the undiscernible Causeless Cause, in a "Golden Egg resplendent as the Sun," as states the *Hindû Classical Dictionary*; Hiranyagarbha meaning the Golden, or rather the Effulgent, Womb or Egg. The meaning tallies awkwardly with the epithet "male." Surely the esoteric meaning of the sentence is clear enough! In the *Rig Veda* it is said—"THAT, the one Lord of all beings ... the one animating principle of gods and men," arose, in the beginning, in the Golden Womb, Hiranyagarbha—which is the Mundane Egg, or Sphere of our Universe. That Being is surely androgynous, and the allegory of Brahmâ separating into two, and creating in one of his halves (the female Vâch) himself as Virâj, is a proof of it.

"The One from the Egg, the Six and the Five," give the number 1065, the value of the First-born (later on the male and female Brahmâ-Prajâpati), who answers to the numbers 7, and 14, and 21 respectively. The Prajâpati, like the Sephiroth are only seven, including the synthetic Sephira of the Triad from which they spring. Thus from Hiranyagarbha, or Prajâpati, the Triune (the primeval Vedic Trimûrti, Agni, Vâyu, and Sûrya), emanate the other seven, or again ten, if we separate the first three which exist in one, and one in three; all, moreover, being comprehended within that one "Supreme," Parama, called Guhya or "Secret," and Sarvâtman, the "Super-Soul." *"The seven Lords of Being lie concealed in Sarvâtman like thoughts in one brain."* So with the Sephiroth. They are either seven when counting from the upper Triad, headed by Kether, or ten—exoterically. In the *Mahâbhârata*, the Prajâpati are 21 in number, or ten, six, and five (1065), thrice seven.

(b) "The Three, the One, the Four, the One, the Five," in their total—Twice Seven, represent 31415—the numerical Hierarchy of the Dhyân Chohans of various orders, and of the inner or circumscribed world. Placed on the boundary of the great Circle, "Pass Not"—called also the Dhyânipâsha, the "Rope of the Angels," the "Rope" that hedges off the phenomenal from the noumenal Cosmos, which does not fall within the range of our present objective consciousness—this number, when not enlarged by permutation and expansion, is ever 31415, anagrammatically and Kabalistically, being both the number of the Circle and the mystic Svastika, the "Twice Seven" once more; for whatever way the two sets of figures are counted, when added separately, one figure after another, whether crossways from right, or from left, they will always yield fourteen. Mathematically they represent the well-known mathematical formula, that the ratio of the diameter of a circle to the circumference is as 1 to 3.1415, or the value of π (pi), as it is called. This set of figures must have the same meaning, since the 1:314,159 and again 1:3.1415927 are worked out in the secret calculations to express the various cycles and ages of the "First-born," or 311,040,000,000,000 with fractions, and yield the same 1.3415 by a process we are not concerned with at present. And it may be shown that Mr. Ralston Skinner, the author of *The Source of Measures*, reads the Hebrew word Alhim in the same number values—by omitting, as said, the ciphers, and by permutation—13514: since א (a) is 1; ל (l) is 3 (30); ה (h) is 5; י (i) is 1 (10); and מ (m) is 4 (40); and anagrammatically—31415, as explained by him.

Thus, while in the metaphysical world, the Circle with the one central Point in it has no number, and is called Anupâdaka—parentless and numberless, for it can fall under no calculation; in the manifested world, the Mundane Egg or Circle is circumscribed within the groups called the Line, the Triangle, the Pentagram, the second Line and the Square (or 13514); and when the Point has generated a Line, and thus becomes a diameter which stands for the androgynous Logos, then the figures become 31415, or a triangle, a line, a square, a second line, and a pentagram. "*When the Son separates from the Mother he becomes the Father,*" the diameter standing for Nature, or the feminine principle. Therefore it is said: "*In the World of Being, the One Point fructifies the Line, the Virgin Matrix of Kosmos, and the immaculate Mother gives birth to the Form that combines all forms.*" Prajâpati is called the first procreating male, and "his mother's husband." This gives the key-note to all the later "Divine Sons" from "Immaculate Mothers." It is strongly corroborated by the significant fact that Anna, the name of the Mother of the Virgin Mary, now represented by the Roman Catholic Church as having given birth to her daughter in an immaculate way ("Mary conceived without sin"), is derived from the Chaldean Ana, Heaven, or Astral Light, Anima Mundi; whence Anaitia, Devî-Durgâ, the wife of Shiva, is also called Annapurna, and Kanyâ, the Virgin; Umâ-Kanyâ being her esoteric name, and meaning the "Virgin of Light," Astral Light in one of its multitudinous aspects.

(c) The Devas, Pitris, Rishis; the Suras and the Asuras; the Daityas and Âdityas; the Dânavas and Gandharvas, etc., etc., have all their synonyms in our Secret Doctrine, as well as in the *Kabalah* and Hebrew Angelology; but it is useless to give their ancient names, as it would only create confusion. Many of these may be now also found even in the Christian Hierarchy of divine and celestial Powers. All those Thrones and Dominions, Virtues and Principalities, Cherubs, Seraphs and Demons, the various denizens of the Sidereal World, are the modern copies of archaic prototypes. The very symbolism in their names, when transliterated and arranged, in Greek and Latin, are sufficient to show it, as will be proved in several cases further on.

(d) The "Sacred Animals" are found in the *Bible* as well as in the *Kabalah*, and they have their meaning—a very profound one, too—on the page of the origins of Life. In the *Sepher Jetzirah* it is stated that: "God engraved in the Holy Four the Throne of his Glory, the Auphanim , the Seraphim, and the Sacred Animals, as Ministering Angels, and from these he formed his habitation."
The following is the literal translation from the IXth and Xth Sections:

Ten numbers without what? One: the Spirit of the living God ... who liveth in eternities! Voice and Spirit and Word, and this is the Holy Spirit. Two: Air out of Spirit. He designed and hewed therewith twenty-two letters of foundation, three mothers, and seven double and twelve single, and one Spirit out of them. Three: Water out of Spirit; he designed and hewed with them the barren and the void, mud and earth. He designed them as a flower-bed, hewed them as a wall, covered them as a paving. Four: Fire out of Water. He designed and hewed therewith the throne of glory and the wheels, and the seraphim and the holy animals as ministering angels, and of the three He founded his dwelling, as it is said, He makes his angels spirits, and his servants fiery flames!

The words "founded his dwelling" show clearly that in the *Kabalah*, as in India, the Deity was considered as the Universe, and was not, in his origin, the extra-cosmic God he now is.

Thus was the world made "through Three Seraphim—Sepher, Saphar, and Sipur," or "through Number, Numbers, and Numbered." With the astronomical key, these "Sacred Animals" become the signs of the Zodiac.

4. THIS WAS THE ARMY OF THE VOICE, THE DIVINE MOTHER OF THE SEVEN. THE SPARKS OF THE SEVEN ARE SUBJECT TO, AND THE SERVANTS OF, THE FIRST, THE SECOND, THE THIRD, THE FOURTH, THE FIFTH, THE SIXTH, AND THE SEVENTH OF THE SEVEN (*a*). THESE ARE CALLED SPHERES, TRIANGLES, CUBES, LINES AND MODELLERS; FOR THUS STANDS THE ETERNAL NIDâNA—THE OI-HA-HOU (*b*).

(a) This Shloka gives again a brief analysis of the Hierarchies of the Dhyân Chohans, called Devas (Gods) in India, or the Conscious Intelligent Powers in Nature. To this Hierarchy correspond the actual types into which Humanity may be divided; for Humanity, as a whole, is in reality a materialized, though as yet imperfect, expression thereof. The "Army of the Voice" is a term closely connected with the mystery of Sound and Speech, as an effect and corollary of the Cause—Divine Thought. As beautifully expressed by P. Christian, the learned author of *Histoire de la Magie* and *L'Homme Rouge des Tuileries*, the words spoken by, as well as the name of, every individual largely determine his future fate. Why? Because:

When our soul creates or evokes a thought, the representative sign of that thought is self-engraved upon the astral fluid, which is the receptacle and, so to say, the mirror of all the manifestations of being.

The sign expresses the thing: the thing is the virtue of the sign.

To pronounce a word is to evoke a thought, and make it present: the magnetic potency of human speech is the commencement of every manifestation in the Occult World. To utter a Name is not only to define a Being, but to place it under, and condemn it through the emission of the Word to the influence of, one or more Occult potencies. Things are, for every one of us, that which it makes them while naming them. The Word or the speech of every man is, quite unconsciously to himself, a *blessing* or a *curse*; this is why our present ignorance about the properties and attributes of the *idea*, as well as about the attributes and properties of *matter*, is often fatal to us.

Yes, names are either *beneficent* or *maleficent*; they are, in a certain sense, either venomous or health-giving, according to the hidden influences attached by Supreme Wisdom to their elements, that is to say, to the *letters* which compose them, and the *numbers* correlative to these letters.

This is strictly true as an esoteric teaching accepted by all the Eastern Schools of Occultism. In the Sanskrit, as also in the Hebrew and all other alphabets, every letter has its occult meaning and its *rationale*: it is a cause and an effect of a preceding cause, and a combination of these very often produces the most magical effect. The vowels, especially, contain the most occult and formidable potencies. The *Mantras* (magical rather than religious invocations, esoterically) are chanted by the Brâhmans, and so are the rest of the *Vedas* and other Scriptures.

The "Army of the Voice" is the prototype of the "Host of the Logos," or the "Word," of the *Sepher Jetzirah*, called in the Secret Doctrine the "One Number issued from No-Number"—the One Eternal Principle. The Esoteric Theogony begins with the One Manifested (therefore not eternal in its presence and being, if eternal in its essence), the Number of the Numbers and Numbered—the latter proceeding from the Voice, the feminine Vâch, "of the hundred forms," Shatarûpâ, or Nature. It is from this Number, 10, or Creative Nature, the Mother (the Occult cypher, or "0," ever procreating and multiplying in union with the unit "1," or the Spirit of Life), that the whole Universe proceeds.

In the *Anugîtâ*, a conversation is given between a Brâhmana and his wife on the origin of Speech and its Occult properties. The wife asks how Speech came into existence, and which was prior to the other, Speech or Mind. The Brâhmana tells her that the Apâna (*inspirational breath*) becoming lord, changes that intelligence, which does not understand Speech or Words, into the state of Apâna, and thus opens the Mind. Thereupon he tells her a story, a dialogue between Speech and Mind. Both went to the Self of Being (*i.e.*, to the individual Higher Self, as Nîlakantha thinks; to Prajâpati, according to the commentator Arjuna Mishra), and asked him to destroy their doubts, and decide which of them preceded and was superior to the other. To this the Lord said: "Mind (is superior)." But Speech answered the Self of Being, by saying: "I verily yield (you) your desires," meaning that by Speech he acquired what he desired. Thereupon again, the Self told her that there are two Minds, the "movable" and the "immovable." "The immovable is with me," he said, "the movable is in your dominion" (*i.e.* of Speech), on the plane of matter. "To that you are superior."

But inasmuch, O beautiful one, as you came personally to speak to me (in the way you did, *i.e.* proudly), therefore, O Sarasvatî! you shall never speak after (hard) exhalation. The goddess Speech , verily, dwelt always between the Prâna and the Apâna. But, O noble one! going with the Apâna wind , though impelled, ... without the Prâna , she ran up to Prajâpati , saying, "Be pleased, O venerable sir!" Then the Prâna appeared again nourishing Speech. And, therefore, Speech never speaks after (hard) exhalation. It is always noisy or noiseless. Of these two, the noiseless is the superior to the noisy (Speech).... The (Speech) which is produced in the body by means of the Prâna, and which then goes into Apâna and then becoming assimilated with the Udâna ... then finally dwells in the Samâna . So Speech formerly spoke. Hence the Mind is distinguished by reason of its being immovable, and the Goddess (Speech) by reason of her being movable.

The above allegory is at the root of the Occult law, which prescribes silence upon the knowledge of certain secret and invisible things, perceptible only to the spiritual mind (the sixth sense), and which cannot be expressed by "noisy" or uttered speech. This chapter of *Anugîtâ* explains, says Arjuna Mishra, Prânâyâma, or regulation of the breath in Yoga practices. This mode, however, without the previous acquisition of, or at least full understanding of, the two higher senses (of which there are seven, as will be shown), pertains rather to the lower Yoga. The Hatha so called was and still is discountenanced by the Arhats. It is injurious to the health, and alone can never develop into Râja Yoga. This story is quoted to show how inseparably connected in the metaphysics of old, are intelligent beings, or

rather "intelligences," with every sense or function, whether physical or mental. The Occult claim that there are seven senses in man, and in nature, as there are seven states of consciousness, is corroborated in the same work, Chapter vii, on Pratyâhâra (the restraint and regulation of the senses, Prânâyâma being that of the "vital winds" or breath). The Brâhmana, speaking of the institution of the seven sacrificial Priests (Hotris), says: "The nose and the eye, and the tongue, and the skin and the ear as the fifth, mind and understanding are the seven sacrificial priests separately
stationed," which "dwelling in a minute space (still) do not perceive each other," on this sensuous plane, none of them except mind. For mind says: "The nose smells not without me, the eye does not take in colour, etc., etc. I am the eternal chief among all elements. Without me, the senses never shine, like an empty dwelling, or like fires the flames of which are extinct. Without me, all beings, like fuel half dried and half moist, fail to apprehend qualities or objects even with the senses exerting themselves."
This, of course, only with regard to *mind on the sensuous plane*. Spiritual Mind, the upper portion or aspect of
the *impersonal* Manas, takes no cognizance of the senses in physical man. How well the ancients were acquainted with the correlation of forces, and all the recently discovered phenomena of mental and physical faculties and functions, and with many more mysteries also—may be found in reading Chapters vii and viii of this priceless work in philosophy and mystic learning. See the quarrel of the senses about their respective superiority and their taking the Brahman, the Lord of all creatures, for their arbiter. "You are all greatest and not greatest. You are all possessed of one another's qualities. All are greatest in their own spheres and all support one another. There is one unmoving . That one is my own Self, accumulated in numerous (forms)."

This Breath, Voice, Self or Wind (Pneuma?), is the Synthesis of the Seven Senses, *noumenally* all minor deities, and esoterically—the *Septenary* and the "Army of the Voice."

(*b*) Next we see Cosmic Matter scattering and forming itself into Elements; grouped into the mystic Four within the fifth Element—Ether, the "lining" of Âkâsha, the Anima Mundi, or Mother of Cosmos. "Dots, Lines, Triangles, Cubes, Circles" and finally "Spheres"—why or how? Because, says the Commentary, such is the first law of Nature, and because Nature geometrizes universally in all her manifestations. There is an inherent law—not only in the primordial, but also in the manifested matter of our phenomenal plane—by which Nature correlates her geometrical forms, and later, also, her compound elements, and in which also there is no place for accident or chance. It is a fundamental law in Occultism, that there is no rest or cessation of motion in Nature. That which seems rest is only the change of one form into another, the change of substance going hand in hand with that of form—so at least we are taught in Occult physics, which thus seem to have anticipated the discovery of the "conservation of matter" by a considerable time. Says the ancient Commentary to Stanza IV:

The Mother is the fiery Fish of Life. She scatters her Spawn and the Breath heats and quickens it. The Grains are soon attracted to each other and form the Curds in the Ocean. The larger lumps coalesce and receive new Spawn—in fiery Dots, Triangles and Cubes, which ripen, and at the appointed time some of the lumps detach themselves and assume spheroidal form, a process which they effect only when not interfered with by the others. After which, Law No. —— comes into operation. Motion becomes the Whirlwind and sets them into rotation.

5. THE OI-HA-HOU, WHICH IS DARKNESS, THE BOUNDLESS, OR THE NO-NUMBER, ÂDI-NIDÂNA SVABHÂVAT, THE :
I. THE ÂDI-SANAT, THE NUMBER, FOR HE IS ONE (*a*).
II. THE VOICE OF THE WORD, SVABHÂVAT, THE NUMBERS, FOR HE IS ONE AND NINE.
III. THE "FORMLESS SQUARE".
AND THESE THREE, ENCLOSED WITHIN THE , ARE THE SACRED FOUR; AND THE TEN ARE THE ARÛPA UNIVERSE (*b*). THEN COME THE SONS, THE SEVEN FIGHTERS, THE ONE, THE EIGHTH LEFT OUT, AND HIS BREATH WHICH IS THE LIGHT-MAKER (*c*).

(*a*) "Âdi-Sanat," translated literally, is the First or "Primeval Ancient," a name which identifies the Kabalistic "Ancient of Days" and the "Holy Aged" (Sephira and Adam Kadmon) with Brahmâ, the Creator, called also Sanat among his other names and titles.

"Svabhâvat" is the mystic Essence, the plastic Root of physical Nature—"Numbers" when manifested; the "Number," in its Unity of Substance, on the highest plane. The name is of Buddhist use and a synonym for the four-fold Anima Mundi, the Kabalistic Archetypal World, from whence proceed the Creative, Formative, and Material Worlds; and the Scintillæ or Sparks—the various other worlds contained in the last three. The Worlds are all subject to Rulers or Regents—Rishis and Pitris with the Hindûs, Angels with the Jews and Christians, Gods with the Ancients in general.

(*b*) "." This means that the "Boundless Circle," the zero, becomes a number, only when one of the other nine figures precedes it, and thus manifests its value and potency; the "Word" or Logos, in union with "Voice" and Spirit (the expression and source of Consciousness), standing for the nine figures, and thus forming, with the cypher, the Decad which contains in itself all the Universe. The Triad forms the Tetraktys, or "Sacred Four," within the Circle, the Square within the Circle being the most potent of all the magical figures.

(*c*) The "One Rejected" is the Sun of our system. The exoteric version may be found in the oldest Sanskrit Scriptures. In the *Rig Veda*, Aditi, the "Boundless" or Infinite Space—translated by Prof. Max Müller, "the visible infinite, visible by the naked eye (!!); the endless expanse beyond the earth, beyond the clouds, beyond the sky"—is the equivalent of "Mother-Space," coëval with "Darkness." She is very properly called the "Mother of the Gods," Deva-Mâtri, as it is from her cosmic matrix that all the heavenly bodies of our system were born—sun and planets. Thus she is described, allegorically, in this wise: "*Eight sons were born from the body of Aditi; she approached the gods with seven, but cast away the eighth,*

Mârttânda," our sun. The seven sons called the Adityas are, cosmically or astronomically, the seven planets; and the sun being excluded from their number shows plainly that the Hindûs may have known, and in fact knew, of a seventh planet, without calling it Uranus. But esoterically and theologically, so to say, the Adityas, in their primitive most ancient meanings, are the eight, and twelve great gods of the Hindû Pantheon. "The Seven allow the mortals to see their dwellings, but show themselves only to the Arhats," says an old proverb; "their dwellings" standing here for the planets. The ancient Commentary gives the following allegory and explains it:

Eight houses were built by Mother: eight houses for her eight Divine Sons; four large and four small ones. Eight brilliant Suns, according to their age and merits. Bal-i-lu was not satisfied, though his house was the largest. He began as the huge elephants do. He breathed into his stomach the vital airs of his brothers. He sought to devour them. The larger four were far away; far, on the margin of their kingdom. They were not robbed, and laughed. Do your worst, Sir, you cannot reach us, they said. But the smaller wept. They complained to the Mother. She exiled Bal-i-lu to the centre of her kingdom, from whence he could not move. he watches and threatens. He pursues them, turning slowly round himself; they turning swiftly from him, and he following from afar the direction in which his brothers move on the path that encircles their houses. From that day he feeds on the sweat of the Mother's body. He fills himself with her breath and refuse. Therefore, she rejected him.

Thus the "Rejected Son" being our Sun, evidently, as shown above, the "Son-Suns" refer not only to our planets but to the heavenly bodies in general. Sûrya, himself only a reflection of the Central Spiritual Sun, is the prototype of all those bodies that evolved after him. In the *Vedas* he is called Loka-Chakshuh, the "Eye of the World" (our planetary world), and he is one of the three chief deities. He is called indifferently the Son of Dyaus or of Aditi, because no distinction is made with reference to, or scope allowed for, the esoteric meaning. Thus he is depicted as drawn by seven horses, and by one horse with

seven heads; the former referring to his seven planets, the latter to their one common origin from the One Cosmic Element.
This "One Element" is called
figuratively "Fire." The *Vedas* teach that "fire verily is all the deities."
The meaning of the allegory is plain, for we have both the Dzyan Commentary and Modern Science to explain it, though the two differ in more than one particular. The Occult Doctrine rejects the hypothesis born of the Nebular Theory, that the (seven) great planets have evolved from the Sun's central mass, of this our visible Sun, at any rate. The first condensation of cosmic matter of course took place about a central nucleus, its parent Sun; but our Sun, it is taught, merely detached itself earlier than all the others, as the rotating mass contracted, and is their elder, bigger "brother" therefore, not their "father." The eight Adityas, the "gods," are all formed from the eternal substance (cometary matter—the Mother), or the "world-stuff," which is both the fifth and the sixth Cosmic Principle, the Upâdhi, or Basis, of the Universal Soul, just as in man, the Microcosm, Manas is the Upâdhi of Buddhi.
There is a whole poem on the pregenetic battles fought by the growing planets before the final formation of Cosmos, thus accounting for the seemingly disturbed position of the systems of several planets; the plane of the satellites of some (of Neptune and Uranus, for instance, of which the ancients knew nothing, it is said) being tilted over, thus giving them an appearance of retrograde motion. These planets are called the Warriors, the Architects, and are accepted by the Roman Church as the leaders of the heavenly Hosts, thus showing the same traditions. Having evolved from Cosmic Space, the Sun, we are taught—before the final formation of the primaries and the annulation of the planetary nebulæ—drew into the depths of his mass all the cosmic vitality he could, threatening to engulf his
weaker "Brothers," before the law of attraction and repulsion was finally adjusted; after which, he began feeding on "the Mother's refuse and sweat"; in other words, on those portions of Æther (the "Breath of the Universal Soul"), of the existence and constitution of which Science is as yet absolutely ignorant. As a theory of this kind has been propounded by Sir William

Grove, who theorizes that the systems "are gradually changing by atmospheric additions or subtractions, or by accretions and diminutions arising from nebular substance," and again that "the sun may condense gaseous matter as it travels in space, and so heat may be produced"—the archaic teaching seems scientific enough, even in this age. Mr. W. Mattieu Williams suggested that the diffused matter or Ether, which is the recipient of the heat radiations of the Universe, is thereby drawn into the depths of the solar mass; expelling thence the previously condensed and thermally exhausted Ether, it becomes compressed and gives up its heat, to be in turn itself driven out in a rarefied and cooled state, to absorb a fresh supply of heat, which he supposes to be in this way taken up by the Ether, and again concentrated and redistributed by the Suns of the Universe.

This is about as close an approximation to the Occult teachings as Science ever imagined; for Occultism explains it by the "dead breath," given back by Mârttânda, and his feeding on the "sweat and refuse" of "Mother Space." What could affect Neptune, Saturn and Jupiter, but little, would have killed such comparatively small "Houses" as Mercury, Venus and Mars. As Uranus was not known before the end of the eighteenth century, the name of the fourth planet mentioned in the allegory must remain to us, so far, a mystery.

The "Breath" of all the "Seven" is said to be Bhâskara, the Light-Maker, because they (the planets) were all comets and suns in their origin. They evolve into manvantaric life from Primeval Chaos (now the noumenon of irresolvable nebulæ), by aggregation and accumulation of the primary differentiations of eternal Matter, according to the beautiful expression in the Commentary, *"Thus the Sons of Light clothed themselves in the fabric of Darkness."* They are called allegorically the "Heavenly Snails," on account of their (to us) formless Intelligences inhabiting unseen their starry and planetary homes, and so to speak, carrying them, as the snails do, along with themselves in their revolution. The doctrine of a common origin for all the heavenly bodies and planets was, as we see, inculcated by the archaic astronomers, before Kepler, Newton, Leibnitz, Kant, Herschel and Laplace. Heat (the "Breath"), Attraction and Repulsion—the three great factors of Motion—are the conditions under which all the members of this primitive family are born, develop, and die; to be reborn after a Night of Brahmâ, during which eternal Matter relapses periodically into its primary undifferentiated state. The most attenuated gases can give no idea of its nature to the modern Physicist. Centres of Forces at first, the invisible Sparks, or primordial Atoms, differentiate into Molecules, and become Suns—passing gradually into objectivity—gaseous, radiant, cosmic, the one "Whirlwind" (or Motion) finally giving the impulse to the form, and the initial motion, regulated and sustained by the never-resting "Breaths"—the Dhyân Chohans.

6. ... THEN THE SECOND SEVEN, WHO ARE THE LIPIKA, PRODUCED BY THE THREE. THE REJECTED SON IS ONE. THE "SON-SUNS" ARE COUNTLESS.

The "Lipika," from the word *lipi*, "writing," means literally the "Scribes." Mystically, these Divine Beings are connected with Karma, the Law of Retribution, for they are the Recorders, or Annalists, who impress on the (to us) invisible tablets of the Astral Light, "the great picture-gallery of eternity"—a faithful record of every act, and even thought, of man; of all that was, is, or ever will be, in the phenomenal Universe. As said in *Isis Unveiled*, this divine and unseen canvas is the *Book of Life*. As it is the Lipika who project into objectivity from the passive Universal Mind the ideal plan of the Universe, upon which the "Builders" reconstruct the Kosmos after every Pralaya, it is they who stand parallel to the Seven Angels of the Presence, whom the Christians recognize in the Seven "Planetary Spirits," or the "Spirits of the Stars"; and thus it is they who are the direct amanuenses of the Eternal Ideation—or, as Plato calls it, the "Divine Thought." The Eternal Record is no fantastic dream, for we meet with the same records in the world of gross matter. As Dr. Draper says:

A shadow never falls upon a wall without leaving thereupon a permanent trace which might be made visible by resorting to proper processes.... The portraits of our friends or landscape-views may be hidden on the sensitive surface from the eye, but they are ready to make their appearance as soon as proper developers are resorted to. A spectre is concealed on a silver or a glassy surface, until, by our necromancy, we make it come forth into the visible world. Upon the walls of our most private apartments, where we think the eye of intrusion is altogether shut out, and our retirement can never be profaned, there exist the vestiges of our acts, silhouettes of whatever we have done.

Drs. Jevons and Babbage believe that every thought displaces the particles of the brain and, setting them in motion, scatters them throughout the universe: they also think that "each particle of the existing matter must be a register of all that has happened." Thus the ancient doctrine has begun to acquire rights of citizenship in the speculations of the scientific world.

The forty "Assessors," who stand in the region of Amenti as the accusers of the Soul before Osiris, belong to the same class of deities as the Lipika, and might stand as parallels, were not the Egyptian gods so little understood in their esoteric meaning. The Hindû Chitragupta who reads out the account of every Soul's life from his register, called Agra-Sandhânî; the Assessors who read theirs from the Heart of the Defunct, which becomes an open book before either Yama, Minos, Osiris, or Karma—are all so many copies of, and variants from, the Lipika and their Astral Records. Nevertheless, the Lipika are not deities connected with Death, but with Life Eternal.

Connected as the Lipika are with the destiny of every man, and the birth of every child, whose life is already traced in the Astral Light—not fatalistically, but only because the Future, like the Past, is ever alive in the Present—they may also be said to exercise an influence on the Science of Horoscopy. We must admit the truth of the latter whether we will or not. For, as observed by one of the modern professors of Astrology:

Now that photography has revealed to us the chemical influence of the sidereal system, by fixing on the sensitized plate of the apparatus milliards of stars and planets that had hitherto baffled the efforts of the most powerful telescopes to discover, it becomes easier to understand how our solar system can, at the birth of a child, influence his brain—

virgin of any impression—in a definite manner and according to the presence on the zenith of such or another zodiacal constellation.

Stanza V.

1. THE PRIMORDIAL SEVEN, THE FIRST SEVEN BREATHS OF THE DRAGON OF WISDOM, PRODUCE IN THEIR TURN FROM THEIR HOLY CIRCUMGYRATING BREATHS THE FIERY WHIRLWIND.

This is, perhaps, the most difficult of all the Stanzas to explain. Its language is comprehensible only to him who is thoroughly versed in Eastern allegory, and its purposely obscure phraseology. The question will surely be asked: Do the Occultists believe in all these "Builders," "Lipika," and "Sons of Light," as Entities, or are they merely imagery? To this the answer is given as plainly: After due allowance for the imagery of personified Powers, we must admit the existence of these Entities, if we would not reject the existence of Spiritual Humanity within physical mankind. For the hosts of these Sons of Light, the Mind-born Sons of the first manifested Ray of the Unknown All, are the very root of Spiritual Man. Unless we want to believe the unphilosophical dogma of a specially created soul for every human birth—a fresh supply of these pouring in daily, since "Adam"—we have to admit the Occult teachings. This will be explained in its place. Let us see, now, what may be the meaning of this Occult Stanza.

The Doctrine teaches that, in order to become a divine, fully conscious God—aye, even the highest—the Spiritual Primeval Intelligences must pass through the human stage. And when we say human, this does not apply merely to our terrestrial humanity, but to the mortals that inhabit any world, *i.e.*, to those Intelligences that have reached the appropriate equilibrium between matter and spirit, as *we* have now, ever since the middle point of the Fourth Root Race of the Fourth Round was passed. Each Entity must have won for itself the right of becoming divine, through self-experience. Hegel, the great German thinker, must have known or sensed intuitively this truth, when he said, that the Unconscious evolved the

Universe only "in the hope of attaining clear self-consciousness," in other words, of becoming Man; for this is also the secret meaning of the oft recurring Purânic phrase, of Brahmâ being constantly "moved by the desire to create." This explains also the hidden Kabalistic meaning of the saying: "The Breath becomes a stone; the stone, a plant; the plant, an animal; the animal, a man; the man, a spirit; and the spirit, a god." The Mind-born Sons, the Rishis, the Builders, etc., were all Men—of whatever forms and shapes—in other worlds and in preceding Manvantaras.

This subject being so very mystical, it is most difficult to explain it in all its details and bearings; for the whole mystery of evolutionary creation is contained therein. A sentence or two in the Shloka vividly recalls to mind similar sentences in the *Kabalah* and the phraseology of the King Psalmist. Both, when speaking of God, show him making the wind his messenger and his "ministers a flaming fire." But in the Esoteric Doctrine it is used figuratively. The "Fiery Whirl-wind" is the incandescent cosmic dust which only follows magnetically, as the iron filings follow the magnet, the directing thought of the "Creative Forces." Yet, this cosmic dust is something more; for every atom in the Universe has the potentiality of self-consciousness in it, and is, like the Monads of Leibnitz, a Universe in itself, and *for* itself. *It is an atom and an angel.*

In this connection it should be noted that one of the luminaries of the modern Evolutionist School, Mr. A. R. Wallace, when discussing the inadequacy of "natural selection" as the sole factor in the development of physical man, practically concedes the whole point here discussed. He holds that the evolution of man was directed and furthered by superior Intelligences, whose agency is a necessary factor in the scheme of Nature. But once the operation of these Intelligences is admitted in one place, it is only a logical deduction to extend it still further. No hard and fast line can be drawn.

2. THEY MAKE OF HIM THE MESSENGER OF THEIR WILL (*a*). THE DZYU BECOMES FOHAT: THE SWIFT SON OF THE DIVINE SONS, WHOSE

Sons are the Lipika, runs circular errands. Fohat is the Steed, and the Thought is the Rider. He passes like lightning through the fiery clouds (*b*); takes Three, and Five, and Seven Strides through the Seven Regions above, and the Seven below. He lifts his Voice, and calls the innumerable Sparks, and joins them together (*c*).

(*a*) This shows the "Primordial Seven" using for their Vehicle, (Vâhana, or the manifested subject which becomes the symbol of the Power directing it) Fohat, called in consequence, the "Messenger of their Will"—the "Fiery Whirlwind."

(*b*) "Dzyu becomes Fohat"—the expression itself shows it. Dzyu is the one Real (Magical) Knowledge, or Occult Wisdom; which, dealing with eternal truths and primal causes, becomes almost omnipotence when applied in the right direction. Its antithesis is Dzyu-mi, that which deals with illusions and false appearances only, as in our exoteric modern sciences. In this case, Dzyu is the expression of the collective Wisdom of the Dhyâni-Buddhas.

As the reader is supposed not to be acquainted with the Dhyâni-Buddhas, it is as well to say at once that, *according to the Orientalists*, there are five Dhyânis who are the Celestial Buddhas, of whom the Human Buddhas are the manifestations in the world of form and matter. Esoterically, however, the Dhyâni-Buddhas are seven, of whom five only have hitherto manifested, and two are to come in the Sixth and Seventh Root-Races. They are, so to speak, the eternal prototypes of the Buddhas who appear on this earth, each of whom has his particular divine prototype. So, for instance, Amitâbha is the Dhyâni-Buddha of Gautama Shâkyamuni, manifesting through him whenever this great Soul incarnates on earth as He did in Tzonkha-pa. As the synthesis of the seven Dhyâni-Buddhas, Avalokiteshvara was the first Buddha (the Logos), and Amitâbha is the inner "God" of Gautama, who, in China, is called Amida (Buddha). They are, as Prof. Rhys Davids correctly states, "the glorious counterparts in the mystic world, free from the debasing conditions of this material life," of every earthly mortal Buddha—the liberated Mânushi-Buddhas appointed to govern the Earth in this Round. They are the "Buddhas of Contemplation," and are all Anupâdaka (parentless), *i.e.*, self-born of the divine essence. The exoteric teaching—which says that every Dhyâni-Buddha has the faculty of creating from himself an equally celestial son, a Dhyâni-Bodhisattva, who, after the decease of the Mânushi-Buddha, has to carry out the work of the latter—rests on the fact that, owing to the highest Initiation performed by one overshadowed by the "Spirit of Buddha"—who is credited by the Orientalists with having created the five Dhyâni-Buddhas!—a candidate becomes virtually a Bodhisattva, created such by the High Initiator.

(*c*) Fohat, being one of the most, if not the most important character in Esoteric cosmogony, should be minutely described. As in the oldest Grecian cosmogony, which differed widely from the later mythology, Eros is the third person in the primeval trinity, Chaos, Gæa, Eros—answering to the Kabalistic Trinity, Ain Suph, the Boundless All (for Chaos is Space, from χαίνω, to open wide, to be void), Shekinah and the Ancient of Days, or the Holy Ghost—so Fohat is one thing in the yet Unmanifested Universe, and another in the phenomenal and Cosmic World. In the latter, he is that occult, electric, vital power, which, under the Will of the Creative Logos, unites and brings together all forms, giving them the first impulse, which in time becomes law. But in the Unmanifested Universe, Fohat is no more this, than Eros is the later brilliant winged Cupid, or Love. Fohat has naught to do with Cosmos yet, since Cosmos is not born, and the Gods still sleep in the bosom of "Father-Mother." He is an abstract philosophical idea. He produces nothing yet by himself; he is simply that potential creative Power, in virtue of whose action the Noumenon of all future phenomena divides, so to speak, but to reunite in a mystic supersensuous act, and emit the creative Ray. When the "Divine Son" breaks forth, then Fohat becomes the propelling force, the active Power which causes the One to become Two and Three—on the cosmic plane of manifestation. The triple One differentiates into the Many, and then Fohat is transformed into that force which brings together the elemental atoms, and makes them aggregate and combine. We find an echo of this primeval teaching in early

Greek mythology. Erebus and Nux are born out of Chaos, and, under the action of Eros, give birth in their turn to Æther and Hemera, the light of the superior and the light of the inferior, or terrestrial, regions. Darkness generates light. Compare in the *Purânas* Brahmâ's Will or "Desire" to create; and in the Phœnician cosmogony of Sanchuniathon the doctrine that Desire, πόθος, is the principle of creation.

Fohat is closely related to the "One Life." From the Unknown One, the Infinite Totality, the Manifested One, or the periodical, Manvantaric Deity, emanates; and this is the Universal Mind, which, separated from its Fountain-Source, is the Demiurge or the Creative Logos of the Western Kabalists, and the Four-faced Brahmâ of the Hindû religion. In its totality, viewed, in the Esoteric doctrine, from the standpoint of manifested Divine Thought, it represents the Hosts of the higher Creative Dhyân Chohans. Simultaneously with the evolution of the Universal Mind, the Concealed Wisdom of Adi-Buddha—the One Supreme and Eternal—manifests itself as Avalokiteshvara (or Manifested Îshvara), which is the Osiris of the Egyptians, the Ahura-Mazda of the Zoroastrians, the Heavenly Man of the Hermetic philosophers, the Logos of the Platonists, and the Âtman of the Vedântins. By the action of the Manifested Wisdom, or Mahat—represented by these innumerable centres of spiritual energy in the Kosmos—the Reflection of the Universal Mind, which is Cosmic Ideation and the Intellectual Force accompanying such Ideation, becomes objectively the Fohat of the Buddhist esoteric philosopher. Fohat, running along the seven principles of Âkâsha, acts upon manifested Substance, or the One Element, as declared above, and, by differentiating it into various centres of energy, sets in motion the law of Cosmic Evolution, which, in obedience to the Ideation of the Universal Mind, brings into existence all the various states of being in the manifested Solar System.

The Solar System, brought into existence by these agencies, consists of Seven Principles, like everything else within these centres. Such is the teaching of the Trans-Himâlayan

Esotericism. Every philosophy, however, has its own way of dividing these principles.

Fohat, then, is the personified electric vital power, the transcendental binding unity of all cosmic energies, on the unseen as on the manifested planes, the action of which resembles—on an immense scale—that of a living Force created by Will, in those phenomena where the seemingly subjective acts on the seemingly objective, and propels it to action. Fohat is not only the living Symbol and Container of that Force, but is looked upon by the Occultists as an Entity; the forces it acts upon being cosmic, human and terrestrial, and exercising their influence on all these planes respectively. On the earthly plane, its influence is felt in the magnetic and active force generated by the strong desire of the magnetizer. On the cosmic, it is present in the constructive power that, in the formation of things—from the planetary system down to the glow-worm and simple daisy—carries out the plan in the mind of Nature, or in the Divine Thought, with regard to the development and growth of a particular thing. It is, metaphysically, the objectivized Thought of the Gods, the "Word made flesh" on a lower scale, and the messenger of cosmic and human Ideation; the active force in Universal Life. In its secondary aspect, Fohat is the Solar Energy, the electric vital fluid, and the preserving Fourth Principle, the Animal Soul of Nature, so to say, or—Electricity.

In 1882, the President of the Theosophical Society, Col. Olcott, was taken to task for asserting in one of his lectures that Electricity is matter. Such, nevertheless, is the teaching of the Occult Doctrine. "Force," "Energy," may be better names for it, so long as European Science knows so little about its true nature; yet matter it is, as much as Ether is matter, since it is as atomic, though indeed several removes from Ether. It seems ridiculous to argue that because a thing is imponderable to Science, therefore it cannot be called matter. Electricity is "immaterial," in the sense that its molecules are not subject to perception and experiment; yet it may be—and Occultism says it is—atomic; therefore it is matter. But even supposing it were unscientific to speak of it in such terms, once Electricity is called in Science a source of Energy, Energy simply, and a Force—

where is that Force or that Energy which can be thought of without thinking of matter? Maxwell, a mathematician and one of the greatest authorities upon Electricity and its phenomena, said, years ago, that Electricity was matter, not motion merely. "If we accept the hypothesis that the elementary substances are composed of atoms, we cannot avoid concluding that electricity also, positive as well as negative, is divided into definite elementary portions, which behave like atoms of electricity." We will go further than this, and assert that Electricity is not only Substance, but that it is an emanation from an Entity, which is neither God nor Devil, but one of the numberless Entities that rule and guide our world, according to the eternal Law of Karma.

To return to Fohat, it is connected with Vishnu and Sûrya in the early character of the former God; for Vishnu is not a high God in the *Rig Veda*. The name Vishnu is from the root *vish*, "to pervade," and Fohat is called the "Pervader" and the Manufacturer, because he shapes the atoms from crude material. In the sacred texts of the *Rig Veda*, Vishnu is also "a manifestation of the Solar Energy, and is described as striding through the seven regions of the Universe in three steps," the Vedic God having little in common with the Vishnu of later times. Therefore the two are identical in this particular feature, and one is the copy of the other.

The Three and Seven "Strides" refer to the seven spheres inhabited by man, in the Esoteric Doctrine, as well as to the seven regions of the Earth. Notwithstanding the frequent objections made by would-be Orientalists, the Seven Worlds, or Spheres, of our Planetary Chain are distinctly referred to in the exoteric Hindû scriptures. But how strangely all these numbers are connected with like numbers in other cosmogonies and with their symbols, can be seen from the comparisons and parallelisms made by students of old religions. The "three strides of Vishnu," through the "seven regions of the Universe," of the *Rig Veda*, have been variously explained by commentators as meaning fire, lightning and the sun, cosmically, and as having been taken in the earth, the atmosphere, and the sky; more philosophically—and in the astronomical sense, very correctly—they are explained by Aurnavâbha as being the various positions of the sun, rising, noon, and setting. Esoteric Philosophy alone explains it clearly, though the *Zohar* has laid it down very philosophically and comprehensively. It is plainly demonstrated therein that in the beginning the Elohim (Alhim) were called Achad, "One," or the "Deity, One in Many," a very simple idea in a pantheistic conception—pantheistic in its philosophical sense, of course. Then came the change, "Jehovah is Elohim," thus unifying the multiplicity and taking the first step towards Monotheism. Now to the query, "How is Jehovah Elohim?" the answer is, "By Three Steps" from below. The meaning is plain. The Steps are symbols, and emblematic, mutually and correlatively, of Spirit, Soul and Body (Man); of the Circle, transformed into Spirit, the Soul of the World and its Body (or Earth). Stepping out of the Circle of Infinity, that no man comprehendeth, Ain Suph—the Kabalistic synonym for Parabrahman, for the Zeroâna Akerne, of the Mazdeans, or for any other "Unknowable"—becomes "One" (the Achad, the Eka, the Ahu); then he (or it) is transformed by evolution into the "One in Many," the Dhyâni-Buddhas or the Elohim, or again the Amshaspends, his third Step being taken into the generation of the flesh, or Man. And from Man, or Jah-Hovah, "male-female," the *inner* divine entity becomes, on the metaphysical plane, once more the Elohim.

The numbers 3, 5, and 7 are prominent in speculative Masonry, as shown in *Isis Unveiled*. A Mason writes:
There are the 3, 5, and 7 steps to show a circular walk. The three faces of 3, 3; 5, 3; and 7, 3; etc., etc. Sometimes it comes in this form: 753/2 = 376.5, and 7535/2 = 3817.5, and the ratio of 20612/6561 feet for cubit measure gives the Great Pyramid measures.

Three, five and seven are mystical numbers, and the last and the first are as greatly honoured by Masons as by Parsis—the Triangle being a symbol of Deity everywhere. As a matter of course, Doctors of Divinity—Cassel, for instance—show the *Zohar* explaining and supporting the Christian Trinity(!). It is the latter, however, that had its origin from the , in the archaic Occultism and Symbology of the Heathen. The Three

Strides relate metaphysically to the descent of Spirit into Matter, of the Logos falling as a ray into the spirit, then into the soul, and finally into the human physical form of man, in which it becomes Life.

The Kabalistic idea is identical with the Esotericism of the archaic period. This Esotericism is the common property of all, and belongs neither to the Âryan Fifth Race, nor to any of its numerous sub-races. It cannot be claimed by the Turanians, so-called, the Egyptians, Chinese, Chaldeans, or by any of the seven divisions of the Fifth Root Race, but really belongs to the Third and Fourth Root Races, whose descendants we find in the Seed of the Fifth, the earliest Âryans. The Circle was with every nation the symbol of the Unknown—"Boundless Space," the abstract garb of an ever present abstraction—the Incognizable Deity. It represents limitless Time in Eternity. The Zeroâna Akerne is also the "Boundless Circle of Unknown Time," from which Circle issues the radiant Light—the Universal Sun, or Ormazd—and the latter is identical with Cronus, in his Æolian form, that of a Circle. For the Circle is Sar and Saros, or Cycle. It was the Babylonian God whose circular horizon was the visible symbol of the invisible, while the Sun was the One Circle from which proceeded the cosmic orbs, of which he was considered the leader. Zeroâna, is the Chakra, or Circle, of Vishnu, the mysterious emblem which is, according to the definition of a Mystic, "a curve of such a nature that as to any, the least possible, part thereof, if the curve be protracted either way, it will proceed and finally reënter upon itself, and form one and the same curve—or that which we call the circle." No better definition could thus be given of the natural symbol and the evident nature of Deity, which having its circumference everywhere (the boundless) has, therefore, its central point also everywhere; in other words, is in every point of the Universe. The invisible Deity is thus also the Dhyân Chohans, or the Rishis, the primitive seven, and the nine, without, and ten, including, their synthetical unit, from which IT steps into Man.

Returning to Commentary 4 of Stanza IV, the reader now will understand why, while the Trans-Himâlayan Chakra has inscribed within it —triangle, first line, square, second line, and a pentacle with a point in the centre, either thus or some other variation—the Kabalistic Circle of the Elohim reveals, when the letters of the word אלהים (Alhim or Elohim) are read numerically, the famous numerals 13514, or anagrammatically 31415—the astronomical π (pi), or the hidden meaning of the Dhyâni-Buddhas, of the Gebers, the Giburim, the Kabeiri, and the Elohim, all signifying "Great Men," "Titans," "Heavenly Men," and, on earth, "Giants."

The Seven was a Sacred Number with every nation; but none applied it to more physiologically materialistic uses than the Hebrews. With them 7 was preëminently the generative number, and 9 the male causative one, forming as shown by the Kabalists the otz, עצ (70, 90), or "the Tree of the Garden of Eden," the "double hermaphrodite rod" of the Fourth Race. This was the symbol of the "Holy of Holies," the 3 and the 4 of sexual separation. Nearly every one of the 22 Hebrew letters are merely phallic symbols. Of the two letters—as shown above—one, the *ayin*, is a negative female letter, symbolically an eye; the the other a male letter, *tzâ*, a *fish*-hook or dart. Whereas with the Hindûs and Âryans generally, the significance was manifold, and related almost entirely to purely metaphysical and astronomical truths. Their Rishis and Gods, their Demons and Heroes, have historical and ethical meanings.
Yet we are told by a Kabalist, who, in a work not yet published, contrasts the *Kabalah* and *Zohar* with Âryan Esotericism, that:

The Hebrew clear, short, terse and exact, modes far and beyond measure surpass the toddling word-talk of the Hindûs—just as by parallelisms the Psalmist says, "My mouth speaks with my tongue, I know not thy numbers" (lxxi., 15).... The Hindû glyph shows by its insufficiency in the large admixture of adventitious sides the same borrowed plumage that the Greeks (the lying Greeks) had, and that Masonry has: which, in the rough monosyllabic (and apparent) poverty of the Hebrew, shows the latter to have come down from a far more remote antiquity than any of these, and to have been the source , or nearer the old original source than any of them.

This is entirely erroneous. Our learned brother and correspondent judges the Hindû religious systems apparently by their *Shâstras* and *Purânas*, probably the latter, and in their modern translations moreover, which disfigure them out of all recognition. It is to their philosophical systems that we have to turn, to their esoteric teaching, if we would make a point of comparison. No doubt the symbology of the *Pentateuch*, and even of the *New Testament*, comes from the same source. But surely the Pyramid of Cheops, whose measurements are all found, by Professor Piazzi Smyth, repeated in Solomon's alleged and mythical Temple, is not of a later date than the Mosaic books? Hence, if there is any such great identity as is claimed, it must be due to servile copying on the part of the Jews, not on that of the Egyptians. The glyphs of the Jews—and even their language, the Hebrew—are not original. They are borrowed from the Egyptians, from whom Moses got his Wisdom; from the Coptic, the probable kinsman, if not parent, of the old Phœnician and from the Hyksos, their (alleged) ancestors, as Josephus shows. Aye; but who are the Hyksos shepherds? And who the Egyptians? History knows nothing of the question, and speculates and theorizes out of the depths of the respective consciousnesses of her historians. "Khamism, or old Coptic, is from Western Asia, and contains some germ of the Semitic, thus bearing witness to the primitive cognate unity of the Âryan and Semitic races," says Bunsen, who places the great events in Egypt 9,000 years B.C. The fact is that in archaic Esotericism and Âryan thought we find a grand philosophy, whereas in the Hebrew records we find only the most surprising ingenuity in inventing apotheoses for phallic worship and sexual theogony.

That the Âryans never made their religion rest solely on physiological symbols, as the old Hebrews have done, may be seen in the exoteric Hindû Scriptures. That these accounts, also, are blinds is shown by their contradicting each other, a different explanation being found in almost every *Purâna* and epic poem. Read esoterically, however, they will all yield the same meaning. Thus one account enumerates seven worlds, exclusive of the nether worlds, also seven in number; these fourteen upper and nether worlds have nothing to do with the classification of the Septenary Chain and belong to the purely ethereal, invisible worlds. These will be noticed elsewhere. Suffice it for the present to show that they are purposely referred to as though they belonged to the Chain. "Another enumeration calls the seven worlds earth, sky, heaven, middle region, place of birth, mansion of the blest, and abode of truth; placing the Sons of Brahmâ in the sixth division, and stating the fifth, or Jana-loka, to be that where animals destroyed in the general conflagration are born again." Some real Esoteric teaching is given in the subsequent chapters on Symbolism. He who is prepared for it will understand the hidden meaning.

3. HE IS THEIR GUIDING SPIRIT AND LEADER. WHEN HE COMMENCES WORK, HE SEPARATES THE SPARKS OF THE LOWER KINGDOM, THAT FLOAT AND THRILL WITH JOY IN THEIR RADIANT DWELLINGS, AND FORMS THEREWITH THE GERMS OF WHEELS. HE PLACES THEM IN THE SIX DIRECTIONS OF SPACE, AND ONE IN THE MIDDLE—THE CENTRAL WHEEL.

"Wheels," as already explained, are the centres of force, around which primordial cosmic matter expands, and, passing through all the six stages of consolidation, becomes spheroidal and ends by being transformed into globes or spheres. It is one of the fundamental dogmas of Esoteric cosmogony, that during the Kalpas (or Æons) of Life, Motion, which, during the periods of Rest, *"pulsates and thrills through every slumbering atom"*—assumes an evergrowing tendency, from the first awakening of Kosmos to a new "Day," to circular movement. "The Deity becomes a Whirlwind." It may be asked, as the writer has not failed to ask: Who is there to ascertain the difference in that Motion, since all Nature is reduced to its primal essence, and there can be no one—not even one of the Dhyâni-Chohans, who are all in Nirvâna—to see it? The answer to this is: Everything in Nature has to be judged by analogy. Though the highest Deities (Archangels or Dhyâni-Buddhas) are unable to penetrate the mysteries which lie too far beyond our Planetary System and the visible Cosmos, yet there were great seers and prophets in olden times who were enabled to perceive the mystery of Breath and Motion retrospectively, when the systems of Worlds were at rest and plunged in their periodic sleep.

The Wheels are also called Rotæ—the moving wheels of the celestial orbs participating in the world's creation—when the meaning refers to the animating principle of the stars and planets; for, in the *Kabalah*, they are represented by the Auphanim, the Angels of the Spheres and Stars, of which they are the informing Souls.

This law of vortical movement in primordial matter is one of the oldest conceptions of Greek philosophy, whose first historical sages were nearly all Initiates of the Mysteries. The Greeks had it from the Egyptians, and the latter from the Chaldeans, who had been the pupils of Brâhmans of the Esoteric school. Leucippus, and Democritus of Abdera—the pupil of the Magi—taught that this gyratory movement of the atoms and spheres existed from eternity. Hicetas, Heraclides, Ecphantus, Pythagoras, and all his pupils, taught the rotation of the earth; and Âryabhata of India, Aristarchus, Seleucus, and Archimedes calculated its revolution as scientifically as the Astronomers do now; while the theory of Elemental Vortices was known to Anaxagoras, and maintained by him 500 years B.C., or nearly 2,000 before it was taken up by Galileo, Descartes, Swedenborg, and finally, with slight modifications, by Sir W. Thomson. All such knowledge, if justice be only done, is an echo of the archaic doctrine, an attempt to explain which is now being made. How men of the last few centuries have come to the same ideas and conclusions that were taught as axiomatic truths in the secrecy of the Adyta, dozens of millenniums ago, is a question that is treated separately. Some were led to it by the natural progress in Physical Science and by independent observation; others—such as Copernicus, Swedenborg, and a few more—their great learning notwithstanding, owed their knowledge far more to intuitive than to acquired ideas, developed in the usual way by a course of study. That Swedenborg, who could not possibly have known anything of the esoteric ideas of Buddhism, independently came near the Occult teaching in his general conceptions, is shown by his essay on the Vortical Theory. In Clissold's translation of it, quoted by Prof. Winchell, we find the following *résumé*:

The first cause is the infinite or unlimited. This gives existence to the first finite or limited. That which produces a limit is analogous to motion. The limit produced is a point, the essence of which is motion; but being without parts, this essence is not actual motion, but only a conatus to it. From this first proceed extension, space, figure, and succession, or time. As in geometry a point generates a line, a line a surface, and a surface a solid, so here the conatus of the point tends towards lines, surfaces and solids. In other words, the Universe is contained *in ovo* in the first natural point.

The Motion toward which the conatus tends is circular, since the circle is the most perfect of all figures…. "The most perfect figure of the motion above described must be the perpetually circular; that is to say, it must proceed from the centre to the periphery and from the periphery to the centre."

This is Occultism pure and simple.

By the "Six Directions of Space" is here meant the "Double Triangle," the junction and blending together of pure Spirit and Matter, of the Arûpa and the Rûpa, of which the Triangles are a Symbol. This Double Triangle is a sign of Vishnu; it is Solomon's Seal, and the Shrî-Antara of the Brâhmans.

4. FOHAT TRACES SPIRAL LINES TO UNITE THE SIXTH TO THE SEVENTH—THE CROWN (*a*). AN ARMY OF THE SONS OF LIGHT STANDS AT EACH ANGLE; THE LIPIKA, IN THE MIDDLE WHEEL (*b*). THEY SAY: "THIS IS GOOD." THE FIRST DIVINE WORLD IS READY; THE FIRST, THE SECOND. THEN THE "DIVINE ARÛPA" REFLECTS ITSELF IN CHHÂYÂ LOKA, THE FIRST GARMENT OF ANUPÂDAKA (*c*).

(*a*) This tracing of "spiral lines" refers to the evolution of Man's as well as of Nature's Principles; an evolution which takes place gradually, as does everything else in Nature. The Sixth Principle in Man (Buddhi, the Divine Soul), though a mere breath, in our conceptions, is still something material when compared with Divine Spirit (Âtmâ), of which it is the carrier or vehicle. Fohat, in his capacity of Divine Love (Eros), the electric power of affinity and sympathy, is shown, allegorically, trying to bring the pure Spirit, the Ray inseparable from the One Absolute, into union with the Soul, the two constituting in Man the Monad, and in Nature the first link between the ever-unconditioned and the manifested. "The First is now the Second"—of the Lipikas—has reference to the same.

(*b*) The "Army" at each angle is the Host of Angelic Beings (Dhyân Chohans), appointed to guide and watch over each respective region, from the beginning to the end of a Manvantara. They are the "Mystic Watchers" of the Christian Kabalists and Alchemists, and relate, symbolically as well as cosmogonically, to the numerical system of the Universe. The numbers with which these Celestial Beings are connected, are extremely difficult to explain, as each number refers to several groups of distinct ideas, according to the particular group of "Angels" which it is intended to represent. Herein lies the *nodus* in the study of symbology, with which so many scholars, unable to untie it, have preferred dealing as Alexander dealt with the Gordian knot; hence erroneous conceptions and teachings, as a direct result.

(*c*) The "First is the Second," because the "First" cannot really be numbered or regarded as such, for the First is the realm of noumena in its primary manifestation, the threshold to the World of Truth, or Sat, through which the direct energy that radiates from the One Reality—the Nameless Deity—reaches us. Here again, the untranslateable term Sat (Be-ness) is likely to lead to an erroneous conception, since that which is manifested cannot be Sat, but is something phenomenal, not everlasting, nor, in truth, even sempiternal. It is coëval and coëxistent with the One Life, "Secondless," but as a manifestation it is still a Mâyâ—like the rest. This "World of Truth," in the words of the Commentary, can be described only as *"a bright star dropped from the Heart of Eternity; the beacon of hope on whose Seven Rays hang the Seven Worlds of Being."* Truly so; since these are the Seven Lights whose reflections are the human immortal Monads—the Âtmâ, or the irradiating Spirit of every creature of the human family. First, this Septenary Light; then the "Divine World"—the countless lights lit at the primeval Light—the Buddhis, or formless Divine Souls, of the last Arûpa (Formless) World, the "Sum Total," in the mysterious language of the old Stanza.

In the Catechism, the Master is made to ask the pupil:

"Lift thy head, O Lanoo; dost thou see one, or countless lights above thee, burning in the dark midnight sky?"
"I sense one Flame, O Gurudeva, I see countless undetached sparks shining in it."
"Thou sayest well. And now look around and into thyself. That light which burns inside thee, dost thou feel it different in anywise from the light that shines in thy brother-men?"
"It is in no way different, though the prisoner is held in bondage by Karma, and though its outer garments delude the ignorant into saying, 'Thy Soul and My Soul'."

The radical unity of the ultimate essence of each constituent part of compounds in Nature—from star to mineral atom, from the highest Dhyân Chohan to the smallest infusorium, in the fullest acceptation of the term, and whether applied to the spiritual, intellectual, or physical worlds—this unity is the one fundamental law in Occult Science. "The Deity is boundless and infinite expansion," says an Occult axiom: hence, the name of Brahmâ, as previously remarked.
There is a deep philosophy underlying the earliest worship in the world, the worship of the Sun and of Fire. Of all the Elements known to Physical Science, Fire is that which has ever eluded definite analysis. It is confidently asserted that air is a mixture containing the gases oxygen and nitrogen. We view the Universe and the Earth as matter composed of definite chemical molecules. We speak of the primitive ten earths, endowing each with a Greek or Latin name. We say that water is, chemically, a compound of oxygen and hydrogen. But what is Fire? It is the effect of combustion, we are gravely answered. It is heat and light and motion, and a correlation of physical and chemical forces in general. And this scientific definition is philosophically supplemented by a theological one in Webster's Dictionary, which explains fire as "the instrument of punishment, or the punishment of the impenitent in another state"—the "state," by the bye, being supposed to be spiritual; but, alas! the presence of fire would seem to be a convincing proof of its material nature.

Yet, speaking of the illusion of regarding phenomena as simple, because they are familiar, Professor Bain says:

Very familiar facts seem to stand in no need of explanation themselves and to be the means of explaining whatever can be assimilated to them. Thus, the boiling and evaporation of a liquid is supposed to be a very simple phenomenon requiring no explanation, and a satisfactory explanation of rarer phenomena. That water should dry up is, to the uninstructed mind, a thing wholly intelligible: whereas to the man acquainted with physical science the liquid state is anomalous and inexplicable. The lighting of a fire by a flame is a *great scientific difficulty*, yet few people think so.

What says the Esoteric teaching with regard to Fire? "*Fire is the most perfect and unadulterated reflection, in Heaven as on Earth, of the One Flame. It is Life and Death, the origin and the end of every material thing. It is divine Substance.*" Thus, not only the Fire-Worshipper, the Parsi, but even the wandering savage tribes of America, which proclaim themselves "born of fire," show more science in their creeds and truth in their superstitions, than all the speculations of modern physics and learning. The Christian who says, "God is a living Fire," and speaks of the Pentecostal "Tongues of Fire" and of the "Burning Bush" of Moses, is as much a fire-worshipper as any other "Heathen." Among the Mystics and Kabalists, the Rosicrucians were those who defined Fire in the most correct way. Procure a sixpenny lamp, keep it only supplied with oil, and you will be able to light at its flame the lamps, candles, and fires of the whole globe without diminishing that flame. If the Deity, the radical One, is an eternal and infinite Substance never consumed ("the Lord thy God is a consuming fire"), then it does not seem reasonable that the Occult teaching should be held as unphilosophical when it says: "Thus were formed the Arûpa and Rûpa : from One Light Seven Lights; from each of the Seven, seven times Seven" etc., etc.

5. FOHAT TAKES FIVE STRIDES (*a*), AND BUILDS A WINGED WHEEL AT EACH CORNER OF THE SQUARE FOR THE FOUR HOLY ONES ... AND THEIR ARMIES (*b*).

(*a*) The "Strides," as already explained in the last Commentary, refer to both the cosmic and the human Principles—the latter of which consist, in the exoteric division, of three (Spirit, Soul and Body), and, in the esoteric calculation, of seven Principles—three Rays of the Essence and four Aspects. Those who have studied Mr. Sinnett's *Esoteric Buddhism* will easily grasp the nomenclature. There are two Esoteric schools beyond the Himâlayas, or rather one school, divided into two sections—one for the inner Lanoos, the other for the outer or semi-lay Chelâs; the first teaching a septenary, the other a six-fold division of the human Principles.

From a cosmic point of view, Fohat taking "Five Strides" refers here to the five upper planes of Consciousness and Being, the sixth and the seventh (counting downwards) being the astral and the terrestrial, or the two lower planes.

(*b*) Four "Winged Wheels at each corner ... for the Four Holy Ones and their Armies (Hosts)." These are the "Four Mahârâjahs," or great Kings, of the Dhyân Chohans, the Devas, who preside each over one of the four cardinal points. They are the Regents, or Angels, who rule over the Cosmical Forces of North, South, East and West, Forces having each a distinct Occult property. These Beings are also connected with Karma, as the latter needs physical and material agents to carry out its decrees, such as the four kinds of winds, for instance, professedly admitted by Science to have their respective evil and beneficent influences upon the health of mankind and every living thing. There is Occult philosophy in the Roman Catholic doctrine which traces the various public calamities, such as epidemics of disease, and wars, and so on, to the invisible "Messengers" from North and West. "The glory of God comes from the way of the East," says Ezekiel; while Jeremiah, Isaiah, and the Psalmist assure their readers that all the evil under the Sun comes from the North and the West—which, when applied to the Jewish nation, sounds like an undeniable prophecy. And this accounts also for St. Ambrose declaring that it is precisely for this reason that "we curse the North Wind, and that during the ceremony of baptism we begin by turning towards the West, to renounce the better him who inhabits it; after which we turn to the East."

Belief in the Four Mahârâjahs—the Regents of the four cardinal points—was universal and is now that of Christians, who call them, after St. Augustine, "Angelic Virtues" and "Spirits," when enumerated by themselves, and "Devils," when named by Pagans. But where is the difference between the Pagans and the Christians in this case? Says the scholarly Vossius:

Though St. Augustine has said that every visible thing in this world had an angelic virtue as an overseer near it, it is not individuals but entire species of things that must be understood, each such species having indeed its particular angel to watch it. He is at one in this with all the philosophers ... For us these angels are spirits separated from the objects.... whereas for the philosophers they were gods.

Considering the Ritual for the "Spirits of the Stars," established by the Roman Catholic Church, these look suspiciously like "gods," but they were no more honoured or worshipped by the ancient, nor are they by the modern, Pagan rabble than they are now at Rome by the highly cultured Catholic Christians.

Following Plato, Aristotle explained that the term στοιχεῖα was understood only as meaning the incorporeal principles placed at each of the four great divisions of our cosmical world, to supervise them. Thus, no more than Christians do Pagans *adore* and *worship* the Elements and the (imaginary) cardinal points, but the "gods" that respectively rule over them. For the Church, there are two kinds of Sidereal Beings, Angels and Devils. For the Kabalist and Occultist, there is but one class, and neither Occultist nor Kabalist makes any difference between the "Rectors of Light" and the "Rectores Tenebrarum," or Cosmocratores, whom the Roman Church imagines and discovers in the "Rectors of Light," as soon as any one of them is called by another name than the one she addresses him by. It is not the Rector, or Mahârâjah, who punishes or rewards, with or without "God's" permission or order, but man himself—his deeds, or Karma, attracting individually and collectively (as in the case of whole nations, sometimes) every kind of evil and calamity. We produce *Causes*, and these awaken the corresponding powers in the Sidereal World, which are magnetically and irresistibly attracted to—and reäct upon—those who produce such causes; whether such persons are practically the evil-doers, or simply "thinkers" who brood mischief. For thought is matter, we are taught by Modern Science; and "every particle of the existing matter must be a register of all that has happened," as Messrs. Jevons and Babbage in their *Principles of Science* tell the profane. Modern Science is every day drawn more into the maëlstrom of Occultism; unconsciously, no doubt, still very sensibly.

"Thought is matter": not of course, however, in the sense of the German Materialist Moleschott, who assures us that "thought is the movement of matter"—a statement of almost unparalleled absurdity. Mental states and bodily states are utterly contrasted as such. But that does not affect the position that every thought, in addition to its physical accompaniment (brain-change), exhibits an objective—though to us supersensuously objective—aspect on the astral plane.
The two main theories of Science as to the relations between Mind and Matter are Monism and Materialism. These two cover the whole ground of negative psychology with the exception of the quasi-occult views of the German Pantheistic schools.

The views of our present-day scientific thinkers as to the relations between mind and matter may be reduced to the following two hypotheses. These show that both views equally exclude the possibility of an independent soul, distinct from the physical brain through which it functions. They are:

(1.) *Materialism*, the theory which regards mental phenomena as the product of molecular change in the brain; *i.e.*, as the outcome of a transformation of motion into feeling (!). The cruder school once went so far as to identify mind with a "peculiar mode of motion" (!!), but this view is now happily regarded as absurd by most of the men of Science themselves.

(2.) *Monism*, or the Single Substance doctrine, is the more subtle form of negative psychology, which one of its advocates,

Professor Bain, ably terms "guarded materialism." This doctrine, which commands a very wide assent, counting among its upholders such men as Lewes, Spencer, Ferrier, and others, while positing thought and mental phenomena generally as radically contrasted with matter, regards them as the two sides, or aspects, of one and the same substance in some of its conditions. Thought as thought, they say, is utterly contrasted with material phenomena, but it must be also regarded as only "the subjective side of nervous motion"—whatever our learned men may mean by this.

To return to the commentary on the Four Mahârâjahs, however, in the Egyptian temples, according to Clemens Alexandrinus, an immense curtain separated the tabernacle from the place for the congregation. The Jews had the same. In both, the curtain was drawn over five pillars (the Pentacle), symbolizing our five senses and five Root Races esoterically, while the four colours of the curtain represented the four cardinal points and the four terrestrial elements. The whole was an allegorical symbol. It is through the four high Rulers over the four points and elements that our five senses may become cognizant of the hidden truths of Nature; and not at all, as Clemens would have it, that it is the elements *per se* that furnished the Pagans with Divine Knowledge or the Knowledge of God. While the Egyptian emblem was spiritual, that of the Jews was purely materialistic, and, indeed, honoured only the blind elements and the imaginary "points." For what was the meaning of the square Tabernacle raised by Moses in the wilderness, if it had not the same cosmical significance? "Thou shalt make an hanging ... of blue, purple, and scarlet ... five pillars of shittim wood for the hanging ... four brazen rings in the four corners thereof ... boards of fine wood for the four sides, North, South, West, and East ... of the Tabernacle ... with Cherubims of cunning work." The Tabernacle and the square courtyard, Cherubim and all, were precisely the same as those in the Egyptian temples. The square form of the Tabernacle meant just the same thing as it still means, to this day, in the exoteric worship of the Chinese and Tibetans—the four cardinal points signifying that which the four sides of the pyramids, obelisks, and other such square erections mean. Josephus takes care to explain the whole thing. He declares that the Tabernacle pillars were the same as those raised at Tyre to the four elements, which were placed on pedestals whose four angles faced the four cardinal points; adding that "the angles of the pedestals had the four figures of the Zodiac" on them, which represented the same orientation. The idea may be traced in the Zoroastrian caves, in the rock-cut temples of India, and in all the sacred square buildings of antiquity that have survived to this day. This is shown definitely by Layard, who finds the four cardinal points, and the four primitive elements, in the religion of every country, under the shape of square obelisks, the four sides of the pyramids, etc., etc. Of these elements and their points the Four Mahârâjahs were the regents and directors.

If the student would know more of them, he has but to compare the Vision of Ezekiel (ch. i.) with what is known of Chinese Buddhism, even in its exoteric teachings, and examine the outward shape of these "Great Kings of the Devas." In the opinion of the Rev. Joseph Edkins, "they preside each over one of the four continents into which the Hindûs divide the world.... Each leads an army of spiritual beings to protect mankind and Buddhism." With the exception of favouritism towards Buddhism, the four Celestial Beings are precisely this. The Hindûs, however, happen to divide the world into seven continents, exoterically as well as esoterically; and their four Cosmic Devas are eight, presiding over the eight points of the compass and not over the continents.

The "Four" are the protectors of mankind and also the agents of Karma on Earth, whereas the Lipika are concerned with Humanity's hereafter. At the same time they are the four living creatures, "who have the likeness of a man," of Ezekiel's vision, called by the translators of the
Bible, "Cherubim," "Seraphim," etc.; by the Occultists, "Winged Globes," "Fiery Wheels"; and in the Hindû Pantheon, by a number of different names. All these Gandharvas, the "Sweet Songsters," the Asuras, Kinnaras, and Nâgas, are the allegorical descriptions of the Four Mahârâjahs. The Seraphim are the fiery Serpents of Heaven which we find in a passage, describing

Mount Meru as "the exalted mass of glory, the venerable haunt of gods and heavenly choristers ... not to be reached by sinful men ... because guarded by Serpents." They are called the Avengers, and the "Winged Wheels."

Their mission and character being explained, let us see what the Christian bible-interpreters say of the Cherubim. "The word signifies in Hebrew, fulness of knowledge; these angels are so called from their exquisite Knowledge, and were therefore used for the punishment of men who affected divine Knowledge." (Interpreted by Cruden in his *Concordance*, from *Genesis* iii. 24.) Very well; and vague as the information is, it shows that the Cherub placed at the gate of the Garden of Eden, after the "Fall," suggested to the venerable interpreters the idea of punishment connected with forbidden Science or divine Knowledge—one that generally leads to another "Fall," that of the gods or "God," in man's estimation. But as the good old Cruden knew nought of Karma, he may be forgiven. Yet the allegory is suggestive. From Meru, the abode of gods, to Eden, the distance is very small, and from the Hindû Serpents to the Ophite Cherubim, the third out of the seven of which was the Dragon, the separation is still smaller, for both watched the entrance to the realm of Secret Knowledge. Ezekiel, moreover, plainly describes the four Cosmic Angels:

I looked, and, behold, a whirlwind, ... a ... cloud and a fire infolding it ... also out of the midst thereof came the likeness of four living creatures ... they had the likeness of a man. And every one had four faces and ... four wings ... the face of a man, and the face of a lion ... the face of an ox, and ... the face of an eagle.... Now as I beheld the living creatures, behold one wheel upon the Earth ... with his four faces ... as it were a wheel in the middle of a wheel ... for the spirit of the living creature was in the wheel.

There are three chief Groups of Builders, and as many of the Planetary Spirits and the Lipika, each Group being again divided into seven sub-groups. It is impossible, even in such a large work as this, to enter into a minute examination of even the three principal Groups, as it would demand an extra volume. The Builders are the representatives of the first "Mind-

Born" Entities, therefore of the primeval Rishi-Prajâpati; also of the Seven great Gods of Egypt, of which Osiris is the chief; of the Seven Amshaspends of the Zoroastrians, with Ormazd at their head; of the "Seven Spirits of the Face"; of the Seven Sephiroth separated from the first Triad, etc., etc. They build, or rather rebuild, every "System" after the "Night." The Second Group of the Builders is the Architect of our Planetary Chain exclusively; and the Third, the Progenitor of our Humanity—the macrocosmic prototype of the microcosm.

The Planetary Spirits are the informing spirits of the Stars in general, and of the Planets especially. They rule the destinies of men who are all born under one or other of their constellations; the Second and Third Groups pertaining to other systems have the same functions, and all rule various departments in Nature. In the Hindû exoteric Pantheon they are the guardian deities who preside over the eight points of the compass—the four cardinal and the four intermediate points—and are called Lokapâlas, "Supporters or Guardians of the World" (in our visible Cosmos), of which Indra (East), Yama (South), Varuna (West), and Kuvera (North) are the chief; their elephants and spouses pertaining of course to fancy and afterthought, though all of them have an Occult significance.

The Lipika, a description of whom is given in Commentary 6 of Stanza IV, are the Spirits of the Universe, whereas the Builders are only our own planetary deities. The former belong to the most Occult portion of cosmogenesis, which cannot be given here. Whether the Adepts—even the highest—know this angelic order in the completeness of its triple degrees, or only the lower one connected with the records of our world, is something which the writer is unprepared to say, and she would rather incline to the latter supposition. Of its highest grade one thing only is taught: the Lipika are connected with Karma—being its direct Recorders. The Symbol for Sacred and Secret Knowledge in antiquity was universally a Tree, by which a Scripture or a Record was also meant. Hence the word Lipika, the Writers or Scribes; the Dragons, symbols of Wisdom, who guard the Trees of Knowledge; the "golden" Apple-Tree of the Hesperides;

the "Luxuriant Trees" and vegetation of Mount Meru, guarded
by Serpents. Juno's giving Jupiter, on her marriage, a Tree with
golden fruit, is another form of Eve offering Adam the apple
from the Tree of Knowledge.

6. THE LIPIKA CIRCUMSCRIBE THE TRIANGLE, THE FIRST ONE, THE
CUBE, THE SECOND ONE, AND THE PENTACLE WITHIN THE EGG (*a*).

IT IS THE RING CALLED "PASS NOT" FOR THOSE WHO DESCEND AND
ASCEND; WHO DURING THE KALPA ARE PROGRESSING TOWARDS THE
GREAT DAY "BE WITH US" (*b*).... THUS WERE FORMED THE ARÛPA
AND THE RÛPA: FROM ONE LIGHT, SEVEN LIGHTS; FROM EACH OF
THE SEVEN, SEVEN TIMES SEVEN LIGHTS. THE WHEELS WATCH THE
RING....

The Stanza proceeds with a minute classification of the Orders
of the Angelic Hierarchy. From the Group of Four and Seven
emanates the Mind-Born Groups of Ten, of Twelve, of Twenty-
one, etc., all these divided again into sub-groups of Heptads,
Enneads, Dodecads, and so on, until the mind is lost in this
endless enumeration of celestial Hosts and Beings, each having
its distinct task in the ruling of the visible Cosmos during its
existence.

(*a*) The Esoteric meaning of the first sentence of the Shloka is,
that those who have been called Lipikas, the Recorders of the
Karmic Ledger, make an impassible barrier between the
personal *Ego* and the impersonal *Self*, the Noumenon and
Parent-Source of the former. Hence the allegory. They
circumscribe the manifested world of matter within the
Ring "Pass Not." This world is the objective symbol of the One
divided into the Many, on the planes of Illusion, of Adi
(the "First") or of Eka (the "One"); and this One is the collective
aggregate, or totality, of the principal Creators or Architects of
this visible Universe. In Hebrew Occultism their name is both
Achath, feminine, "One," and Achad, "One" again, but
masculine. The Monotheists have taken, and are still taking,
advantage of the profound esotericism of the *Kabalah*, to apply
the name by which the One Supreme Essence is known,
to *its* manifestation, the Sephiroth-Elohim, and call it Jehovah.

But this is quite arbitrary and against all reason and logic, as the term Elohim is a plural noun, identical with the plural word Chiim, often compounded with it. The sentence in the *Sepher Yetzirah* and elsewhere, "Achath-Ruach-Elohim-Chiim," denotes the Elohim as androgynous at best, the feminine element almost predominating, as it would read: "ONE is She the Spirit of the Elohim of Life." As said, Achath (or Echath) is feminine, and Achad (or Echad) masculine, both meaning One.

Moreover, in Occult metaphysics, there are, properly speaking, two "Ones"—the One on the unreachable plane of Absoluteness and Infinity, on which no speculation is possible; and the second One on the plane of Emanations. The former can neither emanate nor be divided, as it is eternal, absolute, and immutable; but the second, being, so to speak, the reflection of the first One (for it is the Logos, or Îshvara, in the Universe of Illusion), can do so. It emanates from itself—as the upper Sephirothal Triad emanates the lower seven Sephiroth—the seven Rays or Dhyân Chohans; in other words, the Homogeneous becomes the Heterogeneous, the Protyle differentiates into the Elements. But these, unless they return into their primal Element, can never cross beyond the Laya, or zero-point. This metaphysical tenet can hardly be better described than in T. Subba Row's *Bhagavadgîtâ* Lectures:

Mûlaprakriti acts as the one energy through the Logos. Now Parabrahman ... is the one essence from which starts into existence a centre of energy, which I shall for the present call the Logos.... It is called the Verbum ... by the Christians, and it is the divine Christos who is eternal in the bosom of his Father. It is called Avalokiteshvara by the Buddhists.... In almost every doctrine, they have formulated the existence of a centre of spiritual energy which is unborn and eternal, and which exists in the bosom of Parabrahman at the time of Pralaya, and starts as a centre of conscious energy at the time of cosmic activity....

For, as the lecturer premised by saying, Parabrahman is not this or that, it is not even consciousness, as it cannot be related to matter or anything conditioned. It is not Ego nor is it Non-Ego, nor even Âtmâ, but verily the one source of all manifestations and modes of existence.

Thus in the allegory, the Lipika separate the world (or plane) of pure Spirit from that of Matter. Those who "descend and ascend"—the incarnating Monads, and men striving towards purification and "ascending," but still not having quite reached the goal—may cross the Circle of "Pass Not," only on the Day "Be With Us"; that day when man, freeing himself from the trammels of ignorance, and recognizing fully the non-separateness of the Ego within his Personality—erroneously regarded as his own—from the Universal Ego (Anima Supra-Mundi), merges thereby into the One Essence, to become not only one with "Us," the manifested universal Lives which are *one* Life, but that very Life itself.

Astronomically, the Ring "Pass Not" that the Lipika trace round "the Triangle, the First One, the Cube, the Second One, and the Pentacle," to circumscribe these figures, is thus again shown to contain the symbols of 31415, or the coëfficient constantly used in mathematical tables, the value π (pi), the geometrical figures standing here for numerical figures. According to the general philosophical teachings, this Ring is beyond the region of what are called nebulæ in astronomy. But this is as erroneous a conception as that of the topography and descriptions, given in Purânic and other exoteric Scriptures, about the 1008 worlds of the Deva-loka worlds and firmaments. There are worlds, of course, in the esoteric as well as in the profane scientific teachings, at such incalculable distances that the light of the nearest of them, though it has only just reached our modern "Chaldees," may have left its luminary long before the day on which the words, "Let there be Light," were pronounced; but these are not worlds on the Devalokic plane, but in our Cosmos.

The Chemist goes to the laya or zero-point of the plane of matter with which he deals, and then stops short. The Physicist or the Astronomer counts billions of miles beyond the nebulæ, and then he also stops short. The semi-initiated Occultist also will represent this laya-point to himself as existing on some plane which, if not physical, is still conceivable to the human intellect. But the full Initiate *knows* that the Ring "Pass Not" is neither a locality, nor can it be measured by distance, but that it exists in the absoluteness of Infinity. In this "Infinity" of the full Initiate, there is neither height, breadth nor thickness, but all is fathomless profundity, reaching down from the physical to the "para-metaphysical." In using the word "down," essential depth—"nowhere and everywhere"—is meant, not depth of physical matter.

If one carefully searches through the exoteric and grossly anthropomorphic allegories of popular religions, even in these the doctrine embodied in the Circle of "Pass Not," guarded by the Lipika, may be dimly perceived. Thus one finds it even in the teachings of the Vedântin sect of the Visishthadvaita, the most tenaciously anthropomorphic in all India. For we read of the released soul that, after reaching Moksha—a state of bliss meaning "release from Bandha," or bondage—bliss is enjoyed by it in a place called Paramapada, which place is not material, but made of Suddasattva, the essence, of which the body of Îshvara—the "Lord"—is formed. There, Muktas or Jîvâtmâs (Monads) who have attained Moksha, are never again subject to the qualities of either matter or Karma. "But if they choose, *for the sake of doing good to the world*, they may incarnate on earth." The way to Paramapada, or the immaterial worlds, from this world, is called Devayâna. When a person has attained Moksha and the body dies:

The Jîva (Soul) goes with Sûkshma Sharira from the heart of the body to the Brahmarandra in the crown of the head, traversing Sushumna, a nerve connecting the heart with the Brahmarandra. The Jiva breaks through the Brahmarandra and goes to the region of the Sun (Sûryamandala) through the solar rays. Then it goes, through a dark spot in the Sun, to Paramapada.... The Jîva is directed on its way ... by the Supreme Wisdom acquired by Yoga. The Jîva thus proceeds to Paramapada by the aid of Athivâhikas (bearers in transit), known by the names of Archi Ahas ... Âditya, ... Prajâpati, etc. The Archis, etc., here mentioned, are certain pure Souls, etc., etc.

No Spirits except the "Recorders" (Lipika) have ever crossed the forbidden line of this Ring, nor will any do so until the day of the next Pralaya, for it is the boundary that separates the Finite—however infinite in man's sight—from the truly Infinite. The

Spirits referred to, therefore, as those who "ascend and descend," are the "Hosts" of what are loosely called "Celestial Beings." But they are, in fact, nothing of the kind. They are Entities of higher worlds in the Hierarchy of Being, so immeasurably high that, to us, they must appear as Gods, and collectively—*God*. But so must we, mortal men, appear to the ant, which reasons on the scale of its special capacities. The ant may also, for all we know, see the avenging finger of a Personal God in the hand of the urchin who, under the impulse of mischief, destroys, in one moment, its ant-hill, the labour of many weeks—long years in the chronology of insects. The ant, feeling it acutely, may also, like man, attribute the undeserved calamity to a combination of providence and sin, and see in it the result of the sin of its first parent. Who knows, and who can affirm or deny? The refusal to admit, in the whole Solar System, of any other reasonable and intellectual beings than ourselves on the human plane, is the greatest conceit of our age. All that Science has a right to affirm, is that there are no invisible Intelligences living under the same conditions as we do. It cannot deny point-blank the possibility of there being worlds within worlds, under conditions totally different to those that constitute the nature of our world; nor can it deny that there may be a certain limited communication between some of these worlds and our own. The greatest philosopher of European birth, Emmanuel Kant, assures us that such a communication is in no way improbable.

I confess I am much disposed to assert the existence of immaterial natures in the world, and to place my own soul in the class of these beings. It will hereafter, I know not where, or when, yet be proved that the human soul stands even in this life in indissoluble connection with all immaterial natures in the spirit-world, that it reciprocally acts upon these and receives impressions from them.

To the highest of these worlds, we are taught, belong the seven Orders of the purely divine Spirits; to the six lower ones belong Hierarchies that can occasionally be seen and heard by men, and that do communicate with their progeny of the Earth; a progeny which is indissolubly linked with them, each Principle in man having its direct source in the nature of these great Beings, who furnish us respectively with the invisible elements in us. Physical Science is welcome to speculate upon the physiological mechanism of living beings, and to continue her fruitless efforts in trying to resolve our feelings, our sensations, mental and spiritual, into functions of their organic vehicles. Nevertheless, all that will ever be accomplished in this direction has already been done, and Science can go no farther. She is before a dead wall, on the face of which she traces, as she imagines, great physiological and psychic discoveries, every one of which will be shown later on to be no better than cobwebs, spun by her scientific fancies and illusions. The tissues of our objective framework alone are subservient to the analysis and researches of Physiological Science. The six higher Principles in them will evade for ever the hand that is guided by an animus, which purposely ignores and rejects the Occult Sciences. All that modern physiological research in connection with psychological problems has, and owing to the nature of things could have shown, is that every thought, sensation, and emotion is attended with a re-marshalling of the molecules of certain nerves. The inference drawn by scientists of the type of Büchner, Vogt, and others, that thought is molecular motion, necessitates the fact of our subjective consciousness being made a complete abstraction.

The Great Day "Be With Us," then, is an expression, the only merit of which lies in its literal translation. Its significance is not so easily revealed to a public, unacquainted with the mystic tenets of Occultism, or rather of Esoteric Wisdom or "Budhism." It is an expression peculiar to the latter, and as hazy for the profane as that of the Egyptians, who called the same the Day "Come To Us," which is identical with the former—though the word "be," in this sense, might be still better replaced with either of the two terms "remain" or "rest with us," as it refers to that long period of Rest which is called Paranirvâna. "Le Jour de 'Viens à nous'! C'est le jour où Osiris a dit au Soleil: Viens! Je le vois rencontrant le Soleil dans l'Amenti." The Sun here stands for the Logos (or Christos, or Horus), as the central Essence synthetically, and as a diffused essence of radiated Entities, different in substance, but not in essence. As expressed by the *Bhagavadgîtâ* lecturer, "it must not be supposed that the Logos is but a single centre of energy which is manifested by Parabrahman. There are innumerable others. Their number is almost infinite, in the bosom of Parabrahman." Hence the expressions, "The Day of Come to Us" and "The Day of Be With Us," etc. Just as the Square is the Symbol of the Four sacred Forces or Powers—Tetraktys—so the Circle shows the boundary within the Infinity that no man, even in spirit, or Deva or Dhyân Chohan can cross. The Spirits of those who "descend and ascend," during the course of cyclic evolution, shall cross the "iron-bound world," only on the day of their approach to the threshold of Paranirvâna. If they reach it, they will rest in the bosom of Parabrahman, or the "Unknown Darkness," which shall then become for all of them Light, during the whole period of Mahâpralaya, the "Great Night," namely, 311,040,000,000,000 years of absorption in Brahman. The Day of "Be With Us" is this period of Rest, or Paranirvâna. It corresponds to the Day of the Last Judgment of the Christians, which has been sorely materialized in their religion.

As in the exoteric interpretation of the Egyptian rites, the soul of every defunct person—from the Hierophant down to the sacred bull Apis—became an Osiris, was Osirified (the Secret Doctrine, however, teaching that the real Osirification was the lot of every Monad only after 3,000 cycles of Existences); so in the present case. The Monad, born of the nature and the very Essence of the "Seven" (its highest Principle becoming immediately enshrined in the Seventh Cosmic Element), has to perform its septenary gyration throughout the Cycle of Being and Forms, from the highest to the lowest; and then again from man to God. At the threshold of Paranirvâna, it reässumes its primeval Essence and becomes the Absolute once more.

Stanza VI.

1. BY THE POWER OF THE MOTHER OF MERCY AND KNOWLEDGE (*a*), KWAN-YIN—THE TRIPLE OF KWAN-SHAI-YIN, RESIDING IN KWAN-YIN-TIEN (*b*)—FOHAT, THE BREATH OF THEIR PROGENY, THE SON OF THE SONS, HAVING CALLED FORTH, FROM THE

LOWER ABYSS, THE ILLUSIVE FORM OF SIEN-TCHAN AND THE SEVEN ELEMENTS.

This Stanza is translated from the Chinese text, and the names given as the equivalents of the original terms are preserved. The real Esoteric nomenclature cannot be given, as it would only confuse the reader. The Brâhmanical doctrine has no equivalents for these. Vâch seems, in many an aspect, to approach the Chinese Kwan-Yin, but there is no regular worship of Vâch under this name in India, as there is of Kwan-Yin in China. No exoteric religious system has ever adopted a female Creator, and thus, from the first dawn of popular religions, woman has been regarded and treated as inferior to man. It is only in China and Egypt that Kwan-Yin and Isis are placed on a par with the male gods. Esotericism ignores both sexes. Its highest Deity is as sexless as it is formless, neither Father nor Mother; and its first manifested beings, celestial and terrestrial alike, become only gradually androgynous to finally separate into distinct sexes.

(*a*) "The Mother of Mercy and Knowledge" is called the "Triple" of Kwan-Shai-Yin, because in her correlations, metaphysical and cosmical, she is the "Mother, the Wife and the Daughter" of the Logos, just as in the later theological translations she became the "Father, Son and (female) Holy Ghost"—the Shakti or Energy—the Essence of the Three. Thus in the Esotericism of the Vedântins, Daiviprakriti, the Light manifested through Îshvara, the Logos, is at one and the same time the Mother and also the Daughter of the Logos, or Verbum of Parabrahman; while in that of the Trans-Himâlayan teachings, it is—in the Hierarchy of their allegorical and metaphysical theogony—the "Mother," or abstract ideal Matter, Mûlaprakriti, the Root of Nature; from the metaphysical standpoint, a correlation of Adi-Budha, manifested in the Logos, Avalokiteshvara; and from the purely Occult and cosmical, Fohat, the "Son of the Son," the androgynous energy resulting from this "Light of the Logos," which manifests in the plane of the objective Universe as the hidden, as much as the revealed, Electricity—which is Life. Says T. Subba Row:

Evolution is commenced by the intellectual energy of the Logos, ... not merely on account of the potentialities locked up in Mûlaprakriti. This Light of the Logos is the link ... between objective matter and the subjective Thought of Îshvara . It is called in several Buddhist books Fohat. It is the one instrument with which the Logos works.

(b) "Kwan-Yin-Tien" means the "Melodious Heaven of Sound," the Abode of Kwan-Yin, or the "Divine Voice." This "Voice" is a synonym of the Verbum or Word, "Speech," as the expression of Thought. Thus may be traced the connection with, and even the origin of, the Hebrew Bath-Kol, the "Daughter of the Divine Voice," or Verbum, or the male and female Logos, the "Heavenly Man," or Adam Kadmon, who is at the same time Sephira. The latter was surely anticipated by the Hindû Vâch, the goddess of Speech, or of the Word. For Vâch—the daughter and the female portion, as is stated, of Brahmâ, one "generated by the gods"—is, in company with Kwan-Yin, with Isis (also the daughter, wife and sister of Osiris) and other goddesses, the female Logos, so to speak, the goddess of the *active* forces in Nature, the Word, Voice or Sound, and Speech. If Kwan-Yin is the "Melodious Voice," so is Vâch "the melodious cow who milked forth sustenance and water ... who yields us nourishment and sustenance," as Mother-Nature. She is associated in the work of creation with Prajâpati. She is male and female *ad libitum*, as Eve is with Adam. And she is a form of Aditi—the principle higher than Æther—of Âkâsha, the synthesis of all the forces in Nature. Thus Vâch and Kwan-Yin are both the magic potency of Occult Sound in Nature and Æther—which "Voice" calls forth Sien-Tchan, the illusive form of the Universe out of Chaos and the Seven Elements.

Thus, in *Manu*, Brahmâ (the Logos also) is shown dividing his body into two parts, male and female, and creating in the latter, who is Vâch, Virâj, who is himself, or Brahmâ again. A learned Vedântin Occultist speaks of this "goddess" as follows, explaining the reason why Îshvara (or Brahmâ) is called Verbum or Logos; why in fact it is called Sabda Brahman:

The explanation I am going to give you will appear thoroughly mystical; but if mystical, it has a tremendous significance when properly understood. Our old writers said that Vâch is of four kinds. Vaikharî Vâch is what we utter. Every kind of Vaikharî Vâch exists in its Madhyama, further in its Pashyanti, and ultimately in its Para form. The reason why this Pranava is called Vâch is this, that the four principles of the great cosmos correspond to these four forms of Vâch. Now the whole manifested solar system exists in its Sûkshma form in the light or energy of the Logos, because its energy is caught up and transferred to cosmic matter ... the whole cosmos in its objective form is Vaikharî Vâch, the light of the Logos is the Madhyama form, and the Logos itself the Pashyanti form, and Parabrahman the Para aspect of that Vâch. It is by the light of this explanation that we must try to understand certain statements made by various philosophers to the effect that the manifested cosmos is the Verbum manifested as cosmos.

2. THE SWIFT AND THE RADIANT ONE PRODUCES THE SEVEN LAYACENTRES (*a*), AGAINST WHICH NONE WILL PREVAIL TO THE GREAT DAY "BE WITH US"; AND SEATS THE UNIVERSE ON THESE ETERNAL FOUNDATIONS, SURROUNDING SIEN-TCHAN WITH THE ELEMENTARY GERMS (*b*).

(*a*) The seven Laya Centres are the seven zero-points, using the term zero in the same sense that Chemists do. It indicates, in Esotericism, a point at which the reckoning of differentiation begins. From these Centres—beyond which Esoteric Philosophy allows us to perceive the dim metaphysical outlines of the "Seven Sons" of Life and Light, the Seven Logoi of the Hermetic and all other philosophers—begins the differentiation of the Elements which enter into the constitution of our Solar System. It has often been asked what is the exact definition of Fohat and his powers and functions, for he seems to exercise those of a Personal God as understood in the popular religions. The answer has just been given in the Commentary on Stanza V. As well said in the *Bhagavadgîtâ* Lectures, "The whole cosmos must necessarily exist in the one source of energy from which this light emanates." Whether we count the principles in cosmos and man as seven or only as four, the forces of, and in, physical Nature are Seven; and it is stated by the same authority that, "Prajnâ, or the capacity of perception, exists in seven different aspects corresponding to the seven conditions of matter." For, "just as a human being is composed of seven principles, differentiated matter in the solar system exists in seven different conditions." So does Fohat. Fohat has several meanings, as already shown. He is called the "Builder of the Builders," the Force that he personifies having formed our Septenary Chain. He is One and Seven, and on the cosmic plane is behind all such manifestations as light, heat, sound, adhesion, etc., etc., and is the "spirit" of electricity, which is the Life of the Universe. As an abstraction, we will call it the One Life; as an objective and evident Reality, we speak of a septenary scale of manifestation, which begins at the upper rung with the One Unknowable Causality, and ends as Omnipresent Mind and Life, immanent in every atom of Matter. Thus, while Science speaks of its evolution through brute matter, blind force, and senseless motion, the Occultists point to *Intelligent* Law and *Sentient* Life, and add that Fohat is the guiding Spirit of all this. Yet he is no personal god at all, but the emanation of those other Powers behind him, whom the Christians call the "Messengers" of their God (in reality, of the Elohim, or rather one of the Seven Creators called Elohim), and we the Messenger of the primordial Sons of Life and Light.

(*b*) The "Elementary Germs," with which he fills Sien-Tchan (the Universe) from Tien-Sin (the "Heaven of Mind," or that which is absolute), are the Atoms of Science and the Monads of Leibnitz.

3. OF THE SEVEN—FIRST ONE MANIFESTED, SIX CONCEALED; TWO MANIFESTED, FIVE CONCEALED; THREE MANIFESTED, FOUR CONCEALED; FOUR PRODUCED, THREE HIDDEN; FOUR AND ONE TSANREVEALED, TWO AND ONE HALF CONCEALED; SIX TO BE MANIFESTED, ONE LAID ASIDE (*a*). LASTLY, SEVEN SMALL WHEELS REVOLVING; ONE GIVING BIRTH TO THE OTHER (*b*).

(*a*) Although these Stanzas refer to the whole Universe after a Mahâpralaya (Universal Dissolution), yet this sentence, as any student of Occultism may see, refers also by analogy to the evolution and final formation of the primitive (though compound) seven Elements on our Earth. Of these, four Elements are now fully manifested, while the fifth—Ether—is only partially so, as we are hardly in the second half of the

Fourth Round, and consequently the fifth Element will manifest fully only in the Fifth Round. The Worlds, including our own, as germs, were of course primarily evolved from the One Element in its second stage—"Father-Mother," the Differentiated World's Soul, not what is termed the "Over-Soul" by Emerson—whether we call it, with Modern Science, cosmic dust and fire-mist, or with Occultism, Âkâsha, Jîvâtmâ, Divine Astral Light, or the "Soul of the World." But this first stage of Evolution was in due course of time followed by the next. No World, and no heavenly body, could be constructed on the objective plane, had not the Elements been already sufficiently differentiated from their primeval Ilus, resting in Laya. The latter term is a synonym of Nirvâna. It is, in fact, the Nirvânic dissociation of all substances, merged after a Life-Cycle into the latency of their primary conditions. It is the luminous but bodiless shadow of the Matter that *was*, the realm of negativeness—wherein lie latent during their period of rest the active Forces of the Universe.

Now, speaking of Elements, it is made the standing reproach of the Ancients, that they "supposed their elements simple and undecomposable." The shades of our pre-historic ancestors might return the compliment to modern Physicists, now that new discoveries in Chemistry have led Mr. W. Crookes, F.R.S., to admit, that Science is yet a thousand leagues from a knowledge of the compound nature of the simplest molecule. From him we learn that such a thing as a really simple molecule entirely homogeneous is *terra incognita* in Chemistry. "Where are we to draw the line?" he asks; "is there no way out of this perplexity? Must we either make the elementary examinations so stiff that only 60 or 70 candidates can pass, or must we open the examination doors so wide that the number of admissions is limited only by the number of applicants?" And then the learned chemist gives striking instances. He says:

Take the case of yttrium. It has its definite atomic weight, it behaved in every respect as a simple body, an element, to which we might indeed add, but from which we could not take away. Yet this yttrium, this supposed homogeneous whole, on being submitted to a certain method of fractionation, is resolved into portions not absolutely identical among themselves, and exhibiting a gradation of properties. Or take the case of didymium. Here was a body betraying all the recognized characters of an element. It had been separated with much difficulty from other bodies which approximated closely to it in their properties, and during this crucial process it had undergone very severe treatment and very close scrutiny. But then came another chemist, who, treating this assumed homogeneous body by a peculiar process of fractionation, resolved it into the two bodies praseodymium and neodymium, between which certain distinctions are perceptible. Further, we even now have no certainty that neodymium and praseodymium are simple bodies. On the contrary, they likewise exhibit symptoms of splitting up. Now, if one supposed element on proper treatment is thus found to comprise dissimilar molecules, we are surely warranted in asking whether similar results might not be obtained in other elements, perhaps in all elements, if treated in the right way. We may even ask where the process of sorting-out is to stop—a process which of course presupposes variations between the individual molecules of each species. And in these successive separations we naturally find bodies approaching more and more closely to each other.

Once more this reproach against the Ancients is an unwarrantable statement. Their initiated philosophers at any rate, can hardly come under such an imputation, since it is they who have invented allegories and religious myths from the beginning. Had they been ignorant of the Heterogeneity of their Elements they would have had no personifications of Fire, Air, Water, Earth, and Æther; their cosmic gods and goddesses would never have been blessed with such posterity, with so many sons and daughters, elements born *from* and *within* each respective Element. Alchemy and Occult phenomena would have been a delusion and a snare, even in theory, had the Ancients been ignorant of the potentialities and correlative functions and attributes, of every element that enters into the composition of Air, Water, Earth, and even Fire—the latter a *terra incognita* to this day to Modern Science, which is obliged to call it motion, evolution of light and heat, state of ignition—defining it by its outward aspects in short, in ignorance of its nature.

But what Modern Science seems to fail to perceive, is that, differentiated as may have been those simple chemical atoms—which archaic philosophy called "the creators of their respective parents," fathers, brothers, husbands of their mothers, and these mothers the daughters of their own sons, like Aditi and Daksha, for example—differentiated as these elements were in the beginning, still, they were not the compound bodies known to Science, as they are now. Neither Water, Air, nor Earth (a synonym for solids generally) existed in their present form, representing the only three states of matter recognized by Science; for all these and even Fire are productions already recombined by the atmospheres of completely formed globes, so that in the first periods of the earth's formation they were something quite *sui generis*. Now that the conditions and laws ruling our Solar System are fully developed, and that the atmosphere of our earth, as of every other globe, has become, so to say, a crucible of its own, Occult Science teaches that there is a perpetual exchange taking place, in space, of molecules, or rather of atoms, correlating, and thus changing their combining equivalents on every planet. Some men of Science, and these among the greatest Physicists and Chemists, begin to suspect this fact, which has been known for ages to the Occultists. The spectroscope shows only the probable similarity (on external evidence) of terrestrial and sidereal substance; it is unable to go any farther, or to show whether or not atoms gravitate towards one another in the same way, and under the same conditions, as they are supposed to do on our planet, physically and chemically. The scale of temperature, from the highest degree to the lowest that can be conceived of, may be imagined to be one and the same in and for the whole Universe; nevertheless, its properties, other than those of dissociation and reässociation, differ on every planet; and thus atoms enter into new forms of existence, undreamed of, and incognizable to, Physical Science. As already expressed in *Five Years of Theosophy*, the essence of cometary matter, for instance, "is totally different from any of the chemical or physical characteristics with which the greatest Chemists and Physicists of the earth are acquainted." And even that matter, during rapid passage through our atmosphere, undergoes a certain change in its nature.

Thus not only the elements of our planet, but even those of all its sisters in the Solar System, differ in their combinations as widely from each other, as from the cosmic elements beyond our solar limits. This is again corroborated by the same man of Science in the lecture referred to above, who quotes Clerk Maxwell, saying "that the elements are not absolutely homogeneous." He writes:

It is difficult to conceive of selection and elimination of intermediate varieties, for where can these eliminated molecules have gone to, if, as we have reason to believe, the hydrogen, etc., of the fixed stars is composed of molecules identical in all respects with our own.... In the first place we may call in question this absolute molecular identity, since we have hitherto had no means for coming to a conclusion save the means furnished by the spectroscope, while it is admitted that, for accurately comparing and discriminating the spectra of two bodies, they should be examined under identical states of temperature, pressure, and all other physical conditions. We have certainly seen, in the spectrum of the sun, rays which we have not been able to identify.

Therefore, the elements of our planet cannot be taken as a standard for comparison with the elements in other worlds. In fact each world has its Fohat, which is omnipresent in its own sphere of action. But there are as many Fohats as there are worlds, each varying in power and degree of manifestation. The individual Fohats make one universal, collective Fohat—the aspect-entity of the one absolute Non-Entity, which is absolute Be-ness, Sat. "Millions and billions of worlds are produced at every Manvantara"—it is said. Therefore there must be many Fohats, whom we consider as conscious and *intelligent* Forces. This, no doubt, to the disgust of scientific minds. Nevertheless the Occultists, who have good reasons for it, consider all the forces of Nature as veritable, though supersensuous, states of Matter; and as possible objects of perception to beings endowed with the requisite senses.

Enshrined in its pristine, virgin state within the Bosom of the Eternal Mother, every atom born beyond the threshold of her realm is doomed to incessant differentiation. *"The Mother sleeps, yet is ever breathing."* And every breath sends out into the plane of manifestation her protean products, which, carried on by the wave of efflux, are scattered by Fohat, and driven toward or beyond this or another planetary atmosphere. Once caught by the latter, the atom is lost; its pristine purity is gone for ever, unless fate dissociates it by leading it to a "current of efflux" (an Occult term meaning quite a different process from that which the ordinary word implies), when it may be carried once more to the borderland where it had previously perished, and taking its flight, not into Space *above* but into Space *within*, be brought under a state of differential equilibrium and happily reabsorbed. Were a truly learned Occultist-Alchemist to write the "Life and Adventures of an Atom," he would secure thereby the supreme scorn of the modern Chemist, though perchance also his subsequent gratitude. Indeed, if such an imaginary Chemist happened to be intuitional, and would for a moment step out of the habitual groove of strictly "Exact Science," as the Alchemists of old did, he might be repaid for his audacity. However it may be, *"The Breath of the Father-Mother issues cold and radiant, and gets hot and corrupt, to cool once more and be purified in the eternal bosom of inner Space,"* says the Commentary. Man absorbs cold pure air on the mountain-top, and throws it out impure, hot and transformed. Thus, the higher atmosphere of every globe, being its mouth, and the lower its lungs, the man of our planet breathes only the "refuse of Mother;" therefore, "he is doomed to die thereon." He who would allotropize sluggish oxygen into ozone to a measure of alchemical activity, reducing it to its pure essence (for which there are means), would discover thereby a substitute for an "Elixir of Life" and prepare it for practical use.

(*b*) The process referred to as the "Small Wheels, one giving birth to the other," takes place in the sixth region from above, and on the plane of the most material world of all in the manifested Kosmos—our terrestrial plane. These "Seven Wheels" are our Planetary Chain. By "Wheels" the various spheres and centres of forces are generally meant; but in this case they refer to our septenary Ring.

4. HE BUILDS THEM IN THE LIKENESS OF OLDER WHEELS, PLACING THEM ON THE IMPERISHABLE CENTRES (*a*).

HOW DOES FOHAT BUILD THEM? HE COLLECTS THE FIERY-DUST. HE MAKES BALLS OF FIRE, RUNS THROUGH THEM, AND ROUND THEM,

INFUSING LIFE THEREINTO, THEN SETS THEM INTO MOTION; SOME ONE WAY, SOME THE OTHER WAY. THEY ARE COLD, HE MAKES THEM HOT. THEY ARE DRY, HE MAKES THEM MOIST. THEY SHINE, HE FANS AND COOLS THEM (*b*). THUS ACTS FOHAT FROM ONE TWILIGHT TO THE OTHER, DURING SEVEN ETERNITIES.

(*a*) The Worlds are built "in the likeness of older Wheels"—*i.e.*, of those that had existed in preceding Manvantaras and went into Pralaya; for the Law for the birth, growth, and decay of everything in Kosmos, from the Sun to the glow-worm in the grass, is One. There is an everlasting work of perfection with every new appearance, but the Substance-Matter and Forces are all one and the same. And this Law acts on every planet through minor and varying laws.

The "Imperishable Centres" have a great importance, and their meaning must be fully understood, if we would have a clear conception of the Archaic Cosmogony, whose theories have now passed into Occultism. At present, one thing may be stated. The Worlds are built neither *upon*, nor *over*, nor *in* the Laya Centres, the zero-point being a condition, not a mathematical point.

(*b*) Bear in mind that Fohat, the constructive Force of Cosmic Electricity, is said, metaphorically, to have sprung, like Rudra from the head of Brahmâ, "*from the Brain of the Father and the Bosom of the Mother*," and then to have metamorphosed himself into a male and a female, *i.e.*, polarized himself into positive and negative electricity. He has *Seven Sons* who are his *Brothers*. Fohat is forced to be born, time after time, whenever any two of his "Son-Brothers" indulge in *too close contact*—whether an embrace or a fight. To avoid this, he unites and binds together those of unlike nature, and separates those of similar temperaments. This, as any one can see, relates, of course, to electricity generated by friction, and to the law of attraction between two objects of unlike, and repulsion between those of like polarity. The Seven Son-Brothers, however, represent and personify the seven forms of cosmic magnetism, called in Practical Occultism the "Seven Radicals," whose coöperative and active progeny are, among other energies, Electricity, Magnetism, Sound, Light, Heat, Cohesion, etc. Occult Science defines all these as super-sensuous effects in their hidden behaviour, and as objective phenomena in the world of sense; the former requiring abnormal faculties to perceive them, the latter cognizable by our ordinary physical senses. They all pertain to, and are the emanations of, still more supersensuous spiritual qualities, not personated by, but belonging to, real and conscious Causes. To attempt a description of such Entities would be worse than useless. The reader must bear in mind that, according to our teaching which regards this phenomenal Universe as a Great Illusion, the nearer a body is to the Unknown Substance, the more it approaches Reality, as being the farther removed from this world of Mâyâ. Therefore, though the molecular constitution of these bodies is not deducible from their manifestations, on this plane of consciousness, they nevertheless, from the standpoint of the Adept Occultist, possess a distinctive objective if not material structure, in the relatively noumenal—as opposed to the phenomenal—Universe. Men of science may term them force or forces generated by matter, or "modes of its motion," if they will; Occultism sees in these effects Elementals (Forces), and, in the direct causes producing them, intelligent Divine Workmen. The intimate connection of these Elementals, guided by the unerring hand of the Rulers, with the elements of pure Matter—their correlation we might call it—results in our terrestrial phenomena, such as light, heat, magnetism, etc., etc. Of course we shall never agree with the American Substantialists who call every force and energy—whether light, heat, electricity or cohesion—an "entity"; for this would be equivalent to calling the noise produced by the rolling of the wheels of a vehicle an entity—thus confusing and identifying that "noise" with the "driver" *outside*, and the guiding "Master Intelligence" *within* the vehicle. But we do certainly give that name to the "drivers" and to these guiding "Intelligences," the ruling Dhyân Chohans, as has been shown. The Elementals, the Nature-Forces, are the acting, though invisible, or rather imperceptible, secondary causes, and in themselves the effects of primary causes behind the veil of all terrestrial phenomena. Electricity, light, heat, etc., have been aptly termed the "Ghosts or Shadows of Matter in Motion," *i.e.*, supersensuous states of Matter whose effects only we are able to cognize. To expand, then, the simile given above. The sensation of light is like the sound of the rolling wheels—a purely phenomenal effect, having no existence outside the observer. The proximate exciting cause of the sensation is comparable to the driver—a supersensuous state of matter in motion, a Nature-Force or Elemental. But, behind this—just as the owner of the carriage directs the driver from within—stands the higher and *noumenal* cause, the *Intelligence* from whose essence radiate these States of "Mother," generating the countless milliards of Elementals, or Psychic Nature-Spirits, just as every drop of water generates its physical infinitesimal Infusoria. It is Fohat who guides the transfer of the principles from one planet to the other, from one star to another child-star. When a planet dies, its informing principles are transferred to a laya or sleeping centre, with potential but latent energy in it, which is thus awakened into life and begins to form itself into a new sidereal body.

It is most remarkable that, while honestly confessing their entire ignorance of the true nature of even terrestrial matter—primordial substance being regarded more as a dream than as a sober reality—the Physicists should, nevertheless, set themselves up as judges of that matter, and claim to know what it is able and is not able to do, in various combinations. Scientists know this matter hardly skin-deep, and yet they will dogmatize. It is "a mode of motion" and nothing else! But the "force" that is inherent in a living person's breath, when blowing a speck of dust from the table, is also, undeniably, "a mode of motion." It is as undeniably not a quality of the matter, or the particles of the speck, and it emanates from the living and thinking Entity that breathed, whether the impulse originated consciously or unconsciously. Indeed, to endow matter—something of which nothing is so far known—with an inherent quality called force, of the nature of which still less is known, is to create a far more serious difficulty than that which lies in the acceptation of the intervention of our "Nature-Spirits" in every natural phenomenon.

The Occultists—who, if they would express themselves correctly, do not say that matter, but only the *substance* or *essence* of matter, (*i.e.*, Mûlaprakriti, the Root of all) is indestructible and eternal—assert that all the so-called Forces of Nature, electricity, magnetism, light, heat, etc., etc., far from being modes of motion of material particles, are *in esse, i.e.,* in their ultimate constitution, the differentiated aspects of that Universal Motion which is discussed and explained in the first pages of this volume. When Fohat is said to produce Seven Laya Centres, it means that, for formative or creative purposes, the *Great Law*—Theists may call it God—stays, or rather modifies, its perpetual motion on seven invisible points within the area of the Manifested Universe. "*The Great Breath digs through Space seven holes into Laya, to cause them to circumgyrate during Manvantara,*" says the Occult Catechism. We have said that Laya is what Science may call the zero-point or line; the realm of absolute negativeness, or the one real absolute Force, the *noumenon* of the Seventh State of that which we ignorantly call and recognize as "Force"; or again the noumenon of Undifferentiated Cosmic Substance, which is itself an unreachable and unknowable object for finite perception; the root and basis of all states of objectivity and also subjectivity; the neutral axis, not one of the many aspects, but its centre. It may serve to elucidate the meaning, if we try to imagine a "neutral centre"—the dream of those who would discover perpetual motion. A "neutral centre" is, in one aspect, the limiting point of any given set of senses. Thus, imagine two consecutive planes of matter; each of these corresponding to an appropriate set of perceptive organs. We are forced to admit that between these two planes of matter an incessant circulation takes place; and if we follow the atoms and molecules of, say, the lower in their transformation upwards, they will come to a point where they pass altogether beyond the range of the faculties we are using on the lower plane. In fact, for us the matter of the lower plane there vanishes from our perception—or rather, it passes on to the higher plane, and the state of matter corresponding to such a point of transition must certainly possess special, and not readily discoverable, properties. Seven such "Neutral Centres," then, are produced by Fohat, who, when, as Milton has it:

Fair foundations (are) laid whereon to build ...

quickens matter into activity and evolution.

The Primordial Atom (Anu) cannot be multiplied either in its pregenetic state, or its primogeneity; therefore it is called the "Sum Total," of course, figuratively, as that "Sum Total" is boundless. That which is the abyss of nothingness to the Physicist, who knows only the world of visible causes and effects, is the boundless Space of the Divine Plenum to the Occultist. Among many other objections to the doctrine of an endless evolution and involution, or reäbsorption of the Kosmos, a process which, according to the Brâhmanical and Esoteric Doctrine, is without beginning or end, the Occultist is told that it cannot be, since "by all the admissions of modern scientific philosophy it is a necessity of nature to run down." If the tendency of nature "to run down" is to be considered so forcible an objection to Occult Cosmogony, how, we may ask, do your Positivists and Free-thinkers and Scientists account for the phalanx of active stellar systems around us? They had eternity to "run down" in; why, then, is not the Kosmos a huge inert mass? Even the moon is only hypothetically believed to be a dead planet, "run down," and Astronomy does not seem to be acquainted with many such dead planets. The query is unanswerable. But apart from this, it must be noted that the idea of the amount of "transformable energy" in our little system coming to an end, is based purely on the fallacious conception of a "white-hot, incandescent sun," perpetually radiating away its heat without compensation into space. To this we reply that nature runs down and disappears from the objective plane, only to reëmerge after a time of rest out of the subjective, and to reäscend once more. Our Kosmos and Nature will run down only to reäppear on a more perfect plane after every Pralaya. The Matter of the Eastern philosophers is not the "matter" and Nature of the Western metaphysicians. For what is Matter? And above all, what is our scientific philosophy but that which was so justly and so politely defined by Kant as the "science of the *limits* to our knowledge?" To what have the many attempts made by Science to bind, connect, and define all the phenomena of organic life, by mere physical and chemical manifestations, brought it? To speculation generally—mere soap-bubbles, that have burst one after the other before the men of Science were permitted to discover real facts. All this would have been avoided, and the progress of knowledge would have proceeded with gigantic strides, had only Science and its philosophy abstained from accepting hypotheses merely on the one-sided knowledge of *their* "matter." The behaviour of Uranus and Neptune—whose satellites, four and one in number respectively, revolved, it was thought, in their orbits from East to West, whereas all the other satellites rotate from West to East—is a very good instance, as showing how unreliable are all *à priori* speculations, even when based on the strictest mathematical analysis. The famous hypothesis of the formation of our Solar System out of nebulous rings, put forward by Kant and Laplace, was chiefly based on the assumed fact that all the planets revolved in the same direction. Laplace, relying on this mathematically demonstrated fact in his own time, and calculating on the theory of probabilities, offered to bet three milliards to one that the next planet discovered would have in its system the same peculiarity of motion eastward. The immutable laws of scientific mathematics got "worsted by further experiments and observations." This idea of Laplace's mistake prevails generally to this day; but some Astronomers have finally succeeded in demonstrating (?) that the error has been in accepting Laplace's assertion for a mistake; and steps to correct the *bévue*, without attracting general attention, are now being taken. Many such unpleasant surprises are in store for hypotheses of even a purely physical character. What further disillusions, then, may there not be in questions concerning a transcendental, Occult Nature? At any rate, Occultism teaches that the so-called "reverse rotation" is a fact.

If no physical intellect is capable of counting the grains of sand covering a few miles of sea-shore, or of fathoming the ultimate nature and essence of these grains, when palpable and visible on the palm of the Naturalist, how can any Materialist limit the laws which govern the changes in the conditions and being of the atoms in Primordial Chaos, or know anything certain about the capabilities and potency of the atoms and molecules, before and after their formation into worlds? These changeless and eternal molecules—far more numberless in space than the grains on the ocean shore—may differ in their constitution along the lines of their planes of existence, as the soul-substance differs from its vehicle, the body. Each atom has seven planes of being or existence, we are taught; and each plane is governed by its specific laws of evolution and absorption. Ignorant of any, even approximate, chronological data from which to start, in attempting to decide the age of our planet or the origin of the solar system, Astronomers, Geologists, and Physicists, with each new hypothesis, are drifting farther and farther away from the shores of fact into the fathomless depths of speculative ontology. The Law of Analogy, in the plan of structure between the trans-solar systems and the solar planets, does not necessarily bear upon the finite conditions, to which every visible body is subject, in this our plane of being. In Occult Science, this Law of Analogy is the first and most important key to cosmic physics; but it has to be studied in its minutest details, and "turned seven times," before one comes to understand it. Occult Philosophy is the only science that can teach it. How, then, can anyone hang the truth or the untruth of the Occultist's proposition, "the Kosmos is eternal in its unconditioned collectivity, and finite only in its conditioned manifestations," on this one-sided physical enunciation that "it is a necessity of Nature to run down"?

A Digression.

With this Shloka ends that portion of the Stanzas relating to the cosmogony of the Universe after the last Mahâpralaya, or Universal Dissolution, which, when it comes, sweeps out of Space every differentiated thing, gods as well as atoms, like so many dry leaves. From this verse onwards, the Stanzas are only concerned with our Solar System in general, with the Planetary Chains therein inferentially, and with the history of our Globe (the Fourth and its Chain) especially. All the verses which follow in this Volume refer only to the evolution of, and on, our Earth. With regard to the latter, a strange tenet—strange from the modern scientific standpoint only, of course—is held, which ought to be made known.

But before entirely new and somewhat startling theories are presented to the reader, they must be prefaced by a few words of explanation. This is absolutely necessary, as these theories clash not only with Modern Science, but, on certain points, contradict earlier statements made by other Theosophists, who claim to base their explanations and renderings of these teachings on the same authority as we do.

This may give rise to the idea that there is a decided contradiction between the expounders of the same doctrine; whereas the difference, in reality, arises from the incompleteness of the information given to earlier writers, who thus drew some erroneous conclusions and indulged in premature speculations, in their endeavour to present a complete system to the public. Thus the reader, who is already a student of Theosophy, must not be surprised to find in these pages the rectification of certain statements made in various Theosophical works, and also the explanation of certain points which have remained obscure, because they were necessarily left incomplete. Many are the questions upon which even the author of *Esoteric Buddhism*, the best and most accurate of all such works, has not touched. On the other hand, even he has introduced several mistaken notions, which must now be presented in their true mystic light, as far as the present writer is capable of so doing.

Let us then make a short break between the Shlokas just explained and those which follow, for the cosmic periods which separate them are of immense duration. This will afford us ample time to take a bird's-eye view of some points pertaining to the Secret Doctrine, which have been presented to the public under a more or less uncertain and sometimes mistaken light.

A Few Early Misconceptions Concerning Planets, Rounds, And Man.

Among the eleven Stanzas omitted, there is one which gives a full description of the formation of the Planetary Chains one after another, after the first cosmic and atomic differentiation had commenced in the primitive Acosmism. It is idle to speak of "laws arising when Deity prepares to create," for "laws," or rather Law, are eternal and uncreated; and again Deity is Law, and *vice versà*. Moreover, the one eternal Law unfolds everything in the (to be) manifested Nature on a sevenfold principle; among the rest, the countless circular Chains of Worlds, composed of seven Globes, graduated on the four lower planes of the World of Formation, the three others belonging to the Archetypal Universe. Out of these seven only one, *the lowest and the most material of these Globes*, is within our plane or means of perception, the six others lying outside it and being therefore invisible to the terrestrial eye. Every such Chain of Worlds is the progeny and creation of another, *lower*, and *dead* Chain—its *reïncarnation*, so to say. To make it clearer: we are told that each of the planets—of which *seven only* were called sacred, as being ruled by the highest Regents or Gods, and not at all because the Ancients knew nothing of the others—whether known or unknown, is a septenary, as also is the Chain to which the Earth belongs. For instance, all such planets as Mercury, Venus, Mars, Jupiter, Saturn, etc., etc., or our Earth, are as visible to us as our Globe, probably, is to the inhabitants, if any, of the other planets, because they are all on the same plane; while the superior fellow-globes of these planets are on other planes quite outside that of our terrestrial senses. As their relative positions are given further on, and also in the diagram appended to the comments on Shloka 6 of Stanza VI, a few words of explanation is all that is needed at present. These invisible companions correspond curiously to that which we call the "principles" in man. The seven are on three material planes and one spiritual plane, answering to the three Upâdhis (Material Bases), and one spiritual Vehicle (Vâhana), of our seven Principles in the human division. If, for the sake of a clearer mental conception, we imagine the human Principles to be arranged as in the following scheme, we shall obtain the following diagram of correspondences:

As we are proceeding here from Universals to Particulars, instead of using the inductive or Aristotelean method, the numbers are reversed. Spirit is enumerated the first instead of seventh, as is usually done, but in truth, *ought not to be done.*

The Principles, as usually named after the manner of *Esoteric Buddhism* and other works, are: 1, Âtmâ; 2, Buddhi (Spiritual Soul); 3, Manas (Human Soul); 4, Kâma Rûpa (Vehicle of Desires and Passions); 5, Prâna; 6, Linga Sharîra; 7, Sthûla Sharîra.

The dark horizontal lines of the lower planes are the Upâdhis in the case of the human Principles, and the planes in the case of the Planetary Chain. Of course, as regards the Human Principles, the diagram does not place them quite in order, yet it shows the correspondence and analogy to which attention is now drawn. As the reader will see, it is a case of descent into matter, the adjustment—in both the mystic and the physical sense—of the two, and their interblending for the great coming "struggle for life" that awaits both Entities. "Entity" may be thought a strange term to use in the case of a Globe, but the ancient philosophers, who saw in the Earth a huge "animal," were wiser in their generation than our modern geologists are in theirs; and Pliny, who called the Earth our kind nurse and mother, the only Element which is not inimical to man, spoke more truly than Watts, who fancied that he saw in her the footstool of God. For

Earth is only the footstool of man in his ascension to higher regions; the vestibule—

... to glorious mansions,
Through which a moving crowd for ever press.

But this only shows how admirably Occult Philosophy fits every thing in Nature, and how much more logical are its tenets than the lifeless hypothetical speculations of Physical Science.

Having learned thus much, the Mystic will be better prepared to understand the Occult teaching, though every formal student of Modern Science may, and probably will, regard it as preposterous nonsense. The student of Occultism, however, holds that the theory at present under discussion is far more philosophical and probable than any other. It is more logical, at any rate, than the theory recently advanced which made of the Moon the projection of a portion of our Earth, extruded when the latter was a globe in fusion, a molten plastic mass.

Says Mr. Samuel Laing, the author of *Modern Science and Modern Thought*:

The astronomical conclusions are theories based on data so uncertain, that while in some cases they give results incredibly short, like that of 15 millions of years for the whole past process of formation of the solar system, in others they give results almost incredibly long, as in that which *supposes the moon to have been thrown off when the earth was rotating in three hours*, while the utmost actual retardation obtained from observation would require 600 millions of years to make it rotate in twenty-three hours instead of twenty-four.

And if Physicists persist in such speculations, why should the chronology of the Hindûs be laughed at as exaggerated?

It is said, moreover, that the Planetary Chains having their Days and their Nights—*i.e.*, periods of activity or life, and of inertia or death—behave in heaven as do men on earth: they generate their likes, grow old, and become personally extinct, their spiritual principles only living in their progeny as a survival of themselves.

Without attempting the very difficult task of giving out the whole process in all its cosmic details, enough may be said to give an approximate idea of it. When a Planetary Chain is in its last Round, its Globe A, before finally *dying out*, sends all its energy and principles into a neutral centre of latent force, a laya centre, and thereby informs a new nucleus of undifferentiated substance or matter, *i.e.*, calls it into activity or gives it life. Suppose such a process to have taken place in the Lunar Planetary Chain; suppose again, for argument's sake—though Mr. Darwin's theory quoted below has lately been upset, even if the fact has not yet been ascertained by mathematical calculation—that the Moon is far older than the Earth. Imagine the *six* fellow-globes of the Moon—æons before the first Globe of our seven was evolved—just in the same position in relation to each other as the fellow-globes of our Chain now occupy in regard to our Earth. And now it will be easy to imagine further Globe A of the Lunar Chain informing Globe A of the Terrestrial Chain, and—dying; next Globe B of the former sending its energy into Globe B of the new Chain; then Globe C of the Lunar creating its progeny Sphere C of the Terrene Chain; then the Moon (our satellite) pouring forth into the lowest Globe of our Planetary Chain—Globe D, our Earth—all its life, energy and powers; and, having transferred them to a new centre, becoming virtually a *dead planet*, in which since the birth of our Globe rotation has almost ceased. The Moon is the satellite of our Earth, undeniably, but this does not invalidate the theory that she has given to the Earth all but her corpse. For Darwin's theory to hold good, besides the hypothesis just upset, other still more incongruous speculations had to be invented. The Moon, it is said, has cooled nearly six times as rapidly as the Earth. "The Moon, if the earth is 14,000,000 years old since its incrustation, is only eleven and two-thirds millions of years old since that stage ..." etc. And if our Moon is but a splash from our Earth, why can no similar inference be established for the Moons of other planets? The Astronomers "do not know." Why should Venus and Mercury have no satellites, and by what, when they exist, were they formed? The Astronomers do not know, because, we say, Science has only one key—the key of matter—to open the mysteries of Nature, while Occult Philosophy has seven keys

and explains that which Science fails to see. Mercury and Venus have no satellites, but they had "parents" just as the Earth had. Both are far older than the Earth, and, before the latter reaches her Seventh Round, her mother Moon will have dissolved into thin air, as the Moons of the other planets have, or have not, as the case may be, since there are planets which
have *several* Moons—a mystery again which no Œdipus of Astronomy has solved.

The Moon is now the cold residual quantity, the shadow dragged after the new body, into which her living powers and principles are transfused. She now is doomed for long ages to be ever pursuing the Earth, to be attracted by and to attract her progeny. Constantly *vampirized* by her child, she revenges herself on it, by soaking it through and through with the nefarious, invisible and poisoned influence which emanates from the occult side of her nature. For she is a *dead*, yet a *living body*. The particles of her decaying corpse are full of active and destructive life, although the body which they had formed, is soulless and lifeless. Therefore its emanations are at the same time beneficent and maleficent—a circumstance finding its parallel on earth, in the fact that the grass and plants are nowhere more juicy and thriving than on graves; while at the same time it is the graveyard, or corpse-emanations, which kill. And like all ghouls or vampires, the Moon is the friend of the sorcerers and the foe of the unwary. From the archaic æons and the later times of the witches of Thessaly, down to some of the present Tântrikas of Bengal, her nature and properties have been known to every Occultist, but have remained a closed book for Physicists.

Such is the Moon from the astronomical, geological, and physical standpoints. As to her metaphysical and psychic nature, it must remain an occult secret in this work, as it was in the volume entitled *Esoteric Buddhism*, notwithstanding the rather sanguine statement made therein, that "there is not much mystery left now in the riddle of the eighth sphere." These are topics, indeed, "on which the Adepts are very reserved in their communications to uninitiated pupils," and since they have, moreover, never sanctioned or permitted any published speculations upon them, the less said the better.

Yet, without treading upon the forbidden ground of the "eighth sphere," it may be useful to state some additional facts with regard to the ex-monads of the Lunar Chain—the "Lunar Ancestors"—as they play a leading part in the coming Anthropogenesis. This brings us directly to the Septenary Constitution of man; and as some discussion has arisen of late about the best classification to be adopted for the division of the microcosmic entity, two systems are now appended with a view to facilitate comparison. The subjoined short article is from the pen of Mr. T. Subba Row, a learned Vedântin scholar. He prefers the Brâhmanical division of the Râja Yoga, and from a metaphysical point of view he is quite right. But, as it is a question of simple choice and expediency, we hold in this work to the time-honoured classification of the Trans-Himâlayan "Arhat Esoteric School." The following table and its explanatory text are reprinted from the *Theosophist*, and are also contained in *Five Years of Theosophy*.

The Septenary Division In Different Indian Systems.

We give below in a tabular form the classifications adopted by the Buddhist and Vedântic teachers of the principles of man:

"Esoteric Buddhism."	Vedânta.	Târaka Râja Yoga.
1. Sthûla Sharîra.	Annamayakosha.	Sthûlopâdhi.
2. Prâna.	Prânamayakosha.	Sthûlopâdhi.
3. The Vehicle of Prâna.	Prânamayakosha.	Sthûlopâdhi.
4. Kâma Rûpa.	Mânomayakosha.	Sûkshmopâdhi.
5. Mind (Volitions and feelings); Vijñânam.	Mânomayakosha.	Sûkshmopâdhi.
6. Spiritual Soul.	Ânandamayakosha.	Kâranopâdhi.
7. Âtmâ.	Âtmâ.	Âtmâ.

From the foregoing table it will be seen that the third principle in the Buddhist classification is not separately mentioned in the Vedântic division, as it is merely the vehicle of Prâna. It will also be seen that the fourth principle is included in the third Kosha (Sheath), as the same principle is but the vehicle of will-power, which is but an energy of the mind. It must also be noticed that the Vijñânamayakosha is considered to be distinct from the Mânomayakosha, as a division is made after death between the lower part of the mind, as it were, which has a closer affinity with the fourth principle than with the sixth and its higher part, which attaches itself to the latter, and which is, in fact, the basis for the higher spiritual individuality of man.

We may also here point out to our readers that the classification mentioned in the last column is, for all practical purposes, connected with Râja Yoga, the best and simplest. Though there are seven principles in man, there are but three distinct Upâdhis (Bases), in each of which his Âtmâ may work independently of the rest. These three Upâdhis can be separated by an Adept without killing himself. He cannot separate the seven principles from each other without destroying his constitution.

The student will now be better prepared to see that between the three Upâdhis of the Râja Yoga and its Âtmâ, and our three Upâdhis, Âtmâ, and the additional three divisions, there is in reality but very little difference. Moreover, as every Adept in Cis-Himâlayan or Trans-Himâlayan India, of the Patanjali, the Âryâsanga or the Mahâyâna schools, has to become a Râja Yogî, he must, therefore, accept the Târaka Râja classification in principle and theory, whatever classification he resorts to for practical and Occult purposes. Thus, it matters very little whether one speaks of the *three* Upâdhis, with their *three* Aspects, and Âtmâ, the eternal and immortal synthesis, or calls them the "Seven Principles."

For the benefit of those who may not have read, or, if they have, may not have clearly understood, in Theosophical writings, the doctrine of the septenary Chains of Worlds in the Solar Cosmos, the teaching is briefly as follows.

1. Everything in the metaphysical as in the physical Universe is septenary. Hence every sidereal body, every planet, whether visible or invisible, is credited with six companion Globes. The evolution of life proceeds on these seven Globes or bodies, from the First to the Seventh, in Seven Rounds or Seven Cycles.

2. These Globes are formed by a process which the Occultists call the "rebirth of Planetary Chains (or Rings)." When the Seventh and last Round of one of such Rings has been entered upon, the highest or first Globe, A, followed by all the others down to the last, instead of entering upon a certain time of rest—or "Obscuration," as in the previous Rounds—begins to die out. The Planetary Dissolution (Pralaya) is at hand, and its hour has struck; each Globe has to transfer its life and energy to another planet.

3. Our Earth, as the visible representative of its invisible superior fellow-globes, its "Lords" or "Principles," has to live, as have the others, through seven Rounds. During the first three, it forms and consolidates; during the fourth, it settles and hardens; during the last three, it gradually returns to its first ethereal form: it is spiritualized, so to say.

4. Its Humanity develops fully only in the Fourth—our present Round. Up to this Fourth Life-Cycle, it is referred to as "Humanity" only for lack of a more appropriate term. Like the grub which becomes chrysalis and butterfly, Man, or rather that which becomes Man, passes through all the forms and kingdoms during the First Round, and through all the human shapes during the two following Rounds. Arrived on our Earth at the commencement of the Fourth, in the present series of Life-Cycles and Races, Man is the first form that appears thereon, being preceded only by the mineral and vegetable kingdoms—even the latter having to *develop and continue* its further evolution *through man*. This will be explained in Volume II. During the three Rounds to come, Humanity, like the Globe on which it lives, will be ever tending to reässume its primeval

form, that of a Dhyân Chohanic Host. Man tends to
become *a* God and then—*God*, like every other Atom in the
Universe.

*Beginning so early as with the Second Round, Evolution proceeds
already on quite a different plan. It is only during the first Round
that (Heavenly) Man becomes a human being on Globe A,
(rebecomes) a mineral, a plant, an animal, on Globe B and C, etc.
The process changes entirely from the Second Round; but you have
learned prudence ... and I advise you to say nothing before the time
for saying it has come....*

5. Every Life-Cycle on Globe D (our Earth) is composed of seven
Root-Races. They commence with the ethereal and end with the
spiritual, on the double line of physical and moral evolution—
from the beginning of the Terrestrial Round to its close. One is
a "Planetary Round" from Globe A to Globe G, the seventh; the
other, the "Globe Round," or the Terrestrial.

This is very well described in *Esoteric Buddhism*, and needs no
further elucidation for the time being.

6. The First Root-Race, *i.e.*, the first "Men" on earth (irrespective
of form), were the progeny of the "Celestial Men," rightly called
in Indian philosophy the "Lunar Ancestors" or the Pitris, of
which there are seven Classes or Hierarchies. As all this will be
sufficiently explained in the following sections and in Volume II,
no more need be said of it here.

But the two works already mentioned, both of which treat of
subjects from the Occult doctrine, need particular
notice. *Esoteric Buddhism* is too well known in Theosophical
circles, and even to the outside world, for it to be necessary to
enter at length upon its merits here. It is an excellent book, and
has done still more excellent work. But this does not alter the
fact that it contains some mistaken notions, and that it has led
many Theosophists and lay-readers to form an erroneous
conception of the Eastern Secret Doctrine. Moreover it seems,
perhaps, a little too materialistic.

Man, which came later, was an attempt to present the archaic doctrine from a more ideal standpoint, to translate some visions in and from the Astral Light, to render some teachings partly gathered from a Master's thoughts, but unfortunately misunderstood. This work also speaks of the evolution of the early Races of men on Earth, and contains some excellent pages of a philosophical character. But so far it is only an interesting little mystical romance. It has failed in its mission, because the conditions required for a correct translation of these visions were not present. Hence the reader must not wonder if our volumes contradict these earlier descriptions in several particulars.

Esoteric cosmogony in general, and the evolution of the human Monad especially, differ so essentially in these two books, and in other Theosophical works written independently by *beginners*, that it becomes impossible to proceed with the present work without special mention of these two earlier volumes, for both have a number of admirers—*Esoteric Buddhism* especially. The time has arrived for the explanation of some matters in this direction. Mistakes have now to be checked by the original teachings, and corrected. If one of the said works has too pronounced a bias toward materialistic Science, the other is decidedly too idealistic, and at times is fantastic.

From the doctrine—rather incomprehensible to Western minds—which deals with the periodical Obscurations and successive Rounds of the Globes, along their circular Chains, were born the first perplexities and misconceptions. One of such has reference to the "Fifth-" and even "Sixth-Rounders." Those who knew that a Round was preceded and followed by a long Pralaya, a pause of rest, which created an impassable gulf between two Rounds until the time came for a renewed cycle of life, could not understand the "fallacy" of talking about "*Fifth* and *Sixth*-Rounders" in our *Fourth* Round. Gautama Buddha, it was held, was a "Sixth-Rounder," Plato and some other great philosophers and minds, "Fifth-Rounders." How could it be? One Master taught and affirmed that there were such "Fifth-Rounders" even now on Earth; and though *understood to say* that mankind was yet in the Fourth Round, in another place he *seemed* to say that we were in the Fifth. To this an "apocalyptic answer" was returned by another Teacher: "A few drops of rain do not make a monsoon, though they presage it."... "No, we are not in the Fifth Round, but Fifth Round men have been coming in for the last few thousand years." This was worse than the riddle of the Sphinx! Students of Occultism subjected their brains to the wildest work of speculation. For a considerable time they tried to outvie Œdipus and reconcile the two statements. And as the Masters kept as silent as the stony Sphinx herself, they were accused of "inconsistency," "contradiction," and "discrepancies." But they were simply allowing the speculations to go on, in order *to teach a lesson* which the Western mind sorely needs. In their conceit and arrogance, and in their habit of materializing every metaphysical conception and term, without allowing any margin for Eastern metaphor and allegory, the Orientalists had made a jumble of the Hindû exoteric philosophy, and the Theosophists were now doing the same with regard to Esoteric teachings. To this day it is evident that the latter have utterly failed to understand the meaning of the term "Fifth and Sixth-Rounders." But it is simply this: every Round brings about a new development, and even an entire change, in the mental, psychic, spiritual and physical constitution of man; all these principles evolving on an ever ascending scale. Hence it follows that those persons who, like Confucius and Plato, belonged psychically, mentally and spiritually to the higher planes of evolution, were in our Fourth Round as the average man will be in the Fifth Round, whose mankind is destined to find itself, on this scale of evolution, immensely higher than is our present humanity. Similarly, Gautama Buddha—Wisdom incarnate—was still higher and greater than all the men we have mentioned who are called "Fifth-Rounders," and so Buddha and Shankarâchârya are termed "Sixth Rounders," allegorically. Hence again the concealed wisdom of the remark, pronounced at the time "evasive"—"a few drops of rain do not make a monsoon, *though they presage it.*"

And now the truth of the following remark, in *Esoteric Buddhism*, will be fully apparent:

It is impossible, *when the complicated facts of an entirely unfamiliar science are being presented to untrained minds for the first time*, to put them forward with all their appropriate qualifications ... and abnormal developments.... We must be content to take the broad rules first and deal with the exceptions afterwards, and especially is this the case with a study, in connection with which *the traditional methods of teaching, generally followed, aim at impressing every fresh idea on the memory by provoking the perplexity it at last relieves.*

As the author of the remark was himself, as he says, "an untrained mind" in Occultism, his own inferences, and his better knowledge of modern astronomical speculations than of archaic doctrines, led him, quite naturally, and unconsciously to himself, to commit a few mistakes of detail rather than of any "broad rule." One such will now be noticed. It is a trifling one, still it is calculated to lead many a beginner into erroneous conceptions. But as the mistaken notions of the earlier editions were corrected in the annotations of the fifth edition, so the sixth may be revised and perfected. There were several reasons for such mistakes. They were due to the necessity, under which the Teachers laboured, of giving what were considered as "evasive answers"; the questions being too persistently pressed to be left unnoticed, while, on the other hand, they *could only be partially answered*. This position notwithstanding, the confession that "half a loaf is better than no bread" was but too often misunderstood, and hardly appreciated as it ought to have been. As a result thereof gratuitous speculations were sometimes indulged in by the European lay-chelâs. Among such were the "Mystery of the Eighth Sphere" in its relation to the Moon, and the erroneous statement that two of the superior Globes of the Terrestrial Chain were two of our well-known planets; "besides the earth ... there are *only two other worlds of our chain which are visible* ... Mars and Mercury...."
This was a great mistake. But the blame for it is to be attached as much to the vagueness and incompleteness of the Master's answer as to the question of the learner itself, which was equally vague and indefinite.

It was asked: "What planets, of those known to ordinary Science, besides Mercury, belong to our system of worlds?" Now if by "system of worlds" our *Terrestrial Chain*, or "String," was intended, in the mind of the querist, instead of the "Solar System of Worlds," as it should have been, then of course the answer was likely to have been misunderstood. For the reply was: "*Mars, etc., and, four other planets of which Astronomy knows nothing. Neither A, B, nor Y, Z, are known, nor can they be seen through physical means, however perfected.*" This is plain: (*a*) Astronomy as yet knows nothing in reality of the planets, neither the ancient ones, nor those discovered in modern times. (*b*) No *companion* planets from A to Z, *i.e.*, no upper Globes of any Chain in the Solar System, can be seen; with the exception of course of all the planets which come *fourth* in number, as our Earth, the Moon, etc., etc. As to Mars, Mercury, and "the four other planets," they bear a relation to Earth of which no Master or high Occultist will ever speak, much less explain the nature.

In this same letter the impossibility is distinctly stated by one of the Teachers to the author of *Esoteric Buddhism*: "*Try to understand that you are putting me questions pertaining to the highest Initiation; that I can give you (only) a general view, but that I dare not, nor will I, enter into details....*" Copies of all the letters ever received, or sent, with the exception of a few private ones—"*in which there was no teaching*," the Master says—are with the writer. As it was her duty, in the beginning, to answer and explain certain points not touched upon, it is more than likely that, notwithstanding the many annotations on these copies, the writer, in her ignorance of English and her fear of saying too much, may have bungled the information given. *She takes the whole blame for it upon herself in any and every case.* But it is impossible for her to allow students to remain any longer under erroneous impressions, or to believe that the fault lies with the Esoteric system.

Let it then be now distinctly stated that the theory broached is impossible, with or without the additional evidence furnished by modern Astronomy. Physical Science can supply corroborative, though still very uncertain, evidence, but only as regards heavenly bodies on the same plane of materiality as our objective Universe. Mars and Mercury, Venus and Jupiter, like every hitherto discovered planet, or those still to be discovered, are all, *per se*, the representatives on our plane of such Chains. As distinctly stated in one of the numerous letters of Mr. Sinnett's Teacher: *"there are other and innumerable manvantaric Chains of Globes which bear intelligent Beings, both in and outside our Solar System."* But neither Mars nor Mercury belong to *our* Chain. They are, along with other planets, septenary Units in the great host of Chains of our System, and all are as visible as their *upper* Globes are invisible.

If it is still argued that certain expressions in the Teacher's letters were liable to mislead, the answer comes: Amen; so they were. The author of *Esoteric Buddhism* understood it well when he wrote that such are "the traditional modes of teaching ... by provoking the perplexity," they *do* or *do not relieve*—as the case may be. At all events, if it is urged that this might have been explained earlier, and the true nature of the planets given out as they now are, the answer comes that: It was not found expedient to do so at the time, as it would have opened the way to a series of additional questions *which could never be answered on account of their Esoteric nature*, and thus would only become embarrassing. It had been declared from the first, and has been repeatedly asserted since: (1) That no Theosophist, *not even as an accepted Chelâ*, let alone lay students, could expect to have the secret teachings explained to him *thoroughly and completely*, before *he had irretrievably pledged himself to the Brotherhood and passed through at least one Initiation*, because no figures and numbers could be given to the public, for figures and numbers are the key to the Esoteric system. (2) That what was revealed was merely the Esoteric lining of that which is contained in almost all the exoteric scriptures of the world-religions—preëminently in the *Brâhmanas* and the *Upanishads* of the *Vedas*, and even in the *Purânas*. It was a small portion of what is divulged far more fully now in the present volumes; and even this is very incomplete and fragmentary.

When the present work was commenced, the writer, feeling sure that the speculation about Mars and Mercury was a mistake, applied to the Teachers *by letter* for an explanation and an authoritative version. Both came in due time, and *verbatim* extracts from these are now given.

"... It is quite correct that Mars is in a state of obscuration at present, and Mercury just beginning to get out of it. You might add that Venus is in her last Round.... If neither Mercury nor Venus have satellites, it is because of the reasons ... and also because Mars has two satellites to which he has no right.... Phobos, the supposed 'inner' satellite, is no satellite at all. Thus, this remark of long ago by Laplace and now by Faye do not agree, you see. (Read 'Comptes Rendus,' Tome XC, p. 569.) Phobos keeps a too short periodic time, and therefore there 'must exist some defect in the mother idea of the theory,' as Faye justly observes.... Again, both are septenary Chains, as independent of the Earth's sidereal lords and superiors as you are independent of the 'principles' of Däumling —which were perhaps his six brothers, with or without night-caps.... 'Gratification of curiosity is the end of knowledge for some men,' was said by Bacon, who was as right in postulating this truism, as those who were familiar with it before him, were right in hedging off WISDOM *from Knowledge, and tracing limits to that which is to be given out at one time.... Remember:*
... knowledge dwells
In heads replete with thoughts of other men,
Wisdom in minds attentive to their own...."

"You can never impress it too profoundly on the minds of those to whom you impart some of the Esoteric teachings."

Here are more extracts from another letter written by the same authority. This time it is in answer to some objections laid before the Teachers. They are based upon extremely scientific, and as futile, reasonings about the advisability of trying to reconcile the Esoteric theories with the speculations of Modern Science, were written by a young Theosophist as a warning against the "Secret Doctrine," and in reference to the same subject. He had declared that if there were such companion Earths, "they must be only a wee bit less material than our globe." How then was it that they could not be seen? The answer was:

"... *Were psychic and spiritual teachings more fully understood, it would become next to impossible to even imagine such an incongruity. Unless less trouble is taken to reconcile the irreconcilable—that is to say, the metaphysical and spiritual sciences with physical or natural philosophy, 'natural' being a synonym to them of that matter which falls under the perception of their corporeal senses—no progress can be really achieved. Our Globe, as taught from the first, is at the bottom of the arc of descent, where the matter of our perceptions exhibits itself in its grossest form.... Hence it only stands to reason that the Globes which overshadow our Earth, must be on different and superior planes. In short, as Globes, they are in* COADUNITION *but not in* CONSUBSTANTIALITY *with our Earth, and thus pertain to quite another state of consciousness. Our planet (like all those we see) is adapted to the peculiar state of its human stock, that state which enables us to see with our naked eye the sidereal bodies which are coëssential with our terrene plane and substance, just as their respective inhabitants, the Jovians, Martians and others, can perceive our little world; because our planes of consciousness, differing as they do in degree, but being the same in kind, are on the same layer of differentiated matter.... What I wrote was: 'The minor Pralaya concerns only our little Strings of Globes. (We called Chains "Strings" in those days of lip-confusion.)... To such a String our Earth belongs.' This ought to have shown plainly that the other planets were also 'Strings,' or* CHAINS.... *If he would perceive even the dim silhouette of one of such 'planets' on the higher planes, he has to first throw off even the thin clouds of the astral matter that stand between him and the next plane.*"

It thus becomes patent why we could not perceive, even with the help of the best telescopes, that which is outside our world of matter. Those alone, whom we call Adepts, who know how to direct their mental vision and to transfer their consciousness—

both physical and psychic—to other planes of being, are able to speak with authority on such subjects. And they tell us plainly:

"Lead the life necessary for the acquisition of such knowledge and powers, and Wisdom will come to you naturally. Whenever you are able to attune your consciousness to any of the seven chords of 'Universal Consciousness,' those chords that run along the sounding-board of Kosmos, vibrating from one Eternity to another; when you have studied thoroughly the 'Music of the Spheres,' then only will you become quite free to share your knowledge with those with whom it is safe to do so. Meanwhile, be prudent. Do not give out the great Truths that are the inheritance of the future Races, to our present generation. Do not attempt to unveil the secret of Being and Non-Being to those unable to see the hidden meaning of Apollo's Heptachord, the lyre of the radiant god, in each of the seven strings of which dwelleth the Spirit, Soul and Astral Body of the Kosmos, whose shell only has now fallen into the hands of modern Science.... Be prudent, we say, prudent and wise, and above all take care what those who learn from you believe in; lest by deceiving themselves they deceive others, ... for such is the fate of every truth with which men are, as yet, unfamiliar.... Let rather the Planetary Chains and other super- and sub-cosmic mysteries remain a dreamland for those who can neither see, nor yet believe that others can."

It is to be regretted that few of us have followed the wise advice, and that many a priceless pearl, many a jewel of wisdom, has been cast to an enemy, unable to understand its value, who has turned round and rent us.

"*Let us imagine*"—wrote the same Master to his two "lay chelâs," as he called the author of *Esoteric Buddhism* and another gentleman, his co-student for some time—"*let us imagine that our earth is one of a group of seven planets or man-bearing worlds.... Now the life-impulse reaches A, or rather that which is destined to become A, and which so far is but cosmic dust ...*" etc.

In these early letters, in which terms had to be invented and words coined, the "Rings" very often became "Rounds," and the "Rounds," "Life-Cycles," and *vice versâ*. To a correspondent who called a "Round" a "World-Ring," the Teacher wrote: "*I believe this will lead to a further confusion. A Round we are agreed to call the passage of a Monad from Globe A to Globe G or Z.... The 'World-Ring' is correct.... Advise Mr. ... strongly, to agree upon a nomenclature before going any further.*"

Notwithstanding this agreement, many mistakes, owing to this confusion, crept into the earliest teachings. The "Races" even were occasionally mixed up with the "Rounds" and "Rings," and led to similar mistakes in *Man: Fragments of Forgotten Truth*. From the first the Master had written:

"*Not being permitted to give you the whole truth, or divulge the number of isolated fractions, ... I am unable to satisfy you.*"

This in answer to the questions: "If we are right, then the total existence prior to the man-period is 637," etc., etc. To all the queries relating to figures, the reply was: "*Try to solve the problem of 777 incarnations.... Though I am obliged to withhold information, ... yet if you should work out the problem by yourself, it will be my duty to tell you so.*"

But it never was so worked out, and the results were—never-ceasing perplexity and mistakes.

Even the teaching about the septenary constitution of the sidereal bodies and of the macrocosm—from which the septenary division of the microcosm, or man—has until now been among the most esoteric. In olden times it used to be divulged only at Initiation together with the most sacred figures of the cycles. Now, as stated in one of the Theosophical journals, the revelation of the whole system of cosmogony had not been contemplated, nor even thought for one moment possible, at a time when a few scraps of information were sparingly given out, in answer to letters, written by the author of *Esoteric Buddhism*, in which he put forward a multiplicity of questions. Among these were questions on such problems *as no* MASTER, *however high and independent he might be, would have the right to answer, and thus divulge to the world the most time-honoured and archaic of the mysteries of the ancient college-temples.* Hence only a few of the doctrines were revealed in their broad outlines, while details were constantly withheld, and all the efforts made to elicit more information about them were systematically eluded from the beginning. This was perfectly natural. Of the four Vidyâs, out of the seven branches of Knowledge mentioned in the *Purânas*—namely, Yajna Vidyâ, the performance of religious rites in order to produce certain results; Mahâ Vidyâ, the great (magic) knowledge, now degenerated into Tântrika worship; Guhya Vidyâ, the science of Mantras and their true rhythm or chanting, of mystical incantations, etc.; Âtmâ Vidyâ, or the true *spiritual* and *divine Wisdom*—it is only the last which can throw final and absolute light upon the teachings of the three first named. Without the help of Âtmâ Vidyâ, the other three remain no better than *surface* sciences, geometrical magnitudes having length and breadth, but no thickness. They are like the soul, limbs and mind of a sleeping man, capable of mechanical motions, of chaotic dreams and even sleep-walking, of producing visible effects, but stimulated only by instinctual not intellectual causes, least of all by fully conscious spiritual impulses. A good deal can be given out and explained from the three first-named sciences. But unless the key to their teachings is furnished by Âtmâ Vidyâ, they will remain for ever like the fragments of a mangled text-book, like the adumbrations of great truths, dimly perceived by the most spiritual, but distorted out of all proportion by those who would nail every shadow to the wall.

Then, again, another great perplexity was created in the minds of students by the incomplete exposition of the doctrine of the evolution of the Monads. To be fully realized, both this process and that of the birth of the Globes must be examined far more from their metaphysical aspect, than from what one might call a statistical standpoint, involving figures and numbers which are rarely permitted to be widely used. Unfortunately, there are few who are inclined to handle these doctrines only metaphysically. Even the best of the Western writers upon our doctrine declares in his work, when speaking of the evolution of the Monads, that "on pure metaphysics of that sort we are not now engaged." And in such case, as the Teacher remarks in a letter to him:

"Why this preaching of our doctrines, all this uphill work and swimming 'in adversum flumen'? Why should the West ... learn ... from the East ... that which can never meet the requirements of the special tastes of the œsthetics?" And he draws his correspondent's attention *"to the formidable difficulties encountered by us in every attempt we make to explain our metaphysics to the Western mind."*

And well he may; for *outside* of metaphysics, no Occult philosophy, no Esotericism is possible. It is like trying to explain the aspirations and affections, love and hatred, the most private and sacred workings in the soul and mind of a living man, by an anatomical description of the thorax and brain of his dead body.

Let us now examine two tenets mentioned above, but hardly alluded to in *Esoteric Buddhism*, and supplement them as far as lies in our power.

Additional Facts And Explanations Concerning The Globes And The Monads.

Two statements made in the above work must be noticed and the author's opinions quoted. The first is as follows:

The spiritual Monads ... do not fully complete their mineral existence on Globe A, then complete it on Globe B, and so on. They pass several times round the whole circle as minerals, and then again several times round as vegetables, and several times as animals. We purposely refrain for the present from going into figures, etc., etc.

That was a wise course to adopt in view of the great secrecy maintained with regard to figures and numbers. This reticence is now partially relinquished; but it would perhaps have been better had the real numbers concerning Rounds and evolutional gyrations been either entirely divulged at the time, or entirely withheld. Mr. Sinnett understood this difficulty well when saying:

For reasons which are not easy for the outsider to divine, the possessors of Occult knowledge are especially reluctant to give out numerical facts relating to cosmogony, though it is hard for the uninitiated to understand why they should be withheld.

That there were such reasons is evident. Nevertheless, it is to this reticence that most of the confused ideas of some Eastern as well as Western pupils are due. The difficulties in the way of the acceptance of the particular tenets under consideration seemed great, just because of the absence of any data to go upon. But there it was. For, as the Masters have many times declared, the figures belonging to the Occult calculations cannot be given—outside the circle of pledged Chelâs, and not even these can break the rules.

To make things plainer, without touching upon the mathematical aspects of the doctrine, the teaching given may be expanded and some obscure points solved. As the evolution of the Globes and that of the Monads are so closely interblended, we will make of the two teachings one. In reference to the Monads, the reader is asked to bear in mind that Eastern philosophy rejects the Western theological dogma of a newly-created soul for every baby born, a dogma as unphilosophical as it is impossible in the economy of Nature. There must be a limited number of Monads, evolving and growing more and more perfect, through their assimilation of many successive Personalities, in every new Manvantara. This is absolutely necessary in view of the doctrines of Rebirth and Karma, and of the gradual return of the human Monad to its source—Absolute Deity. Thus, although the hosts of more or less progressed Monads are almost incalculable, they are still finite, as is everything in this Universe of differentiation and finiteness.

As shown in the double diagram of the human Principles and the ascending Globes of the World-Chains, there is an eternal concatenation of causes and effects, and a perfect analogy which runs through, and links together, all the lines of evolution. One begets the other—Globes as Personalities. But, let us begin at the beginning.

The general outline of the process by which the successive Planetary Chains are formed has just been given. To prevent future misconceptions, some further details may be offered which will also throw light on the history of Humanity on our own Chain, the progeny of that of the Moon.

In the accompanying diagram, Fig. 1 represents the Lunar Chain of seven Globes at the outset of its seventh or last Round; while Fig. 2 represents the Earth Chain which will be, but is not yet in existence. The seven Globes of each Chain are distinguished in their cyclic order by the letters A to G, the Globes of the Earth Chain being further marked by a cross, the symbol of the Earth.

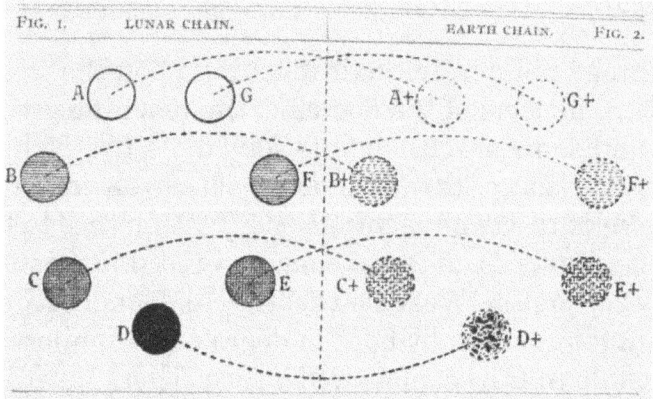

Now, it must be remembered that the Monads cycling round any septenary Chain are divided into seven Classes or Hierarchies, according to their respective stages of evolution, consciousness and merit. Let us follow, then, the order of their appearance on Globe A, in the First Round. The time-spaces between the appearances of these Hierarchies on any one Globe are so adjusted, that when Class 7, the last, appears on Globe A, Class 1, the first, has just passed on to Globe B; and so on, step by step, all round the Chain.

Again, in the Seventh Round of the Lunar Chain, when Class 7, the last, quits Globe A, that Globe, instead of falling asleep, as it had done in previous Rounds, begins to die (to go into its Planetary Pralaya); and in dying it transfers successively, as just said, its principles, or life-elements and energy, etc., one after the other, to a new laya-centre, which commences the formation of Globe A of the Earth Chain. A similar process takes place for each of the Globes of the Lunar Chain, one after the other, each forming a fresh Globe of the Earth Chain. Our Moon was the fourth Globe of the series, and was on the same plane of perception as our Earth. But Globe A of the Lunar Chain is not fully "dead," till the first Monads of the first Class have passed from Globe G or Z, the last of the Lunar Chain, into the Nirvâna which awaits them between the two Chains; and similarly for all the other Globes as stated, each giving birth to the corresponding Globe of the Earth Chain.

Further, when Globe A of the new Chain is ready, the first Class or Hierarchy of Monads from the Lunar Chain incarnate upon it in the lowest kingdom, and so on successively. The result of this is, that it is only the first Class of Monads which attains the human state of development during the first Round, since the second Class, on each Globe, arriving later, has not time to reach that stage. Thus the Monads of Class 2 reach the incipient human stage only in the Second Round, and so on up to the middle of the Fourth Round. But at this point—and on this Fourth Round in which the human stage will be *fully* developed—the "door" into the human kingdom closes; and henceforward the number of "human" Monads, *i.e.*, Monads in the human stage of development, is complete. For the Monads which had not reached the human stage by this point, will, owing to the evolution of Humanity itself, find themselves so far behind, that they will reach the human stage only at the close of the Seventh and last Round. They will, therefore, not be men on this Chain, but will form the Humanity of a future Manvantara, and be rewarded by becoming "men" on a higher Chain altogether, thus receiving their Karmic compensation. To this there is *but one solitary exception*, and for very good reasons, of which we shall speak farther on. But this accounts for the difference in the Races.

It thus becomes apparent how perfect is the analogy between the processes of Nature in the cosmos and in the individual man. The latter lives through his life-cycle, and dies. His higher principles, corresponding in the development of a Planetary Chain to the cycling Monads, pass into Devachan, which corresponds to the Nirvâna and states of rest intervening between two Chains. The man's lower principles are disintegrated in time, and are used by Nature again for the formation of new human principles; the same process also taking place in the disintegration and formation of Worlds. Analogy is thus the surest guide to the comprehension of the Occult teachings.

This is one of the "seven mysteries of the moon," and it is now revealed. The seven "mysteries" are called by the Japanese Yamabooshis, the mystics of the Lao-Tze sect and the ascetic monks of Kioto, the Dzenodoo—the "Seven Jewels"; only, the Japanese and the Chinese Buddhist ascetics and Initiates are, if possible, even more reticent in giving out their "Knowledge" than are the Hindûs.

But the reader must not be allowed to lose sight of the Monads, and must be enlightened as to their nature, as far as permitted, without trespassing upon the highest mysteries, of which the writer does not in any way pretend to know the last or final word.

The Monadic Host may be roughly divided into three great Classes:

1. The most developed Monads—the Lunar Gods or "Spirits," called, in India, the Pitris—whose function it is to pass in the First Round through the whole triple cycle of the mineral, vegetable and animal kingdoms, in their most ethereal, filmy, and rudimentary forms, in order to clothe themselves in, and assimilate, the nature of the newly formed Chain. They are those who first reach the human form—if there can be any form in the realm of the almost subjective—on Globe A, in the First Round. It is they, therefore, who lead and represent the human element during the Second and Third Rounds, and finally evolve their shadows at the beginning of the Fourth Round for the second Class, or those who come behind them.

2. Those Monads that are the first to reach the human stage during the three and a half Rounds, and to become "men."

3. The laggards, the Monads which are retarded, and which will not reach, by reason of Karmic impediments, the human stage at all during this Cycle or Round, save one exception which will be spoken of elsewhere, as already promised.

We are forced to use above the misleading word "men," and this is a clear proof of how little any European language is adapted to express these subtle distinctions.

It stands to reason that these "men" did not resemble the men of to-day, either in form or nature. Why then, it may be asked, call them "men" at all? Because there is no other term, in any Western language, which approximately conveys the idea intended. The word "men" at least indicates that these beings were "*manus*," thinking entities, however they differed in form and intellection from ourselves. But in reality they were, in respect of spirituality and intellection, rather "gods" than "men." The same difficulty of language is met with in describing the "stages" through which the Monad passes. Metaphysically speaking, it is of course an absurdity to talk of the "development" of a Monad, or to say that *it* becomes "man." But any attempt to preserve metaphysical accuracy of language, in the use of such a tongue as the English, would necessitate at least three extra volumes of this work, and would entail an amount of verbal repetition which would be wearisome in the extreme. It stands to reason that a Monad cannot either progress or develop, or even be affected by the changes of state it passes through. *It is not of this world or plane*, and may only be compared to an indestructible star of divine light and fire, thrown down on to our Earth, as a plank of salvation for the Personalities in which it indwells. It is for the latter to cling to it; and thus partaking of its divine nature, obtain immortality. Left to itself the Monad will cling to no one; but, like the plank, be drifted away to another incarnation, by the unresting current of evolution.

Now the evolution of the *external* form, or body, round the *astral*, is produced by the terrestrial forces, just as in the case of the lower kingdoms; but the evolution of the *internal*, or real, *Man* is purely spiritual. It is now no more a passage of the impersonal Monad through many and various forms of matter—endowed at best with instinct and consciousness on quite a different plane—as in the case of external evolution, but a journey of the "Pilgrim-Soul" through various *states* of not only matter, but of self-consciousness and self-perception, or of *perception* from *apperception*.

The Monad emerges from its state of spiritual and intellectual unconsciousness; and, skipping the first two planes—too near the Absolute to permit of any correlation with anything on a lower plane—it gets directly into the plane of Mentality. But there is no plane in the whole universe with a broader margin, or a wider field of action, in its almost endless gradations of perceptive and apperceptive qualities, than this plane, which has in its turn an appropriate smaller plane for every "form," from the Mineral Monad up to the time when that Monad blossoms forth by evolution into the Divine Monad. But all the time it is still one and the same Monad, differing only in its incarnations, throughout its ever succeeding cycles of partial or total obscuration of spirit, or partial or total obscuration of matter—two polar antitheses—as it ascends into the realms of mental spirituality, or descends into the depths of materiality.

To return to *Esoteric Buddhism*. The second statement is with regard to the enormous period intervening between the mineral epoch, on Globe A, and the man epoch, the term "man epoch" being used because of the necessity of giving a name to that fourth kingdom which follows the animal, though in truth the "man" on Globe A, during the First Round, is no man, but only his prototype, or dimensionless image, from the astral regions. The statement runs as follows:

The full development of the mineral epoch on Globe A, prepares the way for the vegetable development, and, as soon as this begins, the mineral life-impulse overflows into Globe B. Then, when the vegetable development on Globe A is complete and the animal development begins, the vegetable life-impulse overflows to Globe B, and the mineral impulse passes on to Globe C. Then finally comes the human life impulse on Globe A.

And so it goes on for three Rounds, when it slackens, and finally stops at the threshold of our Globe, in the Fourth Round; because the human period (of the true physical men to be), the seventh, is now reached. This is evident, for as said:

... There are processes of evolution which precede the mineral kingdom, and thus a wave of evolution, indeed several waves of evolution, precede the mineral wave in its progress round the spheres.

And now we have to quote from another article, "The Mineral Monad," in *Five Years of Theosophy*:

There are seven kingdoms. The first group comprises three degrees of elementals, or nascent centres of forces—from the first stage of differentiation of Mûlaprakriti to its third degree—*i.e.*, from full unconsciousness to semi-perception; the second or higher group embraces the kingdoms from vegetable to man; the mineral kingdom thus forming the central or turning point in the degrees of the "Monadic Essence," considered as an evolving energy. Three stages on the elemental side; the mineral kingdom; three stages on the objective physical side—these are the seven links of the evolutionary chain.

"Preliminary" because they are preparatory, and though belonging in fact to the natural, they would be more correctly described as the sub-natural evolution. This process makes a halt in its stages at the third, at the threshold of the fourth stage, when it becomes, on the plane of natural evolution, the first really manward stage, thus forming with the three elemental kingdoms, the ten, the Sephirothal number. It is at this point that begins:

A descent of spirit into matter equivalent to an ascent in physical evolution; a reäscent from the deepest depths of materiality (the mineral) towards its *status quo ante*, with a corresponding dissipation of concrete organism—up to Nirvâna, the vanishing point of differentiated matter.

Therefore it becomes evident, why that which is pertinently called in *Esoteric Buddhism* "wave of evolution," and "mineral, vegetable, animal and man-impulse," stops at the door of our Globe, at its Fourth Cycle or Round. It is at this point that the Cosmic Monad (Buddhi) will be wedded to, and become the vehicle of, the Âtmic Ray; *i.e.*, Buddhi will awaken to an apperception of it (Âtman), and thus enter on the first step of a new septenary ladder of evolution, which will lead it eventually to the tenth, counting from the lowest upwards, of the Sephirothal Tree, the Crown.

Everything in the Universe follows analogy. "As above, so below"; Man is the microcosm of the Universe. That which takes place on the spiritual plane, repeats itself on the cosmic plane. Concretion follows the lines of abstraction; corresponding to the highest must be the lowest; the material to the spiritual. Thus, corresponding to the Sephirothal Crown, or Upper Triad, there are the three elemental kingdoms, which precede the mineral, and which, using the language of the Kabalists, answer in the cosmic differentiation to the Worlds of Form and Matter, from the Super-Spiritual to the Archetypal.

Now what is a Monad? And what relation does it bear to an Atom? The following reply is based upon the explanations given in answer to these questions in the above-cited article, "The Mineral Monad," written by the author. To the second question it is answered:

None whatever to the atom or molecule as at present existing in the scientific conception. It can neither be compared with the microscopic organisms, once classed among polygastric infusoria, and now regarded as vegetable, and classed among algæ; nor is it quite the *monas* of the Peripatetics. Physically or constitutionally the Mineral Monad differs, of course, from the Human Monad, which is not physical, nor can its constitution be rendered by chemical symbols and elements.

In short, as the Spiritual Monad is One, Universal, Boundless and Impartite, whose Rays, nevertheless, form what we, in our ignorance, call the "Individual Monads" of men, so the Mineral Monad—being at the opposite curve of the circle—is also One, and from it proceed the countless physical atoms, which Science is beginning to regard as individualized.

Otherwise how could one account for, and explain mathematically, the evolutionary and spiral progress of the four kingdoms? The Monad is the combination of the last two principles in man, the sixth and the seventh, and, properly speaking, the term "Human Monad" applies only to the Dual Soul (Âtmâ-Buddhi), not to its highest spiritual vivifying principle, Âtmâ, alone. But since the Spiritual Soul, if divorced from the latter (Âtmâ), could have no existence, no being, it has thus been called.... Now the Monadic, or rather Cosmic, Essence, if such a term be permitted, in the mineral, vegetable and animal, though the same throughout the series of cycles, from the lowest elemental up to the Deva kingdom, yet differs in the scale of progression. It would be very misleading to imagine a Monad as a separate Entity, trailing its slow way in a distinct path through the lower kingdoms, and after an incalculable series of transformations flowering into a human being; in short, that the Monad of a Humboldt dates back to the Monad of an atom of hornblende. Instead of saying a "Mineral Monad," the more correct phraseology in Physical Science, which differentiates every atom, would of course have been to call it "the Monad manifesting in that form of Prakriti called 'the Mineral Kingdom'."The atom, as represented in the ordinary scientific hypothesis, is not a particle of something, animated by a psychic something, destined after æons to blossom into a man. But it is a concrete manifestation of the Universal Energy, which itself has not yet become individualized; a sequential manifestation of the one Universal Monas. The Ocean of Matter does not divide into its potential and constituent drops, until the sweep of the life-impulse reaches the evolutionary stage of man-birth. The tendency towards segregation into individual Monads is gradual, and in the higher animals comes almost to the point. The Peripatetics applied the word Monas to the whole Kosmos, in the pantheistic sense; and the Occultists, while accepting this thought for convenience sake, distinguish the progressive stages of the evolution of the concrete from the abstract, by terms of which the "Mineral, Vegetable, Animal Monad," etc., are examples. The term merely means that the tidal wave of spiritual evolution is passing through that arc of its circuit. The "Monadic Essence" begins to imperceptibly differentiate towards individual consciousness in the vegetable kingdom. As the Monads are uncompounded things, as correctly defined by Leibnitz, it is the Spiritual Essence which vivifies them in their degrees of differentiation, which properly constitutes the Monad—not the atomic aggregation, which is only the vehicle and the substance through which thrill the lower and the higher degrees of intelligence.

Leibnitz conceived of the Monads as elementary and indestructible units, endowed with the power of *giving and receiving* with respect to other units, and thus of determining all spiritual and physical phenomena. It is he who invented the term apperception, which together with nerve- (not perception, but rather) sensation, expresses the state of the Monadic consciousness through all the kingdoms up to Man.

Thus it may be wrong, on strictly metaphysical lines, to call Âtmâ-Buddhi a Monad, since in the materialistic view it is dual and therefore compound. But as Matter is Spirit, and *vice versâ*; and since the Universe and the Deity which informs it are unthinkable apart from each other; so in the case of Âtmâ-Buddhi. The latter being the vehicle of the former, Buddhi stands in the same relation to Âtmâ, as Adam-Kadmon, the Kabalistic Logos, does to Ain Suph, or Mûlaprakriti to Parabrahman.

And now a few words more on the Moon.

What, it may be asked, are the "Lunar Monads," just spoken of? The description of the seven Classes of Pitris will come later, but now some general explanations may be given. It must be plain to everyone that they are Monads, who, having ended their Life-Cycle on the Lunar Chain, which is inferior to the Terrestrial Chain, have incarnated on the latter. But there are some further details which may be added, though they border too closely on forbidden ground to be treated of fully. The last word of the mystery is divulged only to Adepts, but it may be stated that our satellite is only the gross body of its invisible principles. Seeing then that there are seven Earths, so there are seven Moons, the last alone being visible; the same for the Sun, whose visible body is called a Mâyâ, a reflection, just as man's body is. *"The real Sun and the real Moon are as invisible as the real man,"* says an Occult maxim.

And it may be remarked, *en passant*, that those Ancients were not so foolish after all who first started the idea of "Seven Moons." For though this conception is now taken solely as an astronomical measure of time, in a very materialized form, yet underlying the husk there can still be recognized the traces of a profoundly philosophical idea.

In reality the Moon is the satellite of the Earth in one respect only, viz., that physically the Moon revolves round the Earth. But in every other respect, it is the Earth which is the satellite of the Moon, and not *vice versâ*. Startling as the statement may seem, it is not without confirmation from scientific knowledge. It is evidenced by the tides, by the cyclic changes in many forms of disease, which coincide with the lunar phases; it can be traced in the growth of plants, and is very marked in the phenomena of human conception and gestation. The importance of the Moon and its influence on the Earth were recognized in every ancient religion, notably the Jewish, and have been remarked by many observers of psychical and physical phenomena. But, so far as Science knows, the Earth's action on the Moon is confined to the physical attraction, which causes her to circle in her orbit. And should an objector insist, that this fact alone is sufficient evidence that the Moon is truly the Earth's satellite on other planes of action, one may reply by asking whether a mother, who walks round and round her child's cradle, keeping watch over the infant, is the subordinate of her child or dependent upon it? Though in one sense she is its satellite, yet she is certainly older and more fully developed than the child she watches.

It is, then, the Moon that plays the largest and most important part, as well in the formation of the Earth itself, as in the peopling thereof with human beings. The Lunar Monads, or Pitris, the ancestors of man, become in reality man himself. They are the Monads, who enter on the cycle of evolution on Globe A, and who, passing round the Chain of Globes, evolve the human form, as has just been shown. At the beginning of the human stage of the Fourth Round on this Globe, they "ooze out" their astral doubles, from the "ape-like" forms which they had evolved in the Third Round. And it is this subtle, finer form, which serves as the model round which Nature builds physical man. These Monads, or Divine Sparks, are thus the Lunar Ancestors, the Pitris themselves; for these Lunar Spirits have to become "men," in order that their Monads may reach a higher plane of activity and self-consciousness, *i.e.*, the plane of the Mânasa-Putras, those who endow the "senseless" shells, created and informed by the Pitris, with "mind," in the latter part of the Third Root-Race.

In the same way, the Monads, or Egos, of the men of the Seventh Round of our Earth, after our own Globes A, B, C, D, etc., parting with their life-energy, will have informed, and thereby called to life, other laya-centres, destined to live and act on a still higher plane of being—in the same way will the Terrene Ancestors create those who will become their superiors.

It now becomes plain, that there exists in Nature a triple evolutionary scheme for the formation of the three *periodical* Upâdhis; or rather three separate schemes of evolution, which in our system are inextricably interwoven and interblended at every point. These are the Monadic (or Spiritual), the Intellectual, and the Physical Evolutions. These three are the finite aspects, or the reflections on the field of Cosmic Illusion, of Âtmâ, the seventh, the One Reality.

1. The Monadic, as the name implies, is concerned with the growth and development into still higher phases of activity of the Monads, in conjunction with:

2. The Intellectual, represented by the Mânasa-Dhyânis (the Solar Devas, or the Agnishvatta Pitris), the "givers of intelligence and consciousness" to man, and:

3. The Physical, represented by the Chhâyâs of the Lunar Pitris, round which Nature has concreted the present physical body. This body serves as the vehicle for the "growth," to use a misleading word, and the transformations—through Manas, and owing to the accumulation of experiences—of the Finite into the Infinite, of the Transient into the Eternal and Absolute.

Each of these three systems has its own laws, and is ruled and guided by different sets of the highest Dhyânis or Logoi. Each is represented in the constitution of Man, the Microcosm of the great Macrocosm; and it is the union of these three streams in him, which makes him the complex being he now is.

Nature, the physical evolutionary Power, could never evolve Intelligence unaided; she can only create "senseless forms," as will be seen in our Anthropogenesis. The Lunar Monads cannot progress, for they have not yet had sufficient touch with the forms created by "Nature," to allow of their accumulating experiences through its means. It is the Mânasa-Dhyânis who fill up the gap, and they represent the evolutionary power of Intelligence and Mind, the link between Spirit and Matter—in this Round.

Also it must be borne in mind that the Monads which enter upon the evolutionary cycle upon Globe A, in the first Round, are in very different stages of development. Hence the matter becomes somewhat complicated. Let us recapitulate.

The most developed, the Lunar Monads, reach the human germ-stage in the First Round; become terrestrial, though very ethereal, human beings towards the end of the Third Round, remaining on the Globe through the "obscuration" period, as the seed for future mankind in the Fourth Round, and thus become the pioneers of Humanity at the beginning of this, the present Fourth Round. Others reach the human stage only during later Rounds, *i.e.*, in the second, third or first half of the Fourth Round. And finally the most retarded of all—*i.e.*, those still occupying animal forms after the middle turning-point of the Fourth Round—will not become men at all during this Manvantara. They will reach to the verge of Humanity only at the close of the Seventh Round, to be, in their turn, ushered into a new Chain, after Pralaya, by older pioneers, the progenitors of Humanity, or the Seed-Humanity (Shishta), viz., the men who will be at the head of all at the end of these Rounds.

The student scarcely needs any further explanation on the part played by the Fourth Globe and the Fourth Round in the scheme of evolution.

From the preceding diagrams, which are applicable, *mutatis mutandis*, to Rounds, Globes or Races, it will be seen that the fourth member of a series occupies a unique position. Unlike the others, the Fourth has no "sister" Globe on the same plane as itself, and it thus forms the fulcrum of the "balance" represented by the whole Chain. It is the sphere of final evolutionary adjustments, the world of the Karmic scales, the Hall of Justice, where the balance is struck which determines the future course of the Monad during the remainder of its incarnations in the Cycle. And therefore is it that, after this central turning-point has been passed in the Great Cycle—*i.e.*, after the middle point of the Fourth Race in the Fourth Round on our Globe—no more Monads can enter the human kingdom. The door is closed for this Cycle, and the balance struck. For were it otherwise—had there been a new soul created for each of the countless milliards of human beings that have passed away, and had there been no reïncarnation—it would become difficult indeed to provide room for the disembodied "spirits"; nor could the origin and cause of suffering ever be accounted for. It is the ignorance of the Occult tenets, and the enforcement of false conceptions under the guise of religious education, which have created Materialism and Atheism as a protest against the asserted divine order of things.

The only exceptions to the rule just stated are the "dumb races," whose Monads are already within the human stage, in virtue of the fact that these "animals" are later than, and even half descended from, man; their last descendants being the anthropoid and other apes. These "human presentments" are in truth only the distorted copies of the early humanity. But this will receive full attention in the next volume.

As the Commentary, broadly rendered, says:

1. Every Form on earth, and every Speck in Space strives in its efforts towards self-formation to follow the model placed for it in the "Heavenly Man."... Its (the atom's) involution and evolution, its external and internal growth and development, have all one and the same object—Man; Man, as the highest physical and ultimate form on this Earth; the "Monad," in its absolute totality and awakened condition—as the culmination of the divine incarnations on Earth.

2. The Dhyânis are those who have evolved their Bhuta from themselves, which Rûpa has become the vehicle of Monads that had completed their cycle of transmigration in the three preceding Kalpas . Then, they became the men of the first Human Race of the Round. But they were not complete, and were senseless.

This will be explained in the sequel. Meanwhile man—or rather his Monad—has existed on Earth from the very beginning of this Round. But, up to our own Fifth Race, the external shapes which covered those divine Astral Doubles, have changed and consolidated with every sub-race; the form and physical structure of the fauna changing at the same time, as they had to be adapted to the ever-changing conditions of life on this Globe, during the geological periods of its formative cycle. And thus will they go on changing with every Root-Race, and every *chief* sub-race, down to the last one of the Seventh in this Round.

3. The inner, now concealed, man, was then the external man. The progeny of the Dhyânis , he was "the son like unto his father." Like the lotus, whose external shape assumes gradually the form of the model within itself, so did the form of man in the beginning evolve from within without. After the cycle in which man began to procreate his species after the fashion of the present animal kingdom, it became the reverse. The human fœtus follows now in its transformations all the forms that the physical frame of man assumed, throughout the three Kalpas , during the tentative efforts at plastic formation around the Monad, by senseless, because imperfect, matter, in her blind wanderings. In the present age, the physical embryo is a plant, a reptile, an animal, before it finally becomes man, evolving within himself his own ethereal counterpart, in his turn. In the beginning it was that counterpart which, being senseless, got entangled in the meshes of matter.

But this "man" belongs to the Fourth Round. As shown, the Monad had passed through, journeyed and been imprisoned in, every transitional form, throughout every kingdom of nature, during the three preceding Rounds. But the Monad which becomes human, is *not the Man*. In this Round—with the exception of the highest mammals after man, the anthropoids destined to die out in this our race, when their Monads will be liberated and pass into the astral human forms, or the highest elementals, of the Sixth and the Seventh Races, and then into the lowest human forms in the Fifth Round—no units of any of the kingdoms are animated any longer by Monads destined to become human in their next stage, but only by the lower elementals of their respective realms. These "elementals" will become human Monads, in their turn, only at the next great planetary Manvantara.

And in fact the last human Monad incarnated before the beginning of the Fifth Root-Race. Nature never repeats herself; therefore the anthropoids of our day have not existed at any time since the middle of the Miocene period, when, like all cross breeds, they began to show a tendency, more and more marked as time went on, to return to the type of their first parent, the gigantic black and yellow Lemuro-Atlantean. To search for the "missing link" is useless. To the Scientists of the closing Sixth Root-Race, millions and millions of years hence, our modern races, or rather their fossils, will appear as those of small insignificant apes—an extinct species of the *genus homo*.

Such anthropoids form an exception because they were not intended by Nature, but are the direct product and creation of "senseless" man. The Hindûs attribute a divine origin to the apes and monkeys, because the men of the Third Race were gods from another plane, who had become "senseless" mortals. This subject had already been touched upon in *Isis Unveiled*, twelve years ago, as plainly as was then possible. The reader is there referred to the Brâhmans, if he would know the reason of the regard they have for the monkeys.

He would perhaps learn—were the Brâhman to judge him worthy of an explanation—that the Hindû sees in the ape but what Manu desired he should: the transformation of species most directly connected with that of the human family—a bastard branch engrafted on their own stock before the final perfection of the latter. He might learn, further, that in the eyes of the educated "heathen" the spiritual or inner man is one thing, and his terrestrial physical casket another. That physical nature, that great combination of correlations of physical forces, ever creeping on towards perfection, has to avail herself of the material at hand; she models and remodels as she proceeds, and, finishing her crowning work in man, presents him alone as a fit tabernacle for the overshadowing of the Divine Spirit.

Moreover, a German scientific work is mentioned in a footnote on the same page. It says that:

A Hanoverian Scientist has recently published a work entitled, *Ueber die Auflösung der Arten durch Natürliche Zucht-wahl*, in which he shows, with great ingenuity, that Darwin was wholly mistaken in tracing man back to the ape. On the contrary, he maintains that it is the ape which is evolved from man. He shows that, in the beginning, mankind were, morally and physically, the types and prototypes of our present race and of our human dignity, by their beauty of form, regularity of feature, cranial development, nobility of sentiments, heroic impulses, and grandeur of ideal conceptions. This is a purely Brâhmanic, Buddhistic and Kabalistic doctrine. His book is copiously illustrated with diagrams, tables, etc. It asserts that the gradual debasement and degradation of man, morally and physically, can be readily traced throughout ethnological transformations down to our time. And, as one portion has already degenerated into apes, so the civilized man of the present day will at last, under the action of the inevitable law of necessity, be also succeeded by like descendants. If we may judge of the future by the actual present, it certainly does seem possible that so unspiritual and materialistic a race should end as Simia rather than as Seraphs.

But though the apes descend from man, it is certainly not the fact that the human Monad, which has once reached the level of humanity, ever incarnates again in the form of an animal.

The cycle of "metempsychosis" for the human Monad is closed, for we are in the Fourth Round and the Fifth Root-Race. The reader will have to bear in mind—at any rate one who has made himself acquainted with *Esoteric Buddhism*—that the Stanzas which follow in this volume and the next speak of the evolution in our Fourth Round only. The latter is the cycle of the turning-point, after which, matter, having reached its lowest depths, begins to strive onward and to become spiritualized, with every new race and with every fresh cycle. Therefore the student must take care not to see contradiction where there is none, for in *Esoteric Buddhism* Rounds are spoken of in general, while here only the Fourth, or our present Round, is meant. Then it was the work of formation; now it is that of reformation and evolutionary perfection.

Finally, to close this digression anent various, but unavoidable, misconceptions, we must refer to a statement in *Esoteric Buddhism*, which has produced a very fatal impression upon the minds of many Theosophists. One unfortunate sentence, from the work just referred to, is constantly brought forward to prove the materialism of the doctrine. The author, referring to the progress of organisms on the Globes, says that:

The mineral kingdom will no more develop the vegetable … than the Earth was able to develop man from the ape, till it received an impulse.

Whether this sentence renders the thought of the author literally, or is simply, as we believe it is, a *lapsus calami*, may remain an open question.

It is really with surprise that we have ascertained the fact, that *Esoteric Buddhism* was so little understood by some Theosophists, as to have led them into the belief that it thoroughly supported Darwinian evolution, and especially the theory of the descent of man from a pithecoid ancestor. As one member writes: "I suppose you realize that three-fourths of Theosophists and even outsiders imagine that, as far as the evolution of man is concerned, Darwinism and Theosophy kiss one another." Nothing of the kind was ever realized, nor is there any great warrant for it, so far as we know, in *Esoteric Buddhism*. It has been repeatedly stated, that evolution as taught by Manu and Kapila was the groundwork of the modern teachings, but neither Occultism nor Theosophy has ever supported the wild theories of the present Darwinists—least of all the descent of man from an ape. Of this, more hereafter. But one has only to turn to p. 47 of the work named, to find the statement that:

Man belongs to a kingdom distinctly separate from that of the animals.

With such a plain and unequivocal statement before him, it is very strange that any careful student should have been so misled, unless he is prepared to charge the author with a gross contradiction.

Every Round repeats the evolutionary work of the preceding Round, on a higher scale. With the exception of some higher anthropoids, as just mentioned, the Monadic inflow, or inner evolution, is at an end till the next Manvantara. It can never be too often repeated that the full-blown human Monads have to be first disposed of, before the new crop of candidates appears on this Globe at the beginning of the next Cycle. Thus there is a lull; and this is why, during the Fourth Round, man appears on Earth earlier than any animal creation, as will be described.

But it is still urged that the author of *Esoteric Buddhism* has "preached Darwinism" all along. Certain passages would undoubtedly seem to lend countenance to this inference. Besides which, the Occultists themselves are ready to concede *partial* correctness to the Darwinian hypothesis, in later details, bye-laws of evolution, and after the midway point of the Fourth Race. Of that which has taken place, Physical Science can really know nothing, for such matters lie entirely outside of its sphere of investigation. But what the Occultists have never admitted, nor will they ever admit, is that man was *an ape in this or any other Round*; or that he ever could be one, however much he may have been "ape-like." This is vouched for by the very authority from whom the author of *Esoteric Buddhism* got his information.

Thus to those who confront the Occultists with these lines from the above-named volume:

It is enough to show that we may as reasonably—and that we must, if we would talk about these matters at all—conceive a life-impulse giving birth to mineral forms, as of the same sort of impulse concerned to *raise a race of apes into a race of rudimentary men*.

To those who bring this passage forward as showing "decided Darwinism," the Occultists answer by pointing to the explanation of the Master, Mr. Sinnett's Teacher, which would contradict these lines, were they written in the spirit attributed to them. A copy of this letter was sent to the writer, together with others, two years ago (1886), with additional marginal remarks, to quote from, in the *Secret Doctrine*.

It begins by considering the difficulty experienced by the Western student, in reconciling some facts, previously given, with the evolution of man from the animal, *i.e.*, from the mineral, vegetable and animal kingdoms, and advises the student to hold to the doctrine of analogy and correspondences. Then it touches upon the mystery of the Devas, and even Gods, having to pass through states, which it was agreed to refer to as "Immetallization, Inherbation, Inzoönization and finally Incarnation," and explains this by hinting at the necessity of failures even in the ethereal races of Dhyân Chohans. Concerning this it says:

"These 'failures' are too far progressed and spiritualized to be thrown back forcibly from Dhyân Chohanship into the vortex of a new primordial evolution through the lower kingdoms...."

After which, a hint only is given about the mystery contained in the allegory of the fallen Asuras, which will be expanded and explained in Volume II. When Karma has reached them at the stage of human evolution:

"They will have to drink it to the last drop in the bitter cup of retribution. Then they become an active force and commingle with the elementals, the progressed entities of the pure animal kingdom, to develop little by little the full type of humanity."

These Dhyân Chohans, as we see, do not pass through the three kingdoms as do the lower Pitris; nor do they incarnate in man until the Third Root Race. Thus, as the teaching stands:

"Round I. Man in the First Round and First Race on Globe D, our Earth, was an ethereal being (a Lunar Dhyâni, as man), non-

intelligent but super-spiritual; and correspondingly, on the law of analogy, in the First Race of the Fourth Round. In each of the subsequent races and sub-races, ... he grows more and more into an encased or incarnate being, but still preponderatingly ethereal.... He is sexless, and, like the animal and vegetable, he develops monstrous bodies correspondential with his coarser surroundings.

"Round II. He is still gigantic and ethereal, but growing firmer and more condensed in body; a more physical man yet still less intelligent than spiritual (1), for mind is a slower and more difficult evolution than is the physical frame....

"Round III. He has now a perfectly concrete or compacted body, at first the form of a giant-ape, and now more intelligent, or rather cunning, than spiritual. For, on the downward arc, he has now reached a point where his primordial spirituality is eclipsed and overshadowed by nascent mentality (2). In the last half of the Third Round, his gigantic stature decreases, and his body improves in texture, and he becomes a more rational being, though still more an ape than a Deva....

"Round IV. Intellect has an enormous development in this Round. The dumb races acquire our human speech on this Globe, on which, from the Fourth Race, language is perfected and knowledge increases. At this half-way point of the Fourth Round, humanity passes the axial point of the minor manvantaric cycle ... the world teeming with the results of intellectual activity and spiritual decrease...."

This is from the authentic letter; what follows are the later remarks and additional explanations traced by the same hand in the form of footnotes.

"(1) ... The original letter contained general teaching—a 'bird's-eye view'—and particularized nothing.... To speak of 'physical man,' while limiting the statement to the early Rounds, would be drifting back to the miraculous and instantaneous 'coats of skin.'... The first 'Nature,' the first 'body,' the first 'mind' on the first plane

of perception, on the first Globe in the first Round, is what was meant. For Karma and evolution have:
'... centred in our make such strange extremes,
From different Natures marvellously mixed ...'

"(2) Restore: he has now reached the point Third Root Race in the Fourth Round], where his primordial spirituality is eclipsed and overshadowed by nascent human mentality, and you have the true version on your thumb-nail...."

These are the words of the Teacher; text, words and sentences in brackets, and explanatory footnotes. It stands to reason that there must be an enormous difference in such terms as "objectivity" and "subjectivity," "materiality" and "spirituality ," when the same terms are applied to different planes of being and perception. All this must be taken in its relative sense. And therefore there is little to be wondered at, if, left to his own speculations, an author who, however eager to learn, was yet quite inexperienced in these abstruse teachings, has fallen into an error. Nor was the difference between the Rounds and the Races sufficiently defined in the letters received, since nothing of the kind had been required before, as the ordinary Eastern disciple would have found out the difference in a moment. Moreover, to quote from a letter of the Master:

"The teachings were imparted under protest.... They were, so to say, smuggled goods ... and when I remained face to face with only one correspondent, the other, Mr. ... had so far tossed all the cards into confusion, that little remained to be said without trespassing upon law."

Theosophists "whom it may concern" will understand what is meant.

The outcome of all this is, that nothing had ever been said in the letters to warrant the assurance, that the Occult doctrine has ever taught, or any Adept believed in, unless metaphorically, the preposterous modern theory of the descent of man from a common ancestor with the ape—an anthropoid of the actual animal kind. To this day the world is more full of ape-like men than the woods are of men-like apes. The ape is sacred in India because its origin is well known to the Initiates, though concealed under a thick veil of allegory. Hanumâna is the son of Pavana (Vâyu, "God of the wind") by Anjanâ, wife of a monster called Kesarî, though his genealogy varies. The reader who bears this in mind, will find in Volume II, *passim*, the whole explanation of this ingenious allegory. The "men" of the Third Race (who separated) were "Gods," by their spirituality and purity, though senseless, and as yet destitute of mind, as men. These "men" of the Third Race, the ancestors of the Atlanteans, were just such ape-like, intellectually senseless, giants as were those beings, who, during the Third Round, represented Humanity. Morally irresponsible, it was these Third Race "men" who, through promiscuous connection with animal species lower than themselves, created that missing link which became ages later (in the Tertiary period only), the remote ancestor of the real ape, as we find it now in the pithecoid family.

And if this is found clashing with the statement which shows the animal later than man, then the reader is asked to bear in mind that the *placental mammal* only is meant. In those days, there were animals of which Zoölogy does not even dream in our own; *and the modes of reproduction were not identical* with the notions which modern Physiology has upon the subject. It is not altogether convenient to touch upon such questions in public, but there is *no* contradiction or impossibility in this whatever.

Thus the earlier teachings, however unsatisfactory, vague and fragmentary, did not teach the evolution of "man" from the "ape." Nor does the author of *Esoteric Buddhism* assert it anywhere in his work in so many words; but, owing to his inclination towards Modern Science, he uses language which might perhaps justify such an inference. The man who preceded the Fourth, the Atlantean, Race, however much he may have looked physically like a "gigantic ape"—"the counterfeit of man who hath not the life of a man"—was still a thinking and already a speaking man. The Lemuro-Atlantean was a highly civilized Race, and if one accepts tradition, which is better history than the speculative fiction which now passes under that name, he was higher than we are with all our sciences and the degraded civilization of the day: at any rate, the Lemuro-Atlantean of the closing Third Race was so.

And now we may return to the Stanzas.

Stanza VI.
—*Continued.*

5. At the Fourth (*a*), the Sons are told to create their Images. One Third refuses. Two obey.
The Curse is pronounced (*b*); they will be born in the Fourth, suffer and cause suffering. This is the First War (*c*).

The full meaning of this Shloka can only be fully comprehended after reading the additional detailed explanations, in the Anthropogenesis and its Commentaries, in Volume II. Between this Shloka and Shloka 4, extend long ages; and there now gleams the dawn and sunrise of another æon. The drama enacted on our planet is at the beginning of its fourth act; but for a clearer comprehension of the whole play the reader will have to turn back before he can proceed onward. For this verse belongs to the general Cosmogony given in the archaic volumes, whereas Volume II will give a detailed account of
the "creation," or rather formation, of the first human beings, followed by the second humanity, and then by the third; or, as they are called, the First, Second, and the Third Root-Races. As the solid Earth began by being a ball of liquid fire, of fiery dust and its protoplasmic phantom, so did man.

(*a*) That which is meant by the qualification the "Fourth," is explained as the Fourth Round, only on the authority of the Commentaries. It can equally mean Fourth Eternity as Fourth Round, or even our Fourth Globe. For, as will repeatedly be shown, the latter is the fourth sphere, on the fourth or lowest plane of material life. And it so happens that we are in the Fourth Round, at the middle point of which the perfect equilibrium between Spirit and Matter had to take place.

It was, as we shall see, at this period—during the highest point of civilization and knowledge, and also of human intellectuality, of the Fourth, Atlantean Race—that, owing to the final crisis of the physiologico-spiritual adjustment of the races, humanity branched off into two diametrically opposite paths:

the *Right-* and the *Left-hand* Paths of Knowledge or Vidyâ. In the words of the Commentary:

Thus were the germs of the White and the Black Magic sown in those days. The seeds lay latent for some time, to sprout only during the early period of the Fifth .

Says the Commentary explaining the Shloka:

The Holy Youths refused to multiply and create species after their likeness, after their kind. "They are not fit Forms for us. They have to grow." They refuse to enter the Chhâyâs of their inferiors. Thus had selfish feeling prevailed from the beginning, even among the Gods, and they fell under the eye of the Karmic Lipikas.

They had to suffer for it in later births. How the punishment reached the Gods will be seen in Volume II.

It is a universal tradition that, before the physiological "Fall," propagation of one's kind, whether human or animal, took place through the *Will* of the Creators, or of their progeny. This was the Fall of Spirit into generation, not the Fall of mortal Man. It has already been stated that, to become self-conscious, Spirit must pass through every cycle of being, culminating in its highest point on earth in Man. Spirit *per se* is an unconscious negative *abstraction*. Its purity is inherent, not acquired by merit; hence, as already shown, to become the highest Dhyân Chohan, it is necessary for each Ego to attain to full self-consciousness as a human, *i.e.*, conscious, being, which is synthesized for us in Man. The Jewish Kabalists, arguing that no Spirit can belong to the divine Hierarchy unless Ruach (Spirit) is united to Nephesh (Living Soul), only repeat the Eastern Esoteric teaching:

A Dhyâni has to be an Âtmâ-Buddhi; once the Buddhi-Manas breaks loose from the immortal Âtmâ, of which it (Buddhi) is the vehicle, Âtman passes into Non-Being, which is Absolute Being.

This means that the purely Nirvânic state is a passage of Spirit back to the ideal abstraction of Be-ness, which has no relation to the plane on which our Universe is accomplishing its cycle.

(*b*) "The Curse is pronounced" does not mean, in this instance, that any Personal Being, God, or Superior Spirit, pronounced it, but simply that the cause, which could but create bad results, had been generated; and that the effects of this Karmic cause could lead the Beings that counteracted the laws of Nature, and thus impeded her legitimate progress, only to bad incarnations, hence to suffering.

(*c*) "There were many Wars," all referring to struggles of adjustment, spiritual, cosmical and astronomical, but chiefly to the mystery of the evolution of man, as he is now. The Powers or pure Essences that were "told to create," relate to a mystery explained, as already said, elsewhere. It is not only one of the most hidden secrets of Nature—that of generation, over whose solution the Embryologists have vainly put their heads together—but likewise a divine function which involves that great religious, or rather dogmatic, mystery, the so-called "Fall" of the Angels. Satan and his rebellious host, when the meaning of the allegory is explained, will thus prove to have refused to create physical man, only to become the direct Saviours and Creators of divine Man. The symbolical teaching is more than mystical and religious, it is purely scientific, as will be seen later on. For, instead of remaining a mere blind functioning medium, impelled and guided by fathomless Law, the "rebellious" Angel claimed and enforced his right of independent judgment and will, his right of free-agency and responsibility, since Man and Angel are alike under Karmic Law.

Explaining Kabalistic views, the author of *New Aspects of Life* says of the Fallen Angels that:

According to the symbolical teaching, Spirit, from being simply a functionary agent of God, became volitional in its developed and developing action; and, substituting its own will for the divine desire in its regard, so fell. Hence the kingdom and reign of spirits and spiritual action, which flow from and are the product of spirit-volition, are outside, and contrasted with, and in contradiction to, the kingdom of souls and divine action.

So far, so good; but what does the author mean by saying:

When man was created, he was human in constitution, with human affections, human hopes and aspirations. From this state he fell—into the brute and savage.

This is diametrically opposite to our Eastern teaching, and even to the Kabalistic notion, so far as we understand it, and to the *Bible* itself. This looks like Corporealism and Substantialism colouring Positive Philosophy, though it is rather difficult to feel quite sure of the author's meaning. A *fall*, however, "from the natural into the supernatural and the animal"—supernatural meaning the purely spiritual in this case—implies what we suggest.

The *New Testament* speaks of one of these "Wars," as follows:

And there was war in heaven: Michael and his angels fought against the Dragon; and the Dragon fought and his angels, and prevailed not; neither was their place found any more in Heaven. And the great Dragon was cast out, that old serpent, called the Devil and Satan, which deceiveth the whole world.

The Kabalistic version of the same story is given in the *Codex Nazaræus*, the scripture of the Nazarenes, the real mystic Christians of John the Baptist, and the Initiates of Christos. Bahak Zivo, the "Father of the Genii," is ordered to construct creatures—to "create." But, as he is "ignorant of Orcus," he fails to do so, and calls in Fetahil, a still purer spirit, to his aid, who fails still worse. This is a repetition of the failure of the "Fathers," the Lords of Light, who fail one after the other. We will now quote from our earlier volumes:
Then steps on the stage of creation the Spirit (of the Earth so-called, or the Soul, Psyche, which St. James calls "devilish"), the lower portion of the Anima Mundi or Astral Light. With the Nazarenes and the Gnostics this Spirit was *feminine*. Thus the Spirit of the Earth, perceiving that for Fetahil, the newest man (the latest), the splendour was "changed," and that for splendour existed "decrease and

damage," she awakes Karabtanos, "who was frantic and *without sense and judgment*," and says to him: "Arise, see, the Splendour (Light) of the *Newest* Man (Fetahil) has failed (to produce or create men), the decrease of this Splendour is visible. Rise up, come with thy Mother (the Spiritus) and free thee from limits by which thou art held, and those more ample than the whole world." After which, follows the union of the frantic and blind matter, guided by the insinuations of the Spirit (not the *Divine* Breath but the *Astral*Spirit, which by its double essence is already tainted with matter); and the offer of the Mother being accepted, the Spiritus conceives "Seven Figures," and the Seven Stellars (Planets), which represent also the *seven capital sins*, the progeny of an Astral Soul, separated from its divine source (spirit), and *matter*, the blind demon of concupiscence. Seeing this, Fetahil extends his hand towards the abyss of matter, and says: "Let the earth exist, just as the abode of the Powers has existed." Dipping his hand in the chaos, which he condenses, he creates our planet.

Then the *Codex* proceeds to tell how Bahak Zivo was separated from the Spiritus, and the Genii or Angels from the Rebels. Then (the greatest) Mano, who dwells with the greatest Ferho, calls Kebar Zivo (known also by the name of Nebat Iavar bar Iufin Ifafin), the Helm and Vine of the Food of Life—he being the third Life, and commiserating the rebellious and foolish Genii, on account of the magnitude of their ambition, says: "Lord of the Genii (Æons), see what the Genii (the Rebellious Angels) do, and about what they are consulting. They say: 'Let us call forth the world, and let us call the "Powers" into existence. The Genii are the Princes (Principes), the Sons of Light, but Thou art the Messenger of Life'."

And in order to counteract the influence of the seven "badly disposed" principles the progeny of Spiritus, Kebar Zivo (or Cabar Zio), the mighty Lord of Splendour, produces *seven other lives* (the cardinal virtues), who shine in their own form and light "from on high," and thus reëstablish the balance between good and evil, light and darkness.

Here one finds a repetition of the early *allegorical* dual systems, such as the Zoroastrian, and detects a germ of the dogmatic and dualistic religions of the future, a germ which has grown into such a luxuriant tree in ecclesiastical Christianity. It is already the outline of the two "Supremes"—God and Satan. But in the Stanzas no such idea exists.

Most of the Western Christian Kabalists—preëminently Éliphas Lévi—in their desire to reconcile the Occult Sciences with Church Dogmas, did their best to make of the "Astral Light" only and preeminently the Plerôma of the early Church Fathers, the abode of the Hosts of the Fallen Angels, of the Archôns and Powers. But the Astral Light, though only the lower aspect of the Absolute, is still dual. It is the Anima Mundi, and ought never to be viewed otherwise, except for Kabalistic purposes. The difference which exists between its "Light" and its "Living Fire," ought ever to be present in the mind of the Seer and the Psychic. The higher aspect of this "Light," without which only creatures of matter can be produced, is this Living Fire, and its Seventh Principle. It is stated in *Isis Unveiled*, in a complete description of it:

The Astral Light or Anima Mundi is dual and bi-sexual. The (ideal) male part of it is purely divine and spiritual, it is Wisdom, it is Spirit or Purusha; while the female portion (the Spiritus of the Nazarenes) is tainted, in one sense, with matter, *is* indeed matter, and therefore is evil already. It is the life-principle of every living creature, and furnishes the astral soul, the fluidic *perisprit*, to men, animals, fowls of the air, and everything living. Animals have only the latent germ of the highest immortal soul in them. This latter will develop only after a series of countless evolutions; the doctrine of which evolutions is contained in the Kabalistic axiom: "A stone becomes a plant; a plant, a beast; a beast, a man; a man, a spirit; and the spirit, a god."

The seven principles of the Eastern Initiates had not been explained when *Isis Unveiled* was written, but only the three *Kabalistic Faces* of the semi-exoteric *Kabalah*. But these contain the description of the mystic natures of the first Group of Dhyân Chohans in the *regimen ignis*, the region and "rule (or government) of fire," divided into three classes, synthesized by the first, which makes *four* or the "Tetraktys." If one studies the commentaries attentively, he will find the same progression in the angelic natures, *viz.*, from the *passive* down to the *active*; the last of these Beings are as near to the Ahamkâra Element—the region or plane wherein *Egoship*, or the feeling of *I-am-ness*, is beginning to be defined—as the first are near to the undifferentiated Essence. The former are Arûpa, incorporeal; the latter, Rûpa, corporeal.

In Volume II of the same work, the philosophical systems of the Gnostics and the primitive Jewish Christians, the Nazarenes and the Ebionites, are fully considered. They show the views held in those days, outside the circle of Mosaic Jews, about Jehovah. He was identified by all the Gnostics with the evil, rather than with the good principle. For them, he was Ilda-Baoth, the "Son of Darkness," whose mother, Sophia Achamôth, was the daughter of Sophia, the Divine Wisdom—the female Holy Ghost of the early Christians—Âkâsha; Sophia Achamôth personifying the Lower Astral Light or Ether. The Astral Light stands in the same relation to Âkâsha and Anima Mundi, as Satan stands to the Deity. They are one and the same thing *seen from two aspects*, the spiritual and the psychic—the super-ethereal, or connecting link between matter and pure spirit—and the physical. Ilda-Baoth—a compound name, made up of *Ilda* (ילד), child, and *Baoth*; the latter from בהוצ an egg, and בהות, chaos, emptiness, void, or desolation; or the Child born in the Egg of Chaos, like Brahmâ—or Jehovah, is simply one of the Elohim, the Seven Creative Spirits, and one of the lower Sephiroth. Ilda-Baoth produces from himself seven other Gods, "Stellar Spirits," or the Lunar Ancestors, for they are all the same. They are all *in his own image*, the "Spirits of the Face," and the reflections one of the other, who become darker and more material, as they successively recede from their originator. They also inhabit seven regions disposed like a stair, for its steps mount and descend the scale of spirit and matter. With Pagans and Christians, with Hindûs and Chaldeans, with Greek as with Roman Catholics—the texts varying slightly in their interpretations—they all were the Genii of the seven planets, and of the seven planetary spheres of our septenary Chain, of which Earth is the lowest. This connects the "Stellar" and "Lunar" Spirits with the higher planetary Angels, and the Saptarshis, the Seven Rishis of the Stars, of the Hindûs—as subordinate Angels, or Messengers, to these Rishis, their emanations, on the descending scale. Such, in the opinion of the philosophical Gnostics, were the God and the Archangels

now worshipped by the Christians! The "Fallen Angels" and the legend of the "War in Heaven" are thus purely pagan in their origin, and come from India, *viá* Persia and Chaldea. The only reference to them in the Christian canon is found
in *Revelation* xii, as quoted a few pages back.

Thus "Satan," once he ceases to be viewed in the superstitious, dogmatic, unphilosophical spirit of the Churches, grows into the grandiose image of one who makes of a *terrestrial*, a *divine* Man; who gives him, throughout the long cycle of Mahâkalpa, the law of the Spirit of Life, and makes him free from the Sin of Ignorance, hence of Death.

6. THE OLDER WHEELS ROTATED DOWNWARD AND UPWARD (*a*).... THE MOTHER'S SPAWN FILLED THE WHOLE. THERE WERE BATTLES FOUGHT BETWEEN THE CREATORS AND THE DESTROYERS, AND BATTLES FOUGHT FOR SPACE; THE SEED APPEARING AND REÄPPEARING CONTINUOUSLY (*b*).
(*a*) Here, having finished for the time being with our side-issues—which, however they may break the flow of the narrative, are necessary for the elucidation of the whole scheme—we must return once more to Cosmogony. The phrase "Older Wheels" refers to the Worlds, or Globes, of our Chain as they were during the previous Rounds. The present Stanza, when explained esoterically, is found embodied entirely in Kabalistic works. Therein will be found the very history of the evolution of those countless Globes, which evolve after a periodical Pralaya, rebuilt from old material into new forms. The previous Globes disintegrate and reäppear, transformed and perfected for a new phase of life. In the *Kabalah*, worlds are compared to sparks which fly from under the hammer of the great Architect—*Law*, the Law which rules all the smaller Creators.

The following comparative diagram shows the identity between the two systems, the Kabalistic and the Eastern. The three upper are the three higher planes of consciousness, revealed and explained in both schools only to the Initiates; the lower represent the four lower planes—the lowest being our plane, or the visible Universe.

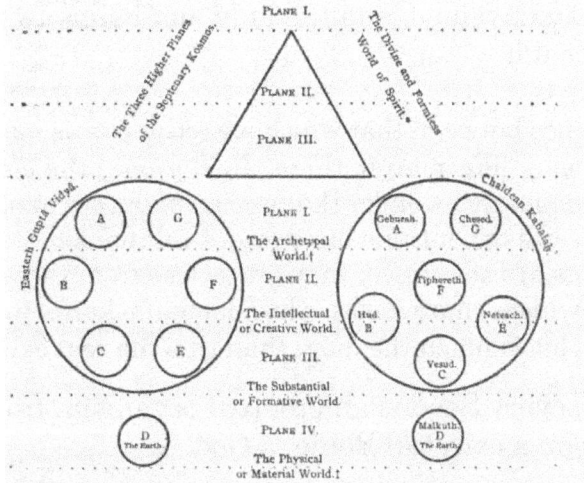

These seven *planes* correspond to the seven *states* of consciousness in man. It remains with him to attune the three higher states in himself to the three higher planes in Kosmos. But before he can attempt to attune, he must awaken the three "seats" to life and activity. And how many are capable of bringing themselves to even a superficial comprehension of Âtmâ Vidyâ (Spirit-Knowledge), or what is called by the Sufis, Rohanee!

(*b*) "The Seed appearing and reäppearing continuously." Here "Seed" stands for the "World-Germ," viewed by Science as material particles in a highly attenuated condition, but in Occult Physics as "spiritual particles," *i.e.*, supersensuous matter existing in a state of primeval differentiation. To see and appreciate the difference—the immense gulf that separates terrestrial matter from the finer grades of supersensuous matter—every Astronomer, every Chemist and Physicist ought to be a *Psychometer*, to say the least; he ought to be able to sense for himself that difference in which he now refuses to believe. Mrs. Elizabeth Denton, one of the most learned, and also one of the most materialistic and sceptical women of her age—the wife of Professor Denton, the well-known American Geologist, and the author of *The Soul of*

Things—was, in spite of her scepticism, one of the most wonderful psychometers. This is what she describes in one of her experiments. A particle of a meteorite was placed on her forehead, in an envelope, and the lady, not being aware of what it contained, said:

What a difference between that which we recognize as matter here and that which seems like matter there! In the one, the *elements are so coarse and so angular*, I wonder that we can endure it at all, much more that we can desire to continue our present relations to it; in the other, all the elements are so refined, they are so free from those great, rough angularities, which characterize the elements here, that I can but regard *that* as by so much the more than this the real existence.

In Theogony, every Seed is an ethereal organism, from which evolves later on a celestial Being, a God.

In the "Beginning," that which is called in mystic phraseology "Cosmic Desire" evolves into Absolute Light. Now light without any shadow would be absolute light; in other words, absolute darkness, as Physical Science tries to prove. This "shadow" appears under the form of primordial matter, allegorized—if you will—in the shape of the Spirit of Creative Fire or Heat. If, rejecting the poetical form and allegory, Science chooses to see in this the primordial "fire-mist," it is welcome to do so. Whether one way or the other, whether Fohat or the famous Force of Science, nameless and as difficult of definition as our Fohat himself, that Something "caused the Universe to move with circular motion," as Plato has it; or, as the Occult teaching expresses it:

The Central Sun causes Fohat to collect primordial dust in the form of balls, to impel them to move in converging lines and finally to approach each other and aggregate.... Being scattered in Space, without order or system, the World-Germs come into frequent collision until their final aggregation, after which they become Wanderers . Then the battles and struggles begin. The older attract the younger, while others repel them. Many perish, devoured by their stronger companions. Those that escape become worlds.

When carefully analyzed and reflected upon, this will be found as scientific as Science can make it, even at our late period.

We have been assured, that there exist several modern works of speculative fancy upon such struggles for life in sidereal heaven, especially in the German language. We rejoice to hear it, for ours is an Occult teaching lost in the darkness of archaic ages. We have treated of it fully in *Isis Unveiled*, and the idea of Darwinian-like evolution, of struggle for life and supremacy, and of the "survival of the fittest," among the Hosts above as of the Hosts below, runs throughout both the volumes of our earlier work, written in 1876. But the idea is not ours, it is that of antiquity. Even the Purânic writers have ingeniously interwoven allegory with cosmic facts and human events. Any symbologist may discern their astro-cosmical allusions, even though he be unable to grasp the whole meaning. The great "wars in heaven," in the *Purânas*; the wars of the Titans, in Hesiod and other classical writers; the "struggles" also between Osiris and Typhon, in the Egyptian myth; and even those in the Scandinavian legends; all refer to the same subject. Northern Mythology refers to it as the battle of the Flames, the sons of Muspel who fought on the field of Wigred. All these relate to Heaven and Earth, and have a double, and often even a triple, meaning and esoteric application to things above as to things below. They severally relate to astronomical, theogonical and human struggles; to the adjustment of orbs, and the supremacy among nations and tribes. The "struggle for existence" and the "survival of the fittest" reigned supreme from the moment that Kosmos manifested into being, and could hardly escape the observant eye of the ancient Sages. Hence the incessant fights of Indra, the God of the Firmament, with the Asuras—degraded from high Gods into cosmic Demons—and with Vritra or Ahi; the battles fought between stars and constellations, between moons and planets—later on incarnated as kings and mortals. Hence also the War in Heaven of Michael and his Host against the Dragon—Jupiter and Lucifer Venus—when a third of the stars of the rebellious Host was hurled down into Space, and "its place was found no more in Heaven." As we wrote long ago:

This is the basic and fundamental stone of the secret cycles. It shows that the Brâhmans and Tanaïm ... speculated on the creation and development of the world quite in a Darwinian way, both anticipating him and his school in the natural selection, gradual development and transformation of species.

There were old worlds that perished, conquered by the new, etc., etc. The assertion that all the worlds (stars, planets, etc.)—as soon as a nucleus of primordial substance, in the laya (undifferentiated) state, is informed by the freed principles of a just *deceased* sidereal body—become first comets, and then suns, to cool down to inhabitable worlds, is a teaching as old as the Rishis.

Thus the Secret Books, as we see, distinctly teach an astronomy that would not be rejected even by modern speculation, could the latter thoroughly understand its teachings.

For archaic astronomy and the ancient physical and mathematical sciences expressed views identical with those of Modern Science, and many of far more momentous import. A "struggle for life" and a "survival of the fittest," in the worlds above and on our planet here below, are distinctly taught. This teaching, however, although it would not be entirely rejected by Science, is sure to be repudiated as an integral whole. For it avers that there are only seven self-born primordial "Gods," emanated from the trinitarian One. In other words, it means that all the worlds, or sidereal bodies—always on strict analogy—are formed one from the other, after the primordial manifestation at the beginning of the Great Age is accomplished.

The birth of the celestial bodies in space is compared to a multitude of pilgrims at the Festival of the Fires. Seven ascetics appear on the threshold of the temple with seven lighted sticks of incense. At the light of these the first row of pilgrims light their incense sticks. After which, every ascetic begins whirling his stick around his head in space, and furnishes the rest with fire. Thus with the heavenly bodies. A laya-centre is lighted and awakened into life by the fires of another "pilgrim," after which, the new "centre" rushes into space and becomes a comet. It is only after losing its velocity, and hence its fiery tail, that the Fiery Dragon settles down into quiet and steady life, as a regular respectable citizen of the sidereal family. Therefore it is said:

Born in the unfathomable depths of Space, out of the homogeneous Element called the World-Soul, every nucleus of cosmic matter, suddenly launched into being, begins life under the most hostile circumstances. Through a series of countless ages, it has to conquer for itself a place in the infinitudes. It circles round and round, between denser and already fixed bodies, moving by jerks, and pulling towards some given point or centre that attracts it, and, like as a ship drawn into a channel dotted with reefs and sunken rocks, trying to avoid other bodies that draw and repel it in turn. Many perish, their mass disintegrating through stronger masses, and, when born within a system, chiefly within the insatiable stomachs of various Suns. Those which move slower, and are propelled into an elliptic course, are doomed to annihilation sooner or later. Others, moving in parabolic curves, generally escape destruction, owing to their velocity.

Some very critical readers will perhaps imagine that this teaching, as to the cometary stage passed through by all heavenly bodies, is in contradiction with the statements just made as to the Moon being the mother of the Earth. They will perhaps fancy that intuition is needed to harmonize the two. But no intuition is in truth required. What does Science know of comets, their genesis, growth, and ultimate behaviour? Nothing—absolutely nothing! And what is there so impossible in that a laya-centre—a lump of cosmic protoplasm, homogeneous and latent—when suddenly animated or fired up, should rush from its bed in space, and whirl throughout the abysmal depths, in order to strengthen its homogeneous organism by an accumulation and addition of differentiated elements? And why should not such a comet settle in life, live, and become an inhabited globe?

"The abodes of Fohat are many"—it is said. *"He places his Four Fiery Sons in the Four Circles"*; these Circles are the equator,

the ecliptic, and the two parallels of declination, or the tropics, to preside over the *climates* of which are placed the Four Mystical Entities. Then again: "*Other Seven are commissioned to preside over the seven hot, and seven cold Lokas at the two ends of the Egg of Matter.*" The seven Lokas are elsewhere also called the "Rings" and the "Circles." The Ancients made the polar circles *seven* instead of two, as do the Europeans; for Mount Meru, which is the North Pole, is said to have seven gold and seven silver steps leading to it.

The strange statements, in one of the Stanzas, that "*The Songs of Fohat and his Sons were* RADIANT *as the noon-tide Sun and the Moon combined,*" and that the Four Sons, on the *middle* Four-fold Circle, "SAW *their Father's Songs and* HEARD *his solar-selenic Radiance,*" are explained, in the Commentary, in these words: "*The agitation of the Fohatic Forces at the two cold ends of the Earth, which results in a multicoloured radiance at night, has in it several of the properties of Âkâsha, Colour and Sound as well.*"

"Sound is the characteristic of Âkâsha: it generates Air, the property of which is Touch; which becomes productive of Colour and Light."
Perhaps the above will be regarded as archaic nonsense, but it will be better comprehended, if the reader remembers the Aurora Borealis and Australis, both of which take place at the very centres of terrestrial electric and magnetic forces. The two Poles are said to be the store-houses, the receptacles and liberators, at the same time, of cosmic and terrestrial Vitality (Electricity), from the surplus of which the Earth, had it not been for these two natural safety-valves, would have been rent to pieces long ago. At the same time it is a theory that has lately become an axiom, that the phenomenon of the polar lights is accompanied by, and productive of, strong sounds, like whistling, hissing and cracking. See Professor Humboldt's works on the Aurora Borealis, and his correspondence regarding this moot question.

7. MAKE THY CALCULATIONS, O LANOO, IF THOU WOULDST LEARN THE CORRECT AGE OF THY SMALL WHEEL. ITS FOURTH SPOKE IS OUR

Mother (a). Reach the Fourth Fruit of the Fourth Path of Knowledge that leads to Nirvâna, and thou shalt comprehend, for thou shalt see (b)....

(a) The "Small Wheel" is our Chain of Spheres, and the "Fourth Spoke" is our Earth, the fourth in the Chain. It is one of those on which the "hot breath of the Sun" has a direct effect.

The seven fundamental transformations of the Globes or heavenly Spheres, or rather of their constituent particles of matter, are described as follows: (1) *homogeneous*; (2) *aëriform* and *radiant*—gaseous; (3) *curd-like* (nebulous); (4) *atomic, ethereal*—beginning of motion, hence of differentiation; (5) *germinal, fiery*—differentiated, but composed of the germs only of the Elements, in their earliest states, they having seven states, when completely developed on our earth; (6) *four-fold, vapoury*—the future Earth; (7) *cold*—and depending on the Sun for life and light.

To calculate its age, however, as the pupil is asked to do in the Stanza, is rather difficult, since we are not given the figures of the Great Kalpa, and are not allowed to publish those of our small Yugas, except as to the approximate duration of these. "*The older Wheels rotated for one Eternity and one-half of an Eternity,*" it says. We know that by "Eternity" the seventh part of 311,040,000,000,000 years, or an Age of Brahmâ is meant. But what of that? We also know that, to begin with, if we take for our basis the above figures, we have first of all to eliminate from the 100 Years of Brahmâ, or 311,040,000,000,000 years, two Years taken up by the Sandhyâs (Twilights), which leaves 98, as we have to bring it to the mystical combination 14 x 7. But *we* have no knowledge at what time precisely the evolution and formation of our little Earth began. Therefore, it is impossible to calculate its age, unless the time of its birth is given—which the Teachers refuse to do, so far. At the close of this Volume and in Volume II, however, some chronological hints will be given. We must remember, moreover, that the law of analogy holds good for the worlds, as it does for man; and that as "*The One becomes Two , and Two becomes Three ,*" etc., so we are taught that the Curds (World-Stuff) become Wanderers (Comets); these become stars; and the stars (the centres of vortices), *our sun and planets*—to put it briefly. This cannot be so very *unscientific*, since Descartes also thought that "the planets rotate on their axes, because they were once lucid stars, the centres of vortices."

(*b*) There are four grades of Initiation mentioned in exoteric works, which are known respectively in Sanskrit as Srotâpanna, Sakridâgâmin, Anâgâmin, and Arhan; the Four Paths to Nirvâna, in this our Fourth Round, bearing the same appellations. The Arhan, though he can see the Past, the Present and the Future, is not yet the highest Initiate; for the Adept himself, the *initiated* candidate, becomes Chelâ (Pupil) to a higher Initiate. Three higher grades have still to be conquered by the Arhan who would reach the apex of the ladder of Arhatship. There are those who have reached it even in this Fifth Race of ours, but the faculties necessary for the attainment of these higher grades will be fully developed, in the average ascetic, only at the end of this Root-Race, and in the Sixth and Seventh. Thus, there will always be Initiates and the Profane until the end of this minor Manvantara, the present Life-Cycle. The Arhats of the "Fire-Mist," of the Seventh Rung, are but one remove from the Root-Base of their Hierarchy, the highest on Earth and our Terrestrial Chain. This "Root-Base" has a name which can only be translated into English by several compound words—the "Ever-Living-Human-Banyan." This "Wondrous Being" descended from a "high region," they say, in the early part of the Third Age, before the separation of sexes in the Third Race.

This Third Race is sometimes called collectively the "Sons of Passive Yoga," *i.e.*, it was produced unconsciously by the Second Race, which, as it was intellectually inactive, is supposed to have been constantly plunged in a kind of blank or abstract contemplation, as required by the conditions of the Yoga state. In the first or earlier portion of the existence of this Third Race, while it was yet in its state of purity, the "Sons of Wisdom," who, as will be seen, incarnated in this Root-Race, produced by

Kriyâshakti a progeny, called the "Sons of Ad," or of the "Fire-Mist," the "Sons of Will and Yoga," etc. They were a conscious production, as a portion of the Race was already animated with the divine spark of spiritual, superior intelligence. This progeny was not a race. It was at first a Wondrous Being, called the "Initiator," and after him a group of semi-divine and semi-human Beings. "Set apart" in archaic genesis for certain purposes, they are those in whom are said to have incarnated the highest Dhyânis—"Munis and Rishis from previous Manvantaras"—*to form the nursery for future human Adepts*, on this Earth and during the present Cycle. These "Sons of Will and Yoga," born, so to speak, in an immaculate way, remained, it is explained, entirely apart from the rest of mankind.

The "Being" just referred to, who has to remain nameless, is the *Tree* from which, in subsequent ages, all the great *historically* known Sages and Hierophants, such as the Rishi Kapila, Hermes, Enoch, Orpheus, etc., have branched off. As objective *man*, he is the mysterious (to the profane—the ever invisible, yet ever present) Personage, about whom legends are rife in the East, especially among the Occultists and the students of the Sacred Science. It is he who changes form, yet remains ever the same. And it is he, again, who holds spiritual sway over the *initiated* Adepts throughout the whole world. He is, as said, the "Nameless One" who has so many names, and yet whose names and whose very nature are unknown. He is *the* "Initiator," called the "GREAT SACRIFICE." For, sitting at the Threshold of LIGHT, he looks into it from within the Circle of Darkness, which he will not cross; nor will he quit his post till the last Day of this Life-Cycle. Why does the Solitary Watcher remain at his self-chosen post? Why does he sit by the Fountain of Primeval Wisdom, of which he drinks no longer, for he has naught to learn which he does not know—aye, neither on this Earth, nor in its Heaven? Because the lonely, sore-footed Pilgrims, on their journey back to their Home, are never sure, to the last moment, of not losing their way, in this limitless desert of Illusion and Matter called Earth-Life. Because he would fain show the way to that region of freedom and light, from which he is a voluntary exile himself, to every prisoner who has succeeded in liberating himself from the bonds of flesh and illusion. Because, in short, he has sacrificed himself for the sake of Mankind, though but a few elect may profit by the GREAT SACRIFICE.

It is under the direct, silent guidance of this *Mahâ-Guru* that all the other less divine Teachers and Instructors of Mankind became, from the first awakening of human consciousness, the guides of early Humanity. It is through these "Sons of God" that infant Humanity learned its first notions of all the arts and sciences, as well as of spiritual knowledge; and it is They who laid the first foundation-stone of those ancient civilizations that so sorely puzzle our modern generation of students and scholars.

Let those who doubt this statement, explain, on any other equally reasonable grounds, the mystery of the extraordinary knowledge possessed by the Ancients—who, some pretend, developed from lower and animal-like savages, the "cave-men" of the palæolithic age! Let them turn, for instance, to such works as those of Vitruvius Pollio of the Augustan age, on architecture, in which all the rules of proportion are those *anciently taught at Initiations*, if they would acquaint themselves with this truly divine art, and understand the *deep esoteric significance hidden in every rule and law of proportion.* No man descended from a palæolithic cave-dweller could ever evolve such a science unaided, even in millenniums of thought and intellectual evolution. It is the pupils of those incarnated Rishis and Devas of the Third Root Race who handed on their knowledge, from one generation to another, to Egypt and to Greece with her now lost *canon of proportion*; just as the disciples of the Initiates of the Fourth, the Atlanteans, handed it over to their Cyclopes, the "Sons of Cycles" or of the "Infinite," from whom the name passed to the still later generations of Gnostic priests.

It is owing to the divine perfection of these architectural proportions that the Ancients could build these wonders of all the subsequent ages, their Fanes, Pyramids, Cave-Temples, Cromlechs, Cairns, Altars, proving they had the powers of machinery and a knowledge of mechanics to which modern skill is like a child's play, and which that skill refers to itself as the "works of hundred-handed giants."

Modern architects may not have altogether neglected these rules, but they have superadded enough empirical innovations to destroy the just proportions. It is Vitruvius who gave to posterity the rules of construction of the Grecian temples erected to the immortal Gods; and the ten books of Marcus Vitruvius Pollio on Architecture, of one, in short, *who was an Initiate*, can only be studied esoterically. The Druidical Circles, the Dolmens, the Temples of India, Egypt and Greece, the Towers, and the 127 towns in Europe which were found "Cyclopean in origin" by the French Institute, are all the work of initiated Priest-Architects, the descendants of those first taught by the "Sons of God," and justly called the "Builders." This is what appreciative posterity says of these descendants:

They used neither mortar nor cement, nor steel, nor iron to cut the stones with; and yet they were so artificially wrought that in many places the joints are hardly seen, though many of the stones, as in Peru, are 38 feet long, 18 feet broad, and 6 feet thick, and in the walls of the fortress of Cuzco there are stones of a still greater size.

Again:

The well of Syene, made 5,400 years ago, when that spot was exactly under the tropic, which it has now ceased to be, was ... so constructed, that at noon, at the precise moment of the solar solstice, the entire disk of the sun was seen reflected on its surface—a work which the united skill of all the astronomers in Europe would not now be able to effect.

Although these matters were barely hinted at in *Isis Unveiled*, it will be well to remind the reader of what was said there concerning a certain Sacred Island in Central Asia, and to refer him for further details to the Section, entitled "The Sons of God and the Sacred Island," attached to Stanza IX of Volume II. A few more explanations, however, though thrown out in a fragmentary form, may help the student to obtain a glimpse into the present mystery.

To state at least one detail concerning these mysterious "Sons of God" in plain words: it is from them, these Brahmaputras, that the high Dvijas, the initiated Brâhmans of old, claimed descent, while the modern Brâhman would have the lower castes believe literally that they (the Brâhmans) issued direct from the mouth of Brahmâ. Such is the Esoteric teaching; and it adds moreover that, although those descended (spiritually, of course) from the "Sons of Will and Yoga" became in time divided into opposite sexes, as their "Kriyâshakti" progenitors did themselves later on; yet even their degenerate descendants have, down to the present day, retained a veneration and respect for the creative function, and still regard it in the light of a religious ceremony, whereas the more civilized nations consider it as a mere animal function. Compare the Western views and practice in these matters with the Institutions of Manu, in regard to the laws of Grihastha, or married life. The true Brâhman is, thus, indeed "he whose seven forefathers have drunk the juice of the Moon-plant (Soma)," and who is a "Trisuparna," for he has understood the secret of the *Vedas*.

And, to this day, such Brâhmans know that, during the early beginnings of this Race, psychic and physical intellect being dormant and consciousness still undeveloped, its spiritual conceptions were quite unconnected with its physical surroundings; that *divine* man dwelt in his animal—though externally human—form; that, if there was instinct in him, no self-consciousness came to enlighten the darkness of the latent Fifth Principle. When the Lords of Wisdom, moved by the law of evolution, infused into him the spark of consciousness, the first feeling it awoke to life and activity was a sense of solidarity, of one-ness with his spiritual creators. As the child's first feeling is for its mother and nurse, so the first aspirations of the awakening consciousness in primitive man were for those whose element he felt within himself, and who were yet outside, and independent of him. *Devotion* arose out of that feeling, and became the first and foremost motor in his nature; for it is the only one which is natural in his heart, which is innate in him, and which we find alike in the human babe and the young of the animal. This feeling of irrepressible, instinctive aspiration in primitive man is beautifully, and one may say intuitively, described by Carlyle, who exclaims:

The great antique heart—how like a child's in its simplicity, like a man's in its earnest solemnity and depth! Heaven lies over him wheresoever he goes or stands on the earth; making all the earth a mystic temple to him, the earth's business all a kind of worship. Glimpses of bright creatures flash in the common sunlight; angels yet hover, doing God's messages among men.... Wonder, miracle, encompass the man; he lives in an element of miracle.... A great law of duty, high as these two infinitudes (heaven and hell), dwarfing all else, annihilating all else—it was a reality, and it is one: the garment only of it is dead; the essence of it lives through all times and all eternity!

It lives undeniably, and has settled in all its ineradicable strength and power in the Asiatic Âryan heart, from the Third Race direct, through its first Mind-born Sons, the fruits of Kriyâshakti. As time rolled on, the holy caste of Initiates produced, but rarely, from age to age, such perfect creatures; beings apart, inwardly, though the same as those who produced them, outwardly.

In the infancy of the Third primitive Race:

A creature of a more exalted kind
Was wanting yet, and therefore was designed;
Conscious of thought, of more capacious breast,
For empire formed and fit to rule the rest.

It was called into being, a ready and perfect vehicle for the incarnating denizens of higher spheres, who took forthwith their abodes in these forms, born of *Spiritual Will* and the natural divine power in man. It was a child of pure spirit, mentally unalloyed with any tincture of earthly element. Its physical frame alone was of time and of life, for it drew its intelligence direct from above. It was the Living Tree of Divine Wisdom; and may therefore be likened to the Mundane Tree of the Norse Legends, which cannot wither and die until the last battle of life shall be fought, while its roots are all the time gnawed by the dragon Nidhogg. For even so, the first and holy Son of Kriyâshakti had his body gnawed by the tooth of time, but the roots of his inner being remained for ever undecaying and strong, because they grew and expanded in heaven, and not on earth. He was the first of the *First*, and he was the Seed of all the others. There were other Sons of Kriyâshakti produced by a second spiritual effort, but the first one has remained to this day the Seed of Divine Knowledge, the One and the Supreme among the terrestrial "Sons of Wisdom." Of this subject we can say no more, except to add that in every age—aye, even in our own—there have been great intellects who have understood the problem correctly.

But how comes our physical body to the state of perfection it is now found in? Through millions of years of evolution, of course, yet never through, or from, animals, as taught by Materialism. For, as Carlyle says:

... The essence of our being, the mystery in us that calls itself "I,"—ah, what words have we for such things?—is a breath of Heaven; the Highest Being reveals himself in man. This body, these faculties, this life of ours, is it not all as a vesture for that Unnamed?

The "breath of Heaven," or rather the breath of Life, called in the *Bible* Nephesh, is in every animal, in every animate speck and in every mineral atom. But none of these has, like man, the consciousness of the nature of that "Highest Being," as none has that divine harmony in its form, which man possesses. It is, as Novalis said, and no one since has said it better, as repeated by Carlyle:

There is but one temple in the Universe, and that is the Body of Man. Nothing is holier than that high form.... We touch Heaven when we lay our hand on a human body! This sounds like a mere flourish of rhetoric; but it is not so. If well meditated, it will turn out to be a scientific fact; the expression ... of the actual truth of the thing. *We* are the miracle of miracles—the great inscrutable Mystery....

Stanza VII.

1. BEHOLD THE BEGINNING OF SENTIENT FORMLESS LIFE (*a*). FIRST, THE DIVINE (*b*), THE ONE FROM THE MOTHER-SPIRIT;THEN, THE SPIRITUAL (*c*); THE THREE FROM THE ONE (*d*), THE FOUR FROM THE ONE (*e*), AND THE FIVE (*f*), FROM WHICH THE THREE, THE FIVE AND THE SEVEN (*g*). THESE ARE THE THREE-FOLD AND THE FOUR-FOLD DOWNWARD; THE MIND-BORN SONS OF THE FIRST LORD, THE

SHINING SEVEN. IT IS THEY WHO ARE THOU, I, HE, O LANOO; THEY WHO WATCH OVER THEE AND THY MOTHER, BHÛMI.

(*a*) The Hierarchy of Creative Powers is divided esoterically into Seven (four and three), within the Twelve great Orders, recorded in the twelve signs of the Zodiac; the Seven of the manifesting scale being connected, moreover, with the Seven Planets. All these are subdivided into numberless Groups of divine spiritual, semi-spiritual, and ethereal Beings.

The chief Hierarchies among these are hinted at in the great Quaternary, or the "four bodies and the three faculties," exoterically, of Brahmâ and the Panchâsya, the five Brahmâs, or the five Dhyâni-Buddhas in the Buddhist system.

The highest Group is composed of the Divine Flames, so called, also spoken of as the "Fiery Lions" and the "Lions of Life," whose esotericism is securely hidden in the zodiacal sign of Leo. It is the *nucleole* of the superior Divine World. They are the Formless Fiery Breaths, identical in one aspect with the upper Sephirothal Triad, which is placed by the Kabalists in the Archetypal World.

The same Hierarchy, with the same numbers, is found in the Japanese system, in the "Beginnings," as taught by both the Shinto and the Buddhist sects. In this system, Anthropogenesis precedes Cosmogenesis, as the divine merges into the human, and creates—midway in its descent into matter—the visible Universe; the legendary personages, remarks reverentially Omoie, "having to be understood as the stereotyped embodiment of the higher doctrine, and its sublime truths." To state this old system at full length would occupy too much of our space; a few words on it, however, cannot be out of place. The following is a short synopsis of this Anthropo-Cosmogenesis, and shows how closely the most separated nations echoed one and the same archaic teaching.

When all was as yet Chaos (Kon-ton), three spiritual Beings appeared on the stage of future creation: (1) Ame no ani naka nushi no Kami, "Divine Monarch of the Central Heaven"; (2)

Taka mi onosubi no Kami, "Exalted, Imperial Divine Offspring of Heaven and Earth"; and (3) Kamu mi musubi no Kami, "Offspring of the Gods," simply.

These were without form or substance—our Arûpa Triad—as neither the celestial nor the terrestrial substance had yet differentiated, "nor had the essence of things been formed."

(*b*) In the *Zohar*—which, as now arranged and reëdited by Moses de Leon, with the help of Syrian and Chaldean Christian Gnostics, in the XIIIth century, and corrected and revised still later by many Christian hands, is only a little less exoteric than the *Bible* itself—this "Divine " no longer appears as it does in the Chaldean *Book of Numbers*. True enough, Ain Suph, the Absolute Endless No-thing, uses also the form of the One, the manifested "Heavenly Man" (the First Cause), as its Chariot (Mercabah, in Hebrew; Vâhana, in Sanskrit) or Vehicle, to descend into, and manifest itself in, the phenomenal world. But the Kabalists neither make it plain how the Absolute can use anything, or exercise any attribute whatever, since, as the Absolute, it is devoid of attributes; nor do they explain that in reality it is the First Cause (Plato's Logos), the original and eternal Idea, that manifests through Adam Kadmon, the Second Logos, so to speak. In the *Book of Numbers*, it is explained that Ain (En, or Aiôr) is the only self-existent, whereas its "Depth," the Bythos of the Gnostics, called Propatôr, is only periodical. The latter is Brahmâ, as differentiated from Brahman or Parabrahman. It is the Depth, the Source of Light, or Propatôr, which is the Unmanifested Logos, or the abstract Idea, and not Ain Suph, whose Ray uses Adam Kadmon—"male and female"—or the Manifested Logos, the objective Universe, as a Chariot, through which to manifest. But in the *Zohar* we read the following incongruity: "*Senior occultatus est, et absconditus; Microprosopus manifestus est, et non manifestus.*" This is a fallacy, since Microprosopus, or the Microcosm, can only exist during its manifestations, and is destroyed during the Mahâpralayas. Rosenroth's *Kabbala* is no guide, but very often a puzzle.

The *First Order* are the Divine. As in the Japanese system, in the Egyptian, and every old cosmogony—at this divine Flame, the "One," are lit the Three descending Groups. Having their potential being in the higher Group, they now become distinct and separate Entities. These are called the Virgins of Life, the Great Illusion, etc., etc., and collectively the six-pointed star. The latter, in almost every religion, is the symbol of the Logos as the first emanation. It is the sign of Vishnu in India, the Chakra, or Wheel; and the glyph of the Tetragrammaton, "He of the Four Letters," in the *Kabalah*, or metaphorically the "Limbs of Microprosopus," which are ten and six respectively.

The later Kabalists, however, especially the Christian Mystics, have played sad havoc with this magnificent symbol. Indeed, the Microprosopus—who is, philosophically speaking, quite distinct from the unmanifested eternal Logos, "one with the Father"—has finally been brought, by centuries of incessant efforts of sophistry and of paradoxes, to be considered as one with Jehovah, or the *one* living God (!), whereas Jehovah is no better than Binah, a female Sephira. This fact cannot be too frequently impressed upon the reader. For the "Ten Limbs" of the Heavenly Man are the ten Sephiroth; but the first Heavenly Man is the unmanifested Spirit of the Universe, and ought never to be degraded into Microprosopus, the Lesser Face or Countenance, the prototype of man on the terrestrial plane. The Microprosopus is, as just said, the Logos manifested, and of such there are many. Of this, however, later on. The six-pointed star refers to the six Forces or Powers of Nature, the six planes, principles, etc., etc., all synthesized by the seventh, or the central point in the star. All these, the upper and lower Hierarchies included, emanate from the Heavenly or Celestial Virgin, the Great Mother in all religions, the Androgyne, the Sephira Adam Kadmon. Sephira is the Crown, Kether, in the abstract principle only, as a mathematical x, the unknown quantity. On the plane of differentiated nature, she is the female counterpart of Adam Kadmon, the first Androgyne.

The *Kabalah* teaches that the words *"Fiat Lux"* referred to the formation and evolution of the Sephiroth, and not to light as opposed to darkness. Rabbi Simeon says:

O companions, companions, man as an emanation was both man and woman, Adam Kadmon verily, and this is the sense of the words, "Let there be Light, and there was Light." And this is the two-fold man.

In its Unity, Primordial Light is the seventh, or highest, principle, Daiviprakriti, the Light of the Unmanifested Logos. But in its differentiation, it becomes Fohat, or the "Seven Sons." The former is symbolized by the central point in the Double Triangle; the latter by the Hexagon itself, or the "Six Limbs" of Microprosopus, the Seventh being Malkuth, the "Bride" of the Christian Kabalists, or our Earth. Hence the expressions:

The first after the One is Divine Fire; the second, Fire and Ether; the third is composed of Fire, Ether and Water; the fourth of Fire, Ether, Water, and Air. The One is not concerned with Man-bearing Globes, but with the inner, invisible Spheres. The First-Born are the LIFE, *the Heart and Pulse of the Universe; the Second are its* MIND *or Consciousness.*

These Elements of Fire, Air, etc., are not our compound elements; and this "Consciousness" has no relation to our consciousness. The Consciousness of the "One Manifested," if not absolute, is still unconditioned. Mahat, the Universal Mind, is the first production of the Brahmâ-Creator, but also of Pradhâna, Undifferentiated Matter.

(c) The *Second Order* of Celestial Beings, those of Fire and Ether, corresponding to Spirit and Soul, or Âtmâ-Buddhi, whose names are legion, are still formless, but more definitely "substantial." They are the first differentiation in the Secondary Evolution or "Creation"—a misleading word. As the name shows, they are the Prototypes of the incarnating Jîvas or Monads, and are composed of the Fiery Spirit of Life. It is through these that passes, like a pure solar beam, the Ray which is furnished by them with its future Vehicle, the Divine Soul, Buddhi. These are directly concerned with the Hosts of the higher World of *our* System. From these Two-fold Units emanate the "Three-fold."

In the cosmogony of Japan, when, out of the chaotic mass, an egg-like nucleus appears, having within itself the germ and potency of all universal as well as of all terrestrial life, it is the Three-fold just named, which differentiate. The male ethereal principle (Yo) ascends, and the female grosser or more material principle (In) is precipitated into the universe of substance, when a separation occurs between the celestial and the terrestrial. From this, the female, the Mother, the first rudimentary objective being is born. It is ethereal, without form or sex, and yet it is from it and the Mother that the Seven Divine Spirits are born, from whom will emanate the seven "creations"; just as in the *Codex Nazaræus* from Karabtanos and the Mother Spiritus the seven "evilly disposed" (material) spirits are born. It would be too long to give here the Japanese names, but in translation they stand in this order:

(1.) The "Invisible Celibate," which is the Creative Logos of the non-creating "Father," or the creative potentiality of the latter made manifest.

(2.) The "Spirit of the rayless Depths," which becomes differentiated matter, or the world-stuff; also the mineral realm.
(3.) The "Spirit of the Vegetable Kingdom," of the "Abundant Vegetation."

(4.) The "Spirit of the Earth" and "the Spirit of the Sands"; a Being of dual nature, the former containing the potentiality of the male element, the latter that of the female element. These two were one, as yet unconscious of being two.

In this duality were contained (*a*) Isu no gai no Kami, the male, dark and muscular Being; and (*b*) Eku gai no Kami, the female, fair and weaker or more delicate Being. Then:
(5 and 6.) The Spirits who were androgynous or dual-sexed.

(7.) The Seventh Spirit, the last emanated from the "Mother," appears as the first divine human form distinctly

male and female. It was the seventh "creation," as in
the *Purânas*, wherein man is the seventh creation of Brahmâ.

These, Tsanagi-Tsanami, descended into the Universe by the
Celestial Bridge, the Milky Way, and "Tsanagi, perceiving far
below a chaotic mass of cloud and water, thrust his jewelled
spear into the depths, and dry land appeared. Then the two
separated to explore Onokoro, the newly-created island-
world." (Omoie.)

Such are the Japanese exoteric fables, the rind that conceals the
kernel of the same one truth of the Secret Doctrine.

(*d*) The *Third Order* correspond to Âtmâ-Buddhi-Manas, Spirit,
Soul and Intellect; and are called the "Triads."

(*e*) The *Fourth Order* are substantial Entities. This is the
highest Group among the Rûpas (Atomic Forms). It is the
nursery of the human, conscious, spiritual Souls. They are called
the "Imperishable Jîvas," and constitute, through the Order
below their own, the first Group of the first Septenary Host—the
great mystery of human, conscious and intellectual Being. For
the latter is the field wherein lies concealed, *in its privation*, the
Germ that will *fall into generation*. That Germ will become the
spiritual potency in the physical cell, that guides the
development of the embryo, and that is the cause of the
hereditary transmission of faculties, and all the inherent
qualities in man. The Darwinian theory, however, of the
transmission of acquired faculties is neither taught nor accepted
in Occultism. Evolution, in the latter, proceeds on quite other
lines; the physical, according to Esoteric teaching, evolving
gradually from the spiritual, mental, and psychic. This inner
soul of the physical cell—the "spiritual plasm" that dominates
the germinal plasm—is the key that must open one day the
gates of the *terra incognita* of the Biologist, now called the dark
mystery of Embryology. It is worthy of notice that Modern
Chemistry, while rejecting, as a superstition of Occultism and
Religion as well, the theory of substantial and invisible Beings,
called Angels, Elementals, etc.—without, of course, having ever
looked into the philosophy of these incorporeal Entities, or

thought over them—should, owing to observation and discovery, have been unconsciously forced to recognize and adopt the same ratio of progression and order, in the evolution of chemical atoms, as Occultism does for both its Dhyânis and Atoms—analogy being its first law. As seen above, the very first Group of the Rûpa Angels is quaternary, an element being added to each in descending order. So also are the atoms, in the phraseology of Chemistry, monatomic, diatomic, triatomic, tetratomic, etc., progressing downwards.

Let it be remembered that the Fire, Water, and Air of Occultism, or the "Elements of Primary Creation" so-called, are not the compound elements they are on earth, but noumenal homogeneous Elements—the Spirits of the former. Then follow the Septenary Groups or Hosts. Placed on parallel lines with the atoms in a diagram, the natures of these Beings would be seen to correspond, in their downward scale of progression, to composite elements in a mathematically identical manner as to analogy. This refers, of course, only to diagrams made by Occultists; for were the scale of Angelic Beings to be placed on parallel lines with the scale of the chemical atoms of Science—from the hypothetical Helium down to Uranium—they would of course be found to differ. For the latter have, as correspondents on the Astral Plane, only the four lowest orders—the three higher principles in the atom, or rather molecule, or chemical element, being perceptible to the initiated Dangma's eye alone. But then, if Chemistry desired to find itself on the right path, it would have to correct its tabular arrangement by that of the Occultists—which it might refuse to do. In Esoteric Philosophy, every physical particle corresponds to, and depends on, its higher noumenon—the Being to whose essence it belongs; and, above as below, the Spiritual evolves from the Divine, the Psycho-mental from the Spiritual—tainted from its lower plane by the Astral—the whole animate and (seemingly) inanimate Nature evolving on parallel lines, and drawing its attributes from above as well as below.

The number seven, as applied to the term Septenary Host, above mentioned, does not imply only seven Entities, but seven Groups or Hosts, as explained before. The highest Group, the Asuras born in Brahmâ's first body, which turned into "Night," are septenary, *i.e.*, divided like the Pitris into seven Classes, three of which are bodiless (arûpa) and four with bodies. They are in fact more truly our Pitris (Ancestors) than the Pitris who projected the first physical man.

(*f*) The *Fifth Order* is a very mysterious one, as it is connected with the microcosmic pentagon, the five-pointed star, representing man. In India and Egypt, these Dhyânis were connected with the Crocodile, and their abode is in Capricornus. But these are convertible terms in Indian Astrology, for the tenth sign of the Zodiac, which is called Makara, is loosely translated "Crocodile." The word itself is occultly interpreted in various ways, as will be shown further on. In Egypt, the Defunct—whose symbol is the pentagram, or the five-pointed star, the points of which represent the limbs of a man—was shown emblematically transformed into a crocodile. Sebekh, or Sevekh (or "Seventh"), as Mr. Gerald Massey says, showing it to be the type of intelligence, is a dragon in reality, not a crocodile. He is the "Dragon of Wisdom," or Manas, the Human Soul, Mind, the Intelligent Principle, called in our Esoteric Philosophy the *Fifth* Principle.

Says the defunct "Osirified," in the *Book of the Dead*, or *Ritual*, under the glyph of a mummiform God with a crocodile's head:

I am the crocodile presiding at the fear, I am the God-crocodile, at the arrival of his Soul among men. I am the God-crocodile brought for destruction.

An allusion to the destruction of divine spiritual purity when man acquires the knowledge of good and evil; also to the "fallen" Gods, or Angels of every theogony.

I am the fish of the great Horus. I am merged in Sekhem.

This last sentence gives the corroboration, and repeats the doctrine of esoteric "Buddhism," for it alludes directly to the Fifth Principle (Manas), or the most spiritual part of its essence rather, which merges into, is absorbed by, and made one with

Âtmâ-Buddhi, after the death of man. For Sekhem is the residence, or Loka, of the God Khem (Horus-Osiris, or Father and Son); hence the Devachan of Âtmâ-Buddhi. In the *Book of the Dead*, the Defunct is shown entering into Sekhem, with Horus-Thot, and "emerging from it as pure spirit." Thus the Defunct says:

I see the forms of men transforming eternally.... I know this . He who knows it ... takes all kinds of living forms.

And addressing in magic formula that which is called, in Egyptian Esotericism, the "ancestral heart," or the reïncarnating principle, the permanent Ego, the Defunct says:

O my heart, my ancestral heart, necessary for my transformations, ... do not separate thyself from me before the guardian of the scales. Thou art my personality within my breast, divine companion *watching over my fleshes* .

It is in Sekhem that lies concealed the "Mysterious Face," or the real Man concealed under the false personality, the triple-crocodile of Egypt, the symbol of the higher Trinity, or human Triad, Âtmâ, Buddhi and Manas.

One of the explanations of the real though hidden meaning of this Egyptian religious glyph is easy. The crocodile is the first to await and meet the devouring fires of the morning sun, and very soon came to personify the solar heat. When the sun arose, it was like the arrival on earth, and among men, of the "divine soul which informs the Gods." Hence the strange symbolism. The mummy donned the head of a crocodile to show that it was a Soul arriving from the earth.

In all the ancient papyri, the crocodile is called Sebekh (Seventh); water also symbolizes the fifth principle esoterically; and, as already stated, Mr. Gerald Massey shows that the crocodile was the "seventh Soul, the supreme one of seven—the Seer unseen." Even exoterically Sekhem is the residence of the God Khem, and Khem is Horus avenging the death of his father Osiris, hence punishing the sins of man, when he becomes a disembodied Soul. Thus the defunct Osirified became the God

Khem, who "gleans the field of Aanroo"; that is, he gleans either his reward or punishment, for that field is the celestial locality (Devachan), where the Defunct is given *wheat*, the food of divine justice. The Fifth Group of Celestial Beings is supposed to contain in itself the dual attributes of both the spiritual and physical aspects of the Universe; the two poles, so to say, of Mahat, the Universal Intelligence, and the dual nature of man, the spiritual and the physical. Hence its number Five, doubled and made into Ten, connecting it with Makara, the tenth sign of the Zodiac.

(*g*) The *Sixth* and *Seventh Orders* partake of the lower qualities of the Quaternary. They are conscious ethereal Entities, as invisible as Ether, which are shot out, like the boughs of a tree, from the first central Group of the Four, and shoot out in their turn numberless side Groups, the lower of which are the Nature-Spirits, or Elementals, of countless kinds and varieties; from the formless and unsubstantial—the ideal Thoughts of their creators—down to atomic, though, to human perception, invisible organisms. The latter are considered as the "spirits of atoms," for they are the first remove (backwards) from the physical atom—sentient, if not intelligent creatures. They are all subject to Karma, and have to work it out through every cycle. For, as the Doctrine teaches, there are no such privileged Beings in the Universe, whether in our own or in other Systems, in the outer or the inner Worlds, as the Angels of the Western Religion and the Judean. A Dhyân Chohan has to become one; he cannot be born or appear suddenly on the plane of life as a full-blown Angel. The Celestial Hierarchy of the present Manvantara will find itself transferred, in the next Circle of Life, into higher superior Worlds, and will make room for a new Hierarchy, composed of the elect ones of our mankind. Being is an endless cycle within the One Absolute Eternity, wherein move numberless inner cycles finite and conditioned. Gods, created as such, would evince no personal merit in being Gods. Such a class of Beings—perfect only by virtue of the special immaculate nature inherent in them—in the face of suffering and struggling humanity, and even of the lower creation, would be the symbol of an eternal injustice quite Satanic in character, an ever present crime. It is an anomaly and an impossibility in Nature. Therefore the "Four" and the "Three" have to incarnate as all other beings have. This Sixth Group, moreover, remains almost inseparable from man, who draws from it all but his highest and lowest principles, or his spirit and body; the five middle human principles being the very essence of those Dhyânis. Paracelsus calls them the Flagæ; the Christians, the Guardian Angels; the Occultists, the Ancestors, the Pitris. They are the Six-fold Dhyân Chohans, having the six spiritual Elements in the composition of their bodies—in fact, men, minus the physical body.

Alone, the Divine Ray, the Âtman, proceeds directly from the One. When asked how this can be? How is it possible to conceive that these "Gods," or Angels, can be at the same time their own emanations and their personal selves? Is it in the same sense as in the material world, where the son is, in one way, his father, being his blood, the bone of his bone and the flesh of his flesh? To this the Teachers answer: Verily it is so. But one has to go deep into the mystery of Being, before one can fully comprehend this truth.

2. THE ONE RAY MULTIPLIES THE SMALLER RAYS. LIFE PRECEDES FORM, AND LIFE SURVIVES THE LAST ATOM. THROUGH THE COUNTLESS RAYS THE LIFE-RAY, THE ONE, LIKE A THREAD THROUGH MANY BEADS.

This shloka expresses the conception—a purely Vedântic one, as already explained elsewhere—of a Life-Thread, Sûtrâtmâ, running through successive generations. How, then, can this be explained? By resorting to a simile, to a familiar illustration, though necessarily imperfect, as all our available analogies must be. Before resorting to it, however, I would ask, whether it seems unnatural, least of all "supernatural," to any one of us, when we consider the process of the growth and development of a fœtus into a healthy baby weighing several pounds? Evolving from what? From the segmentation of an infinitesimally small ovum and a spermatozoön! And afterwards we see the baby develop into a six-foot man! This refers to the atomic and physical expansion, from the microscopically small into something exceedingly large; from the unseen, to the naked eye, into the visible and objective. Science has provided for all this; and, I dare say, her theories, embryological, biological and physiological, are correct enough, so far as exact observation of the material goes. Nevertheless, the two chief difficulties of the science of Embryology—namely, what are the forces at work in the formation of the fœtus, and the *cause* of "hereditary transmission" of likeness, physical, moral or mental—have never been properly answered; nor will they ever be solved, till the day when Scientists condescend to accept the Occult theories. But if this physical phenomenon astonishes no one, except in so far as it puzzles the Embryologists, why should our intellectual and inner growth, the evolution of the Human-Spiritual to the Divine-Spiritual, be regarded as, or seem, more impossible than the other?

The Materialists and the Evolutionists of the Darwinian school would be ill-advised to accept the newly worked-out theories of Professor Weissmann, the author of *Beiträge zur Descendenzlehre*, with regard to one of the two mysteries of Embryology, as above specified, which he seems to think he has solved; for, when it is fully solved, Science will have stepped into the domain of the truly Occult, and passed for ever out of the realm of transformation, as taught by Darwin. The two theories are irreconcilable, from the standpoint of Materialism. Regarded from that of the Occultists, however, the new theory solves all these mysteries. Those who are not acquainted with the discovery of Professor Weissmann—at one time a fervent Darwinist—ought to hasten to repair the deficiency. The German embryologist-philosopher—stepping over the heads of the Greek Hippocrates and Aristotle, right back into the teachings of the old Âryans—shows one infinitesimal cell, out of millions of others at work in the formation of an organism, alone and unaided determining, by means of constant segmentation and multiplication, the correct image of the future man, or animal, in its physical, mental and psychic characteristics. It is this cell which impresses on the face and form of the new individual the features of the parents, or of some distant ancestor; it is this cell, again, which transmits to him the intellectual and mental idiosyncracies of his sires, and so on. This Plasm is the immortal portion of our bodies, developing by means of a process of successive assimilations. Darwin's theory, viewing the embryological cell as the essence or extract from all other cells, is set aside; it is incapable of accounting for hereditary transmission. There are but two ways of explaining the mystery of heredity: either the substance of the germinal cell is endowed with the faculty of crossing the whole cycle of transformations that lead to the construction of a separate organism, and then to the reproduction of identical germinal cells; or, *these germinal cells do not have their genesis at all in the body of the individual, but proceed directly from the ancestral germinal cell passed from father to son through long generations.* It is the latter hypothesis that Weissmann has adopted and worked upon, and it is to this cell that he traces the immortal portion of man. So far, so good; and when this almost correct theory is accepted, how will Biologists explain the first appearance of this everlasting cell? Unless man "grew" like the immortal "Topsy," and was not born at all, but fell from the clouds, how was that embryological cell generated in him?

Complete the Physical Plasm, mentioned above, the "Germinal Cell" of man with all its material potentialities, with the "Spiritual Plasm," so to say, or the fluid that contains the five lower principles of the Six-principled Dhyâni—and you have the secret, if you are spiritual enough to understand it.

Now to the promised simile.

When the seed of the animal man is cast into the soil of the animal woman, that seed cannot germinate unless it has been fructified by the five virtues of the Six-fold Heavenly Man. Wherefore the Microcosm is represented as a Pentagon, within the Hexagon Star, the Macrocosm.
The functions of Jiva on this Earth are of a five-fold character. In the mineral atom, it is connected with the lowest principles of the Spirits of the Earth (the Six-fold Dhyânis); in the vegetable particle, with their second—the Prâna (Life); in the animal, with all these plus the third and the fourth; in man, the germ must

receive the fruitage of all the five. Otherwise he will be born no higher than an animal.

Thus in man alone the Jîva is complete. As to his seventh principle, it is but one of the Beams of the Universal Sun, for each rational creature receives the temporary loan only of that which has to return to its source. As to his physical body, it is shaped by the lowest terrestrial Lives, through physical, chemical and physiological evolution; "the Blessed Ones have nought to do with the purgations of matter," says the Kabalah in the Chaldean *Book of Numbers*.

It comes to this: Mankind, in its first prototypal, shadowy form, is the offspring of the Elohim of Life, or Pitris; in its qualitative and physical aspect, it is the direct progeny of the "Ancestors," the lowest Dhyânis, or Spirits of the Earth; for its moral, psychic and spiritual nature, it is indebted to a Group of divine Beings, the name and characteristics of which will be given in Volume II. Collectively, men are the handiwork of Hosts of various Spirits; distributively, the tabernacles of those Hosts; and occasionally and individually, the vehicles of some of them. In our present all-material Fifth Race, the earthly Spirit of the Fourth is still strong in us; but we are approaching the time when the pendulum of evolution will direct its swing decidedly upwards, bringing Humanity back on a parallel line with the primitive Third Root-Race in spirituality. During its childhood, mankind was wholly composed of that Angelic Host, who were the indwelling Spirits that animated the monstrous and gigantic tabernacles of clay of the Fourth Race, built by and composed of countless myriads of Lives, as our bodies are also now. This sentence will be explained later on in the present Commentary. Science, dimly perceiving the truth, may find bacteria and other infinitesimals in the human body, and see in them only occasional and abnormal visitors, to which diseases are attributed. Occultism—which discerns a Life in every atom and molecule, whether in a mineral or human body, in air, fire or water—affirms that our whole body is built of such Lives; the smallest bacterium under the microscope being to them in comparative size like an elephant to the tiniest infusoria.

The "tabernacles" mentioned above have improved in texture and symmetry of form, growing and developing with the Globe that bears them; but the physical improvement has taken place at the expense of the spiritual Inner Man and of Nature. The three middle principles, in earth and man, became with every Race more material; the Soul stepping back to make room for the Physical Intellect; the essence of the Elements becoming the material and composite elements now known.

Man is not, nor could he ever be, the complete product of the "Lord God"; but he *is* the child of the Elohim, so arbitrarily changed into the singular number and masculine gender. The first Dhyânis, commissioned to "create" man in their image, could only throw off their Shadows, as a delicate model for the Nature Spirits of matter to work upon. Man is, beyond any doubt, formed physically out of the dust of the Earth, but his creators and fashioners were many. Nor can it be said that the "Lord God breathed into his nostrils the Breath of Life," unless that God is identified with the "One Life," omnipresent though invisible, and unless the same operation is attributed to "God" on behalf of every "Living Soul," which is the *Vital* Soul (Nephesh), and not the Divine Spirit (Ruach) which ensures to man alone a divine degree of immortality, that no animal, as such, could ever attain in this cycle of incarnation. It is owing to the inadequate distinctions made by the Jews, and now by our Western metaphysicians, who are unable to understand, and hence to accept, more than a triune man—Spirit, Soul, Body—that the "Breath of Life" has been confused with the immortal "Spirit." This applies also directly to the Protestant theologians, who in translating a certain verse in the Fourth Gospel have entirely perverted its meaning. This mistranslation runs, "the *wind* bloweth where it listeth," instead of "the *spirit* goeth where it willeth," as in the original, and also in the translation of the Greek Eastern Church.

The learned and very philosophical author of *New Aspects of Life* would impress upon his reader that the Nephesh Chiah (Living Soul), according to the Hebrews:

Proceeded from, or was produced by, the infusion of the Spirit or Breath of Life into the quickening body of man, and was to supersede and take the place of that Spirit in the thus constituted Self, so that the Spirit passed into, was lost sight of, and disappeared in the Living Soul.

The human body, he thinks, ought to be viewed as a matrix in which, and from which, the Soul, which he seems to place higher than the Spirit, is developed. Considered *functionally* and from the standpoint of activity, the Soul stands undeniably higher, in this finite and conditioned world of Mâyâ. The Soul, he says, "is ultimately produced from the animated body of man." Thus the author identifies "Spirit" (Âtmâ) with the "Breath of Life" simply. The Eastern Occultists will demur to this statement, for it is based on the erroneous conception that Prâna and Âtmâ, or Jîvâtmâ, are one and the same thing. The author supports the argument, by showing that with the ancient Hebrews, Greeks, and even Latins, Ruach, Pneuma and Spiritus meant Wind—with the Jews undeniably, and with the Greeks and Romans very probably; the Greek word Anemos (Wind) and the Latin Animus (Soul) having a suspicious relation.

This is very far fetched. But a legitimate battle-field for deciding this question is hardly to be found, since Dr. Pratt seems to be a practical, matter-of-fact metaphysician, a kind of Kabalist-Positivist, whereas the Eastern metaphysicians, especially the Vedântins, are all Idealists. The Occultists also are of the extreme Esoteric Vedântin school, and though they call the One Life (Parabrahman) the Great Breath and the Whirlwind, they disconnect the seventh principle entirely from matter, and deny that it has any relation to, or connection with it.

Thus the philosophy of man's psychic, spiritual and mental relations with his physical functions is in almost inextricable confusion. Neither the old Âryan nor the Egyptian psychology is now properly understood; nor can they be assimilated, without accepting the Esoteric septenary, or, at any rate, the Vedântic quinquepartite division of the human inner principles. Failing which, it will be for ever impossible to understand the metaphysical and purely psychic, and even physiological, relations between the Dhyân Chohans, or Angels, on the one plane, and Humanity on the other. No Eastern (Âryan) Esoteric works are so far published, but we possess the Egyptian papyri, which speak clearly of the seven principles, or the "Seven Souls of Man." The *Book of the Dead* gives a complete list of the "transformations" that every Defunct undergoes, while divesting himself, one by one, of all these principles— materialized for the sake of clearness into ethereal entities or bodies. We must, moreover, remind those who try to show that the Ancient Egyptians did not teach Reïncarnation, that the "Soul" (the Ego or Self) of the Defunct is said to be living in Eternity: it is immortal, "coëval with, and disappearing with, the Solar Boat," that is, for the Cycle of Necessity.

This "Soul" *emerges* from the Tiaou, the Realm of the *Cause of Life*, and joins the living on Earth by *day*, to return to Tiaou every *night*. This expresses the periodical existences of the Ego. The Shadow, the Astral Form, is annihilated, "devoured by the Uræus," the Manes will be annihilated; the two Twins (the Fourth and Fifth Principles) will be scattered; but the Soul-Bird, "the Divine Swallow, and the Uræus of Flame" (Manas and Âtmâ-Buddhi) will live in the eternity, for they are their mother's husbands.

Another suggestive analogy between the Âryan, or Brâhmanical, and the Egyptian Esotericism. The former call the Pitris the "Lunar Ancestors" of men, and the Egyptians make of the Moon-God, Taht-Esmun, the first human ancestor.

This Moon-God "expressed the Seven nature-powers that were prior to himself, and were summed up in him as his seven souls, of which he was the manifestor as the Eighth One. ... The seven rays of the Chaldean ... Heptakis or Iao, on the Gnostic stones, indicate the same septenary of souls.... The first form of the mystical Seven was seen to be figured in heaven, by the seven large stars of the Great Bear, the constellation assigned by the Egyptians to the Mother of Time, and of the seven Elemental Powers."

As well known to every Hindû, this same constellation represents in India the Seven Rishis, and is called Riksha, and Chitrashikandinas.

Like alone produces like. The Earth gives Man his body, the Gods (Dhyânis) give him his five inner principles, the psychic Shadow, of which these Gods are often the animating principle. Spirit (Âtman) is one, and indiscrete. It is not in the Tiaou.

For what is the Tiaou? The frequent allusion to it in the *Book of the Dead* contains a mystery. Tiaou is the path of the Night-Sun, the inferior hemisphere, or the infernal region of the Egyptians, placed by them on the *concealed side of the Moon.* The human being, in their Esotericism, came out from the Moon—a triple mystery, astronomical, physiological and psychical, at once; he crossed the whole cycle of existence, and then returned to his birth-place, before issuing from it again. Thus the Defunct is shown arriving in the West, receiving his judgment before Osiris, resurrecting as the God Horus, and circling round the sidereal heavens, which is an allegorical assimilation to Ra, the Sun; then having crossed the Noot, the Celestial Abyss, returning once more to Tiaou; an assimilation to Osiris, who, as the God of life and reproduction, inhabits the Moon.
Plutarch shows the Egyptians celebrating a festival called "The Ingress of Osiris into the Moon." In the *Ritual*, life is promised after death; and the renovation of life is placed under the patronage of Osiris-Lunus, because the Moon was the symbol of life-renewals or reïncarnations, owing to its growth, waning, dying, and reäppearance every month. In the *Dankmoe*, it is said: "O Osiris-Lunus, that renews to thee thy renewal." And Sabekh says to Seti I: "Thou renewest thyself as the God Lunus, when a babe." It is still better explained in a Louvre papyrus: "Couplings and conceptions abound when he is seen in heaven on that day." Says Osiris: "O sole radiant beam of the Moon! I issue from the circulating multitudes .... Open me the Tiaou, for Osiris N. I will issue by day to do what I have to do amongst the living"—*i.e.*, to produce conceptions.

Osiris was "God manifest in generation," because the ancients knew, far better than the moderns, the real occult influences of the lunar body upon the mysteries of conception. In the oldest systems we find the Moon always male. Thus Soma, with the Hindûs, is a kind of sidereal Don Juan, a "King," and the father, albeit illegitimate, of Budha—Wisdom. This relates to Occult Knowledge, a wisdom gathered through a thorough acquaintance with lunar mysteries, including those of sexual generation. And later, when the Moon became connected with the female Goddesses, with Diana, Isis, Artemis, Juno, etc., this connection was also due to a thorough knowledge of physiology and female nature, physical as much as psychic.

If, instead of being taught in Sunday Schools useless lessons from the *Bible*, the armies of the ragged and poor were taught Astrology—so far, at any rate, as the occult properties of the Moon and its hidden influences on generation are concerned—then, there would be little need to fear increase of the population, or to resort to the questionable literature of the Malthusians for its arrest. For it is the Moon and her conjunctions that regulate conceptions, and every Astrologer in India knows it. During the previous Races, and at least at the beginning of the present one, those who indulged in marital relations during certain lunar phases that made those relations sterile, were regarded as sorcerers and sinners. But now even these sins of old, which arose from the abuse of Occult knowledge, would appear preferable to the crimes of to-day, which are perpetrated because of the complete ignorance of such Occult influences.

But, primarily, the Sun and Moon were the only visible and, by their effects, so to say, *tangible*, psychic and physiological deities—the Father and the Son—while Space or Air in general, or that expanse of heaven called Noot by the Egyptians, was the concealed Spirit or Breath of the two. The Father and Son were interchangeable in their functions, and worked together harmoniously in their effects upon terrestrial nature and humanity; hence they were regarded as *one*, though *two* as personified Entities. They were both males, and both had their distinct though collaborative work in the causative generation of humanity. So much from the astronomical and cosmic standpoints, viewed and expressed in symbolical language, which became in our last races theological and dogmatic. But behind this veil of cosmic and astrological symbols, there were the occult mysteries of anthropography and the primeval genesis of man. And in this, no knowledge of symbols, or even the key to the post-diluvian symbolical language of the Jews, will or can help, save only with reference to that which has been laid down in national scriptures for exoteric uses; the sum of which, however cleverly veiled, was but the smallest portion of the real primitive history of each people, and often, moreover, as in the Hebrew Scriptures, related merely to the terrestrial human, and not to the divine life of that nation. That psychic and spiritual element belonged to the MYSTERIES and INITIATION. There were things never recorded in scrolls, but which, as in Central Asia, were engraved on rocks and in subterranean crypts.

Nevertheless, there was a time when the whole world was "of one lip and of one knowledge," and man knew more of his origin than he does now; and thus knew that the Sun and Moon, however large a part they may play in the constitution, growth and development of the human body, were not the direct causative agents of his appearance on Earth; for these agents, in truth, are the living and intelligent Powers which the Occultists call Dhyân Chohans.

As to this, a very learned admirer of the Jewish Esotericism tells us that:

The *Kabalah* says expressly that Elohim is a "general abstraction"; what we call in mathematics "a constant coëfficient," or a "general function," entering into all construction, not particular; that is, by the general ratio 1 to 31415, the Elohistic figures.

To this the Eastern Occultist replies: Quite so; they are an abstraction to our physical senses. To our spiritual perceptions, however, and to our inner spiritual eye, the Elohim, or Dhyânis, are no more an abstraction than our soul and spirit are to us. Reject the one and you reject the other, since that which is the *surviving* Entity *in us*, is partly the direct emanation from, and partly those celestial Entities *themselves*. One thing is certain; the Jews were perfectly acquainted with sorcery and various maleficent forces: but, with the exception of some of their great prophets and seers like Daniel and Ezekiel—Enoch belonging to a far distant race, as a generic character, and not to any nation but to all—they knew little of, nor would they deal with, the real divine Occultism; their national character being averse to anything which had no direct bearing upon their own ethnical, tribal and individual benefits—witness their own prophets, and the curses thundered by them against the "stiff-necked race." But even the *Kabalah* plainly shows the direct relation between the Sephiroth, or Elohim, and men.

Therefore, when it is proved to us that the Kabalistic identification of Jehovah with Binah, a female Sephira, has still another, a sub-occult, meaning in it, then and then only will Occultists be ready to pass the palm of perfection to the Kabalist. Until then, it is asserted that, as Jehovah, in the abstract sense of a "one living God," is a single number, a metaphysical figment, and a reality only when put in his proper place as an emanation and a Sephira—we have a right to maintain that the *Zohar*, as witnessed by the *Book of Numbers*, at any rate, gave out originally, before the Christian Kabalists had disfigured it, and still gives out, the same doctrine that we do; that is, it makes Man emanate, not from one Celestial Man, but from a Septenary Group of Celestial Men, or Angels, just as in *Pymander, the Thought Divine*.

3. WHEN THE ONE BECOMES TWO, THE THREE-FOLD APPEARS (*a*). THE THREE ARE ONE; AND IT IS OUR THREAD, O LANOO, THE HEART OF THE MAN-PLANT, CALLED SAPTAPARNA (*b*).

(*a*) "When the One becomes Two, the Three-fold appears": to wit, when the One Eternal drops its reflection into the region of Manifestation, that reflection, the Ray, differentiates the Water of Space; or, in the words of the *Book of the Dead*: "Chaos ceases, through the effulgence of the Ray of Primordial Light dissipating total darkness, by the help of the great magic power of the Word of the Sun." Chaos becomes male-female, and Water, incubated by Light, and the Three-fold Being issues as its "First-born." "Ra creates his own Limbs , by creating the Gods destined to personify his phases," during the Cycle. The Egyptian Ra, issuing from the Deep, is the Divine Universal Soul in its manifested aspect, and so is Nârâyana, the Purusha, "concealed in Âkâsha, and present in Ether."

This is the metaphysical explanation, and refers to the very beginning of Evolution, or, as we would rather say, of Theogony. The meaning of the Stanza, when explained from another standpoint in its reference to the mystery of man and his origin, is still more difficult to comprehend. In order to form a clear conception of what is meant by the One becoming Two, and then being transformed into the Three-fold, the student has to make himself thoroughly acquainted with what we call Rounds. If he refers to *Esoteric Buddhism*—the first attempt to sketch out an approximate outline of archaic cosmogony—he will find that by a Round is meant the serial evolution of nascent material Nature, of the seven Globes of our Chain, with their mineral, vegetable and animal kingdoms; man being included in the latter and standing at the head of it, during the whole period of a Life-Cycle, which latter would be called by the Brâhmans a "Day of Brahmâ." It is, in short, one revolution of the "Wheel" (our Planetary Chain), which is composed of seven Globes, or seven separate "Wheels," in another sense this time. When evolution has run downward into matter from Globe A to Globe G, it is one Round. In the middle of the fourth revolution, which is our present Round, "Evolution has reached its acme of physical development, crowned its work with the perfect physical man, and, from this point, begins its work spiritward." All this needs little repetition, as it is well explained in *Esoteric Buddhism*. That which was hardly touched upon, however, and of which the little that was said has misled many, is the origin of man, and it is upon this that a little more light may now be thrown, just enough to make the Stanza more comprehensible, as the process will be fully explained only in its legitimate place, in Volume II.

Now every Round, on the descending scale, is but a repetition in a more concrete form of the Round which preceded it, just as every Globe, down to our Fourth Sphere the actual Earth, is a grosser and more material copy of the more shadowy Sphere which precedes it, each in order, on the three higher planes. On its way upwards, on the ascending arc, Evolution spiritualizes and etherealizes, so to speak, the general nature of all, bringing it on to a level with the plane on which the twin Globe on the opposite arc is placed; the result being, that when the seventh Globe is reached, in whatever Round, the nature of everything that is evolving returns to the condition it was in at its starting point—*plus*, every time, a new and superior degree in the states of consciousness. Thus it becomes clear that the "origin of man," so-called, in this our present Round, or Life-Cycle, on this Planet, must occupy the same place in the same order—save details based on local conditions and time—as in the preceding Round. Again, it must be explained and remembered that, as the work of each Round is said to be apportioned to a different Group of so-called Creators, or Architects, so is that of every Globe; that is, it is under the supervision and guidance of special Builders and Watchers—the various Dhyân Chohans.

"Creators" is an incorrect word to use, as no other religion, not even the sect of the Visishthadvaitîs in India, one which anthropomorphizes even Parabrahman, believes in creation *ex nihilo*, as Christians and Jews do, but only in evolution out of preëxisting materials.

The Group of the Hierarchy which is commissioned to "create" men is a special Group, then; yet it evolved shadowy man in this Cycle, just as a higher and still more spiritual Group evolved him in the Third Round. But as it is the Sixth, on the downward scale of Spirituality—the last and Seventh being the Terrestrial Spirits (Elementals), which gradually form, build and condense his physical body—this Sixth Group evolves no more than the future man's shadowy form, a filmy, hardly visible, transparent copy of themselves. It becomes the task of the Fifth Hierarchy—the mysterious Beings that preside over the constellation Capricornus, Makara, or "Crocodile," in India and in Egypt—to inform the empty and ethereal animal form, and make of it the Rational Man. This is one of those subjects upon which very little may be said to the general public. It is a Mystery truly, but only to him who is prepared to reject the existence of intellectual and conscious Spiritual Beings in the Universe, and to limit full Consciousness to man alone, and that only as a "function of the brain." Many are those among the Spiritual Entities, who have incarnated bodily in man, since his first appearance, and who, for all that, still exist as independently as they did before, in the infinitudes of Space.

To put it more clearly, such an invisible Entity may be bodily present on earth without, however, abandoning its status and functions in the supersensuous regions. If this needs explanation, we can do no better than remind the reader of like cases in so-called "Spiritualism"; though such cases are very rare, at least as regards the nature of the Entity incarnating, or taking temporary possession of a medium. For the so-called "spirits" that may occasionally possess themselves of the bodies of mediums are not the Monads, or Higher Principles, of disembodied Personalities. Such "spirits" can only be either Elementaries, or—Nirmânakâyas. Just as certain persons, whether by virtue of a peculiar organization, or through the power of acquired mystic knowledge, can be seen in their "double" in one place, while their body is many miles away; so the same thing can occur in the case of superior Beings.

Man, philosophically considered, is, in his outward form, simply an animal, hardly more perfect than his pithecoid-like ancestor of the Third Round. He is a living Body, not a living Being, since the realization of existence, the "*Ego Sum*," necessitates self-consciousness, and an animal can only have direct consciousness, or instinct. This was so well understood by the ancients, that even the Kabalists made of soul and body two Lives, independent of each other. In the *New Aspects of Life*, the author states the Kabalistic teaching:

They held that, functionally, Spirit and Matter, of corresponding opacity and density, tended to coalesce; and that the resultant created Spirits, in the disembodied state, were constituted on a scale in which the differing opacities and transparencies of elemental or uncreated Spirit were reproduced. And that these Spirits, in the disembodied state, attracted, appropriated, digested and assimilated elemental Spirit and elemental Matter whose condition was conformed to their own.... They therefore taught that there was a wide difference in the conditions of created Spirits; and that, in the intimate association between the Spirit-world and the world of Matter, the more opaque Spirits, in the disembodied state, were drawn towards the more dense parts of the material world, and therefore tended towards the centre of the Earth, where they found the conditions most suited to their state; while the more transparent Spirits passed into the surrounding aura of the planet, the most rarefied finding their home in its satellite.

This relates exclusively to our Elemental Spirits, and has naught to do with either the Planetary, Sidereal, Cosmic or Inter-Etheric Intelligent Forces, or "Angels" as they are termed by the Roman Church. The Jewish Kabalists, especially the practical Occultists who dealt with Ceremonial Magic, busied themselves solely with the Spirits of the Planets and the "Elementals" so-called. Therefore the above covers only a portion of the Esoteric teaching.

The Soul, whose body-vehicle is the astral, ethereo-substantial envelope, could die and man be still living on earth. That is to say, the Soul could free itself from and quit the tabernacle for various reasons, such as insanity, spiritual and physical depravity, etc. The possibility of the "Soul"—that is, the eternal Spiritual Ego—dwelling in the unseen worlds, while its body goes on living on Earth, is a preeminently Occult doctrine, especially in Chinese and Buddhist philosophy. Many are the *soulless* men among us, for the occurrence is found to take place in wicked materialists as well as in persons "who advance in holiness and never turn back."

Therefore, that which living men (Initiates) can do, the Dhyânis, who have no physical body to hamper them, can do still better. This was the belief of the antediluvians, and it is fast becoming that of modern intellectual society in "Spiritualism," as well as in the Greek and Roman Churches, which teach the ubiquity of their Angels. The Zoroastrians regarded their Amshaspends as dual entities (Ferouers), applying this duality—in Esoteric philosophy, at any rate—to all the spiritual and invisible denizens of the numberless worlds in space, which are visible to our eye. In a note of Damascius (sixth century) on the Chaldean Oracles, we have ample evidence of the universality of this doctrine, for he says: "In these Oracles, the seven Cosmocratores of the World , mentioned likewise by St. Paul, are double; one set being commissioned to rule the superior worlds, the spiritual and the sidereal, and the other to guide and watch over the worlds of matter." Such is also the opinion of Jamblichus, who makes an evident distinction between the Archangels and the Archontes.

The above may be applied, of course, to the distinction made between the degrees or orders of Spiritual Beings, and it is in this sense that the Roman Catholic Church tries to interpret and teach the difference; for while the Archangels are in her teaching divine and holy, she denounces their "Doubles" as Devils. But the word Ferouer is not to be understood in this sense, for it means simply the reverse or the opposite side of some attribute or quality. Thus when the Occultist says that the "Demon is the inverse of God"—evil, the reverse of the medal—he does not mean two separate actualities, but two aspects or facets of the same Unity. But the best man living, side by side with an Archangel—as described in Theology—would appear a fiend. Hence a certain reason in depreciating a lower "Double," immersed far deeper in matter than its original. But still there is as little cause to regard them as Devils, and this is precisely what the Roman Catholics maintain against all reason and logic.

This identity between the Spirit and its material "Double"—in man it is the reverse—explains still better the confusion, already alluded to in this work, in the names and individualities, as well as in the numbers, of the Rishis and Prajâpatis; especially of those of the Satya Yuga and the Mahâbhâratan Period. It also throws additional light on what the Secret Doctrine teaches with regard to the Root- and the Seed-Manus. Not only these Progenitors of our mankind, but every human being, we are taught, has his prototype in the Spiritual Spheres, which prototype is the highest essence of his Seventh Principle. Thus the seven Manus become fourteen, the Root-Manu being the Prime Cause, and the Seed-Manu its

Effect; and from the Satya Yuga (the first stage) to the Heroic Period, these Manus or Rishis become twenty-one in number.

(*b*) The concluding sentence of this shloka shows how archaic is the belief and the doctrine that man is seven-fold in his constitution. The "Thread" of Being, which animates man, and passes through all his Personalities, or Rebirths on this Earth— an allusion to Sûtrâtmâ—the Thread on which moreover all his "Spirits" are strung, is spun from the essence of the Threefold, the Four-fold and the Five-fold which contain all the preceding. Panchâshikha, agreeably to *Padma Purâna*, is one of the seven *Kumâras* who go to Shveta Dvîpa to worship Vishnu. We shall see, further on, what connection there is between the "celibate" and chaste Sons of Brahmâ, who refuse "to multiply," and terrestrial mortals. Meanwhile, it is evident that the "Man-Plant, Saptaparna," thus refers to the seven principles, and that man is compared to this seven-leaved plant, which is so sacred among Buddhists. The Egyptian allegory, in the *Book of the Dead*, that relates to the "reward of the Soul," is as suggestive of our septenary doctrine as it is poetical. The Deceased is allotted a piece of land in the field of Aanroo, wherein the Manes, the deified shades of the dead, glean, as the harvest they have sown by their actions in life, the corn seven cubits high, which grows in a territory divided into seven and fourteen portions. This corn is the food on which they will live and prosper, or that will kill them, in Amenti, the realm of which the Aanroo-field is a domain. For, as said in the hymn, the Deceased is either destroyed therein, or becomes pure spirit for the Eternity, in consequence of the "seven times seventy-seven lives" passed, or to be passed, on Earth. The idea of the corn reaped as the "fruit of our actions" is very graphic.

4. IT IS THE ROOT THAT NEVER DIES, THE THREE-TONGUED FLAME OF THE FOUR WICKS (*a*)... THE WICKS ARE THE SPARKS, THAT DRAW FROM THE THREE-TONGUED FLAME, SHOT OUT BY THE SEVEN, THEIR FLAME; THE BEAMS AND SPARKS OF ONE MOON, REFLECTED IN THE RUNNING WAVES OF ALL THE RIVERS OF THE EARTH (*b*).

(*a*) The "Three-tongued Flame that never dies" is the immortal spiritual Triad, the Âtmâ, Buddhi and Manas, or rather the fruitage of the last, assimilated by the first two after every terrestrial life. The "Four Wicks," that go out and are extinguished, are the Quaternary, the four lower principles, including the body.

"I am the Three-wicked Flame and my Wicks are immortal," says the Defunct. "I enter into the domain of Sekhem hand sows the seed of action produced by the disembodied soul], and I enter the region of the Flames who have destroyed their adversaries ."
"The Three-tongued Flame of the Four Wicks" corresponds to the four Unities and the three Binaries of the Sephirothal tree.

(*b*) Just as milliards of bright sparks dance on the waters of an ocean, above which one and the same moon is shining, so our evanescent Personalities—the illusive envelopes of the immortal Monad-Ego—twinkle and dance on the waves of Mâyâ. They appear and, as the thousands of sparks produced by the moon-beams, last only so long as the Queen of the Night radiates her lustre on the "Running Waves" of Life, the period of a Manvantara; and then they disappear, the "Beams"—symbols of our eternal Spiritual Egos—alone surviving, remerged in, and being, as they were before, one with the Mother-Source.

5. THE SPARK HANGS FROM THE FLAME BY THE FINEST THREAD OF FOHAT. IT JOURNEYS THROUGH THE SEVEN WORLDS OF MÂYÂ (*a*). IT STOPS IN THE FIRST, AND IS A METAL AND A STONE; IT PASSES INTO THE SECOND, AND BEHOLD—A PLANT; THE PLANT WHIRLS THROUGH SEVEN FORMS AND BECOMES A SACRED ANIMAL (*b*).
FROM THE COMBINED ATTRIBUTES OF THESE, MANU, THE THINKER, IS FORMED.

WHO FORMS HIM? THE SEVEN LIVES, AND THE ONE LIFE (*c*). WHO COMPLETES HIM? THE FIVE-FOLD LHA. AND WHO PERFECTS THE LAST BODY? FISH, SIN AND SOMA (*d*).

(*a*) The phrase, "through the Seven Worlds of Mâyâ," refers here to the seven Globes of the Planetary Chain and the seven Rounds, or the forty-nine stations of active existence that are before the "Spark," or Monad, at the beginning of every Great Life-Cycle, or Manvantara. The "Thread of Fohat" is the Thread of Life before referred to.

This relates to the greatest problem of philosophy—the physical and substantial nature of Life, the independent nature of which is denied by Modern Science, because that Science is unable to comprehend it. The reïncarnationists and believers in Karma alone dimly perceive, that the whole secret of Life is in the unbroken series of its manifestations, whether in, or apart from, the physical body. Because even if:

Life, like a dome of many-coloured glass,
Stains the white radiance of Eternity—

yet it is itself part and parcel of that Eternity; for Life alone can understand Life.

What is that "Spark" which "hangs from the Flame"? It is Jîva, the Monad in conjunction with Manas, or rather its aroma—that which remains from each Personality, when worthy, and hangs from Âtmâ-Buddhi, the Flame, by the Thread of Life. In whatever way it is interpreted, and into whatever number of principles the human being is divided, it may be easily shown that this doctrine is supported by all the ancient religions, from the Vedic to the Egyptian, from the Zoroastrian to the Jewish. In the case of the last-mentioned, the Kabalistic works offer abundant proof of this statement. The entire system of the Kabalistic numerals is based on the divine Septenary hanging from the Triad, thus forming the Decad, and its permutations 7, 5, 4, and 3, which, finally, all merge into the *One* itself; an endless and boundless Circle.

As says the *Zohar*:

The Deity manifests itself through the *ten* Sephiroth, which are its radiating witnesses. The Deity is like the sea from which outflows a stream called Wisdom, the waters of which fall into a lake named Intelligence. From the basin, like seven channels, issue the Seven Sephiroth.... For *ten* equal *seven*: the Decad contains *four* Unities and *three* Binaries.

The Ten Sephiroth correspond to the Limbs of Man.

When I framed Adam Kadmon, the Spirit of the Eternal shot out of his Body, like a sheet of lightning that radiated at once on the billows of the *seven* millions of skies, and my *ten* Splendours were his Limbs.

But neither the Head nor the Shoulders of Adam Kadmon can be seen; therefore we read in the *Siphra Dtzenioutha*, the "Book of the Concealed Mystery":

In the beginning of Time, after the Elohim had shaped out of the eternal Essence the Heavens and the Earth, they formed the worlds six by six.

The seventh being Malkuth, which is our Earth on its plane, and the lowest on all the other planes of conscious existence. The Chaldean *Book of Numbers* contains a detailed explanation of all this.

The first triad of the Body of Adam Kadmon cannot be seen before the Soul stands in the presence of the Ancient of Days.

The Sephiroth of this upper Triad are: "1. Kether (the Crown), represented by the brow of Macroprosopus; 2. Chokmah (Wisdom, a male Principle), by his right shoulder; and 3. Binah (Intelligence, a female Principle), by the left shoulder." Then come the *seven* Limbs, or Sephiroth, on the planes of manifestation; the totality of these four planes being represented by Microprosopus, the Lesser Face, or Tetragrammaton, the "four-lettered" Mystery. "The *seven* manifested and the *three* concealed Limbs are the Body of the Deity."

Thus our Earth, Malkuth, is both the *seventh* and the *fourth* World; the former when counting from the first Globe above, the latter if reckoned by the planes. It is generated by the sixth Globe or Sephira, called Yezud, "Foundation," or, as said in the *Book of Numbers*, "by Yezud, He fecundates the primitive Heva ." Rendered in mystic language, this is the explanation why Malkuth, called the Inferior Mother, Matrona, Queen, and the Kingdom of the Foundation, is shown as the Bride of Tetragrammaton, or Microprosopus (the Second Logos), the Heavenly Man. When free from all impurity, she will become united with the Spiritual Logos, *i.e.*, in the Seventh Race of the Seventh Round—after the regeneration, on the day of "Sabbath." For the "*Seventh* Day" again has an occult significance undreamed of by our theologians.

When Matronitha, the Mother, is separated and brought face to face with the King, in the excellence of the Sabbath, all things become one body.

"Become one body" means, that all is reäbsorbed once more into the One Element, the spirits of men becoming Nirvânîs, and the elements of everything else becoming again what they were before—Protyle or Undifferentiated Substance. "Sabbath" means Rest, or Nirvâna. It is not the "*seventh* day" after *six* days, but a period the duration of which equals that of the seven "days," or any period made up of seven parts. Thus a Pralaya is equal in duration to a Manvantara, or a Night of Brahmâ is equal to his Day. If the Christians will follow Jewish customs, they ought to adopt the spirit and not the dead letter thereof. They should work one week of seven days and *rest* seven days. That the word "Sabbath" had a mystic significance, is disclosed in the contempt shown by Jesus for the Sabbath day, and by what is said in *Luke*. Sabbath is there taken for the *whole week*. See the Greek text where the week is called "Sabbath." Literally, "I fast twice in the Sabbath." Paul, an Initiate, knew it well when referring to the eternal rest and felicity in Heaven, as Sabbath: "and their happiness will be eternal, for they will ever be with the Lord, and will enjoy *an eternal Sabbath*."

The difference between the Kabalah and the archaic Esoteric Vidyâ—taking the Kabalah as contained in the Chaldean *Book of Numbers*, not as misrepresented by its now disfigured copy, the *Kabalah* of the Christian Mystics—is very small indeed, being confined to unimportant divergences of form and expression. Thus Eastern Occultism refers to our Earth as the

Fourth World, the lowest of the Chain, above which run upward on both curves the six Globes, three on each side. The *Zohar*, on the other hand, calls the Earth the lower, or the *seventh*, adding that upon the six depend all things which are in it (Microprosopus). The "Smaller Face is formed of *six* Sephiroth," says the same work. "Seven Kings come and *die in the thrice-destroyed World*. And their reign will be broken up." This relates to the Seven Races, *five* of which have already appeared, and *two* more have still to appear in this Round.

The Shinto allegorical accounts of cosmogony and the origin of man, in Japan, hint at the same belief.

Captain C. Pfoundes, who studied the religion underlying the various sects of the land, for nearly nine years in the monasteries of Japan, says:

The Shinto idea of creation is as follows: Out of Chaos (Konton) the Earth (In) was the sediment precipitated, and the Heavens (Yo) the ethereal essences which ascended: Man (Jin) appeared between the two. The first man was called Kuni-to ko tatchino-mikoto, and *five other names were given to him*, and then the human race appeared, male and female. Isanagi and Isanami begat Tenshoko doijin, the first of the five Gods of the Earth.

These "Gods" are simply our Five Races, Isanagi and Isanami being the two kinds of "Ancestors," the two preceding Races which give birth to animal and to rational man.

It will be shown in Volume II, that the number seven, as well as the doctrine of the septenary constitution of man, was preëminent in all the secret systems. It plays as important a part in Western Kabalah as in Eastern Occultism. Éliphas Lévi calls the number seven "the key to the Mosaic creation and the symbols of every religion." He shows the Kabalah faithfully following even the septenary division of man, for the diagram he gives in his *Clef des Grands Mystères* is septenary. This may be seen at a glance, however cleverly the correct thought is veiled. One needs also only to look at the diagram, the "Formation of the Soul," in Mathers' *Kabbalah Unveiled*, from the above mentioned, work of Lévi, to find the same, though with a different interpretation.

Thus it stands with both the Kabalistic and Occult names attached:

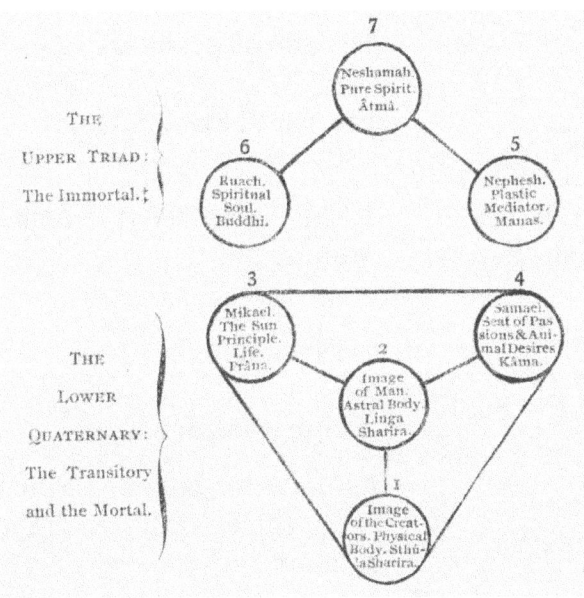

Lévi calls Nephesh that which we name Manas, and *vice versâ*. Nephesh is the Breath of (animal) Life in man—the Breath of Life, *instinctual* in the animal; and Manas is the Third Soul—the human in its light side, and animal, in its connection with Samaël or Kâma. Nephesh is really the "Breath of (animal) Life" breathed into Adam, the Man of Dust; it is consequently the Vital Spark, the informing Element. Without Manas, the "Reasoning Soul," or Mind, which in Lévi's diagram is miscalled Nephesh, Âtmâ-Buddhi is irrational on this plane and cannot act. It is Buddhi which is the Plastic Mediator; not Manas, the intelligent medium between the upper Triad and the lower Quaternary. But there are many such strange and curious transformations to be found in the Kabalistic works—a convincing proof that this literature has become a sad jumble. We do not accept the classification, except in this one particular, in order to show the points of agreement.

We will now give in tabular form what the very cautious Éliphas Lévi says in explanation of his diagram, and what the Esoteric Doctrine teaches—and compare the two. Lévi, too, makes a distinction between Kabalistic and Occult Pneumatics.

Says Éliphas Lévi, the Kabalist: KABALISTIC PNEUMATICS.	Say the Theosophists: ESOTERIC PNEUMATICS.
1. The Soul (or Ego) is a clothed light; and this light is triple.	1. The same; for it is Âtmâ-Buddhi-Manas.
2. Neshamah—pure Spirit.	2. The same.
3. Ruach—the Soul or Spirit.	3. Spiritual Soul.
4. Nephesh—Plastic Mediator.	4. Mediator between Spirit and Man, the Seat of Reason, the Mind, in man.
5. The garment of the Soul is the rind of the Image.	5. Correct.
6. The Image is double, because it reflects the good and the bad.	6. Too uselessly apocalyptic. Why not say that the Astral reflects the good as well as the bad man; man, who is ever tending to the upper Triad, or else disappears with the Quaternary.
7.	7. The Earthly Image.
OCCULT PNEUMATICS. (As given by Éliphas Lévi.)	OCCULT PNEUMATICS. (As given by the Occultists.)
1. Nephesh is immortal, because it renews its life by the destruction of forms.	1. Manas is immortal, because after every new incarnation it adds to Âtmâ-Buddhi something of itself; and thus, assimilating

2. Ruach progresses by the evolution of ideas (!?).

3. Neshamah is progressive, without oblivion and destruction.

4. The Soul has three dwellings.

5. These dwellings are: the Plane of Mortals; the Superior Eden; and the Inferior Eden.

6. The Image is a sphinx that offers the riddle of birth.

7. The fatal Image endows Nephesh with its aptitudes; but Ruach is able to substitute for it the Image conquered in accordance with the inspirations of Neshamah.

itself to the Monad, shares its immortality.

2. Buddhi becomes conscious by the accretions it gets from Manas, on the death of man after every new incarnation.

3. Âtmâ neither progresses, forgets, nor remembers. It does not belong to this plane; it is but the Ray of Light eternal which shines upon, and through, the darkness of matter—when the latter is willing.

4. The Soul—collectively, as the Upper Triad—*lives* on three planes, besides its fourth, the terrestrial sphere; and it *is* eternally on the highest of the three.

5. These dwellings are: Earth for the physical man, or Animal Soul; Kâma Loka (Hades, the Limbo) for the disembodied man, or his Shell; Devachan for the Higher Triad.

6. Correct.

7. The Astral, through Kâma (Desire), is ever drawing Manas down into the sphere of material passions and desires. But if the *better* Man, or Manas, tries to escape the fatal attraction, and turns its aspirations to Âtmâ (Neshamah), then Buddhi (Ruach) conquers, and carries Manas with it to the realm of eternal Spirit.

It is very evident that the French Kabalist either did not sufficiently know the real tenet, or distorted it to suit himself and his objects. Thus he says again, treating upon the same subject, as follows; and we Occultists answer the late Kabalist and his admirers also as follows:

1. The Body is the mould of Nephesh; Nephesh the mould of Ruach; Ruach the mould of the *garment* of Neshamah.

1. The Body follows the whims, good or bad, of Manas; Manas tries to follow the Light of Buddhi, but often fails. Buddhi is the mould of the "garments" of Âtmâ; for Âtmâ is no body, or shape, or anything, and because Buddhi is only *figuratively* its Vehicle.

2. Light personifies itself in clothing itself; and personality endures only when the garment is perfect.

2. The Monad becomes a personal Ego when it incarnates; and something remains of that Personality through Manas, when the latter is perfect enough to assimilate Buddhi.

3. The Angels aspire to become men; a Perfect Man, a Man-God, is above all the Angels.

3. Correct.

4. Every 14,000 years the soul rejuvenates, and rests in the jubilean sleep of oblivion.

4. Within a period, a Great Age, or a Day of Brahmâ, 14 Manus reign; after which comes Pralaya, when all the Souls (Egos) rest in Nirvâna.

Such are the distorted copies of the Esoteric Doctrine in the *Kabalah*.

But to return to Shloka 5 of Stanza VII.

(*b*) The well-known Kabalistic aphorism runs: "A stone becomes a plant; a plant, a beast; the beast, a man; a man, a spirit; and the spirit, a god." The "Spark" animates all the kingdoms, in turn, before it enters into and informs Divine Man, between whom and his predecessor animal man, there is all the difference in the world. *Genesis* begins its anthropology at the wrong end—evidently for a blind—and lands nowhere. The introductory chapters of *Genesis* were never meant to represent even a remote allegory of the creation of *our* Earth. They embrace a metaphysical conception of some indefinite period, in eternity, when successive attempts were being made by the law of evolution at the formation of universes. The idea is plainly stated in the *Zohar*:

There were old Worlds, which perished as soon as they came into existence, were formless, and were called Sparks. Thus, the smith, when hammering the iron, lets the sparks fly in all directions. The Sparks are the primordial Worlds, which could not continue because the Sacred Aged (Sephira) had not as yet assumed its form (of androgyne, or opposite sexes) of King and Queen (Sephira and Kadmon), and the Master was not yet at his work.

Had *Genesis* begun as it ought, one would have found in it, first, the Celestial Logos, the "Heavenly Man," which evolves as a Compound Unit of Logoi, out of which, after their pralayic sleep—a sleep that gathers the Numbers scattered on the mâyâvic plane into One, as the separate globules of quicksilver on a plate blend into one mass—the Logoi appear in their totality as the first "Male and Female," or Adam Kadmon, the "Fiat Lux" of the *Bible*, as we have already seen. But this transformation did not take place on our Earth, nor on any material plane, but in the Spacial Depths of the first differentiation of the eternal Root-Matter. On our nascent Globe, things proceed differently. The Monad or Jîva, as said in *Isis Unveiled*, is, first of all, shot down by the Law of Evolution into the lowest form of matter—the mineral. After a sevenfold gyration encased in the stone, or that which will become mineral and stone in the Fourth Round, it creeps out of it, say, as a lichen. Passing thence, through all the forms of vegetable matter, into what is termed animal matter, it has now reached the point at which it has become the germ, so to speak, of the animal, that will become the physical man. All this, up to the Third Round, is formless, as matter, and senseless, as consciousness. For the Monad, or Jîva, *per se*, cannot be called even Spirit: it is a Ray, a Breath of the Absolute, or the ABSOLUTENESS rather; and the Absolute Homogeneity, having no relations with the conditioned and relative finiteness, is unconscious on our plane. Therefore, besides the material which will be needed for its future human form, the Monad requires (*a*) a spiritual model, or prototype, for that material to shape itself into; and (*b*) an intelligent consciousness, to guide its evolution and progress, neither of which is possessed by the homogeneous Monad, or by senseless though living matter. The Adam of dust requires the Soul of Life to be breathed into him: the two middle Principles, which are the *sentient* Life of the irrational animal and the Human Soul, for the former is irrational without the latter. It is only when, from a potential androgyne, man has become separated into male and female, that he will be endowed with this conscious, rational, individual Soul (Manas), "the principle, or the intelligence, of the Elohim," to receive which, he has to eat of the fruit of Knowledge from the Tree of Good and Evil. How is he to obtain all this? The Occult Doctrine teaches that while the Monad is cycling on downward into matter, these very Elohim, or Pitris—the lower Dhyân Chohans—are evolving, *pari passu* with it, on a higher and more spiritual plane, descending also relatively into matter, on their own plane of consciousness, when, after having reached a certain point, they will meet the incarnating senseless Monad, encased in the lowest matter, and blending the two potencies, Spirit and Matter, the union will produce that terrestrial symbol of the "Heavenly Man" in space—PERFECT MAN. In the Sânkhya Philosophy, Purusha (Spirit) is spoken of as something impotent unless it mounts on the shoulders of Prakriti (Matter), which, left alone, is—senseless. But in the Secret Philosophy they are viewed as graduated. Spirit and Matter, though one and the same thing in their origin, when once they are on the plane of differentiation, begin each of them their evolutionary progress in contrary directions—Spirit falling gradually into Matter, and the latter ascending to its original condition, that of a pure spiritual Substance. Both are inseparable, yet ever separated. On the physical plane, two like poles will always repel each other, while the negative and the positive are mutually attracted; so do Spirit and Matter stand to each other—the two poles of the same homogeneous Substance, the Root-Principle of the Universe.

Therefore, when the hour strikes for Purusha to mount on Prakriti's shoulders for the formation of the Perfect Man—rudimentary man of the first Two and a Half Races being only the *first*, gradually evolving into the *most perfect, of mammals*—the Celestial Ancestors (Entities from preceding Worlds, called in India the Shishta) step in on this our plane, and incarnate in the physical or animal man, as the Pitris had stepped in before them for the formation of the latter. Thus the two processes for the two "creations"—the animal and the divine man—differ greatly. The Pitris shoot out from their ethereal bodies still more ethereal and shadowy similitudes of themselves, or what we should now call "doubles," or "astral forms," in their own likeness. This furnishes the Monad with its first dwelling, and blind matter with a model around and upon which to build henceforth. But *Man is still incomplete.* From Svâyambhuva Manu, from whom descended the seven primitive Manus, or Prajâpatis, each of whom gave birth to a primitive Race of men, down to the *Codex Nazarœus*, in which Karabtanos, or Fetahil, blind concupiscent Matter, begets on his Mother, Spiritus, seven Figures, each of which stands as the progenitor of one of the primeval seven Races—this doctrine has left its impress on every archaic scripture.

"Who forms Manu and who forms his body? The Life and the Lives. Sin and the Moon." Here Manu stands for the spiritual, heavenly Man, the real and non-dying Ego in us, which is the direct emanation of the "One Life," or the Absolute Deity. As to our outward physical bodies, the house of the tabernacle of the Soul, the Doctrine teaches a strange lesson; so strange that unless thoroughly explained, and as thoroughly comprehended, it is only the exact science of the future that is destined to fully vindicate the theory.

It has been stated before now that Occultism does not accept anything inorganic in the Kosmos. The expression employed by Science, "inorganic substance," means simply that the latent life, slumbering in the molecules of so-called "inert matter," is incognizable. ALL IS LIFE, and every atom of even mineral dust is a LIFE, though beyond our comprehension and perception, because it is outside the range of the laws known to those who reject Occultism. "The very atoms," says Tyndall, "seem instinct with a desire for life." Whence, then, we would ask, comes the tendency "to run into organic form"? Is it in any way explicable except according to the teachings of Occult Science?

The Worlds, to the profane, are built up of the known Elements. To the conception of an Arhat, these Elements are themselves, collectively, a Divine Life; distributively, on the plane of manifestations, the numberless and countless crores of Lives. Fire alone is ONE, *on the plane of the One Reality: on that of manifested, hence illusive, Being, its particles are fiery Lives which live and have their being at the expense of every other Life that they consume. Therefore they are named the "*DEVOURERS.*" ... Every visible thing in this Universe was built by such* LIVES, *from conscious and divine primordial man down to the unconscious agents that construct matter.... From the* ONE LIFE, *formless and uncreate, proceeds the Universe of Lives. First was manifested from the Deep cold luminous Fire, which formed the Curds in Space ... These fought, and a great heat was developed by the encountering and collision, which produced rotation. Then came the first manifested* MATERIAL *Fire, the hot Flames, the Wanderers in Heaven. Heat generates moist vapour; that forms solid water; then dry mist, then liquid mist, watery, that puts out the luminous brightness of the Pilgrims, and forms solid watery Wheels. Bhümi appears with six sisters. These produce by their continuous motion the inferior fire, heat, and an aqueous mist, which yields the third World-Element—* WATER; *and from the breath of all* AIR *is born. These four are the* *four Lives of the first four Periods of Manvantara. The three last will follow.*

The Commentary first speaks of the "numberless and countless crores of Lives." Is Pasteur, then, unconsciously taking the first step toward Occult Science, in declaring that, if he dared express his ideas fully upon this subject, he would say, that the organic cells are endowed with a vital potency that does not cease its activity with the cessation of a current of oxygen towards them, and does not, on that account, break off its relations with life itself, which is supported by the influence of that gas? "I would add," continues Pasteur, "that the evolution of the germ is accomplished by means of complicated phenomena, among which we must class processes of fermentation"; and life, according to Claude Bernard and Pasteur, is nothing else than a process of fermentation. That there exist in Nature Beings, or Lives, that can live and thrive without air, even on our Globe, has been demonstrated by the same Scientists. Pasteur found that many of the lower lives, such as vibriones, and other microbes and bacteria, could exist without air, which, on the contrary, killed them. They derived the oxygen necessary for their multiplication from the various substances that surrounded them. He calls them *œrobes*, living on the tissues of our matter, when the latter has ceased to form a part of an integral and living whole (then called very unscientifically by Science "dead matter"), and *anœrobes*. The one kind binds oxygen, and contributes greatly to the destruction of animal life and vegetable tissues, furnishing to the atmosphere materials which enter, later on, into the constitution of other organisms; the other finally destroys, or rather annihilates, the so-called organic substance; ultimate decay being impossible without their participation. Certain germ-cells, such as those of yeast, develop and multiply in air, but when deprived of it, they will adapt themselves to life without air and become ferments, absorbing oxygen from substances coming in contact with them, and thereby ruining the latter. The cells in fruit, when lacking free oxygen, act as ferments and stimulate fermentation. "Therefore the vegetable cell, in this case, manifests its life as an anærobic being. Why, then, should an organic cell form, in this case, an exception?" asks Professor Bogolubof. Pasteur shows that in the substance of our tissues and organs, the cell, not finding sufficient oxygen for itself, stimulates fermentation in the same way as the fruit-cell, and Claude Bernard thought that Pasteur's idea of the formation of ferments found its application and corroboration in the fact that urea increases in the blood during strangulation. LIFE therefore is everywhere in the Universe, and, Occultism teaches us, it is also in the atom.

"Bhûmi appears with six sisters," says the Commentary. It is a Vedic teaching that "there are three Earths, corresponding to three Heavens, and our Earth is called Bhûmi." This is the explanation given by our exoteric Western Orientalists. But the esoteric meaning, and allusion to it in the *Vedas*, is that it refers to our Planetary Chain; "three Earths" on the descending arc, and "three Heavens," which are three Earths or Globes also, only far more ethereal, on the ascending or spiritual arc. By the first three we descend into Matter, by the other three we ascend into Spirit; the lowest one, Bhûmi, our Earth, forming the turning point, so to say, and containing, *potentially*, as much of Spirit as it does of Matter. But we shall treat of this hereafter.

The general teaching of the Commentary, then, is that every new Round develops one of the Compound Elements, as now known to Science, which rejects the primitive nomenclature, preferring to subdivide them into constituents. If Nature is the "Ever-Becoming" on the manifested plane, then these Elements are to be regarded in the same light: they have to evolve, progress, and increase to the manvantaric end.

Thus the First Round, we are taught, developed but one Element, and a nature and humanity in what may be spoken of as one aspect of Nature—called by some, very unscientifically, though it may be so *de facto*, "one-dimensional space."

The Second Round brought forth and developed two Elements, Fire and Earth; and *its* humanity, adapted to this condition of Nature, if we can give the name humanity to beings living under conditions now unknown to men, was—to use again a familiar phrase in a strictly figurative sense, the only way in which it can be used correctly—a "two-dimensional" species.

The processes of natural development which we are now considering will at once elucidate and discredit the fashion of speculating on the attributes of *two*, *three*, and *four* or more *dimensional* space; but, in passing, it is worth while to point out the real significance of the sound, but incomplete, intuition that has prompted—among Spiritualists and Theosophists, and several great men of Science, for the matter of that—the use of the modern expression, the "fourth dimension of space." To begin with, the superficial absurdity of assuming that Space itself is measurable in any direction is of little consequence. The familiar phrase can only be an abbreviation of the fuller form—the "*fourth dimension of matter, in Space.*" But even thus expanded, it is an unhappy phrase, because while it is perfectly true that the progress of evolution may be destined to introduce us to new characteristics of matter, those with which we are already familiar are really more numerous than the three dimensions. The qualities, or what is perhaps the best available term, the characteristics of matter, must clearly bear a direct relation always to the senses of man. Matter has extension, colour, motion (molecular motion), taste and smell, corresponding to the existing senses of man, and the next characteristic it develops—let us call it for the moment "Permeability"—will correspond to the next sense of man, which we may call "Normal Clairvoyance." Thus, when some bold thinkers have been thirsting for a fourth dimension, to explain the passage of matter through matter, and the production of knots upon an endless cord, they have been in want of a *sixth characteristic* of matter. The three dimensions belong really to only one attribute, or characteristic, of matter—extension; and popular common sense justly rebels against the idea that, under any condition of things, there can be more than three of such dimensions as length, breadth and thickness. These terms, and the term "dimension" itself, all belong to one plane of thought, to one stage of evolution, to one characteristic of matter. So long as there are foot-rules within the resources of cosmos, to apply to matter, so long will they be able to measure it three ways and no more; just as, from the time the idea of measurement first occupied a place in the human understanding, it has been possible to apply measurement in three directions and no more. But these considerations do not in any way militate against the certainty that, in the progress of time, as the faculties of humanity are multiplied, so will the characteristics of matter be multiplied also. Meanwhile, the expression is far more incorrect than even the familiar phrase of the sun's "rising" or "setting."

We now return to the consideration of material evolution through the Rounds. Matter in the Second Round, it has been stated, may be figuratively referred to as two-dimensional. But here another *caveat* must be entered. This loose and figurative expression may be regarded—on one plane of thought, as we have just seen—as equivalent to the second characteristic of matter, corresponding to the second perceptive faculty or sense of man. But these two linked scales of evolution are concerned with the processes going on within the limits of a single Round. The succession of primary aspects of Nature, with which the succession of Rounds is concerned, has to do, as already indicated, with the development of the Elements—in the Occult sense—Fire, Air, Water, Earth. We are only in the Fourth Round, and our catalogue so far stops short. The order in which these Elements are mentioned, in the last sentence but one, is the correct one for Esoteric purposes and in the Secret Teachings. Milton was right when he spoke of the "Powers of Fire, Air, Water, Earth"; the Earth, such as we know it now, had no existence before the Fourth Round, hundreds of millions of years ago, the commencement of our geological Earth. The Globe, says the Commentary, was *"fiery, cool and radiant, as its ethereal men and animals, during the First Round"*—a contradiction or paradox in the opinion of our present Science—*"luminous and more dense and heavy, during the Second Round; watery during the Third."* Thus are the Elements reversed.

The centres of consciousness of the Third Round, destined to develop into humanity as we know it, arrived at a perception of the third Element, Water. If we had to frame our conclusions according to the *data* furnished us by Geologists, then we would say that there was no real water, even during the Carboniferous Period. We are told that gigantic masses of carbon, which existed formerly spread in the atmosphere, as carbonic acid, were absorbed by plants, while a large proportion of that gas was mixed in the water. Now, if this be so, and we have to believe that all the carbonic acid which went to compose those plants that formed bituminous coal, lignite, etc., and went towards the formation of lime-stone, and so on, that all this was at that period in the atmosphere in gaseous form, then, there must have been seas and oceans of liquid carbonic acid! But how then could the Carboniferous Period be preceded by the Devonian and Silurian Ages—those of fishes and molluscs—on that assumption? Barometric pressure, moreover, must have exceeded several hundred times the pressure of our present atmosphere. How could organisms, even so simple as those of certain fishes and molluscs, stand that? There is a curious work by Blanchard, on the Origin of Life, wherein he shows some strange contradictions and confusions in the theories of his colleagues, and which we recommend to the reader's attention.

Those of the Fourth Round have added Earth as a state of matter to their stock, as well as the three other Elements in their present transformation.

In short, none of the so-called Elements were, in the three preceding Rounds, as they are now. For all we know, FIRE may have been *pure* Âkâsha, the First Matter of the "Magnum Opus" of the Creators and Builders, that Astral Light which the paradoxical Éliphas Lévi calls in one breath the "Body of the Holy Ghost," and in the next "Baphomet," the "Androgyne Goat of Mendes"; AIR, simply Nitrogen, the "Breath of the Supporters of the Heavenly Dome," as the Mahometan Mystics call it; WATER, that primordial fluid which was required, according to Moses, to make a "Living Soul." And this may account for the flagrant discrepancies and unscientific statements found in *Genesis*. Separate the first from the second chapter; read the former as a scripture of the Elohists, and the latter as that of the far later Jehovists; still one finds, if one reads between the lines, the same order in which created things appear; namely, Fire (Light), Air, Water, and Man (or Earth). For the sentence of the first chapter (the Elohistic), "In the beginning God created the heaven and the earth," is a mistranslation; it is not "the heaven and the earth," but the duplex, or dual, Heaven, the *upper* and the *lower* Heavens, or the separation of Primordial Substance that was light in its upper, and dark in its lower portions (the manifested Universe), in its duality of the *invisible* (to the senses), and the *visible* to our perceptions. "God divided the light from the darkness"; and then made the firmament (Air). "Let there be a firmament in the midst of the waters, and let it divide the waters from the waters," *i.e.*, "the waters which were under the firmament from the waters which were *above* the firmament ." In the second chapter (the Jehovistic), plants and herbs are created before water, just as in the first, *light* is produced before the *sun*. "God made the earth and the heavens, and every plant of the field *before it was in the earth*, and every herb of the field *before it grew*; for the Lord God had not caused it to rain upon the earth, etc."—an absurdity unless the esoteric explanation is accepted. The plants *were* created before they were in the earth—*for there was no earth then such as it is now*; and the herb of the field was in existence before it grew as it does now, in the Fourth Round.

Discussing and explaining the nature of the invisible Elements and the "Primordial Fire" mentioned above, Éliphas Lévi invariably calls it the "Astral Light": with him it is the "Grand Agent Magique." Undeniably it is so, but—only so far as *Black* Magic is concerned, and on the lowest planes of what we call Ether, the noumenon of which is Âkâsha; and even this would be held incorrect by orthodox Occultists. The "Astral Light" is simply the older "Sidereal Light" of Paracelsus; and to say that "everything which exists has been evolved from it, and it preserves and reproduces all forms," as he does, is to enunciate truth only in the second proposition. The first is erroneous; for if all that exists was evolved *through* (or *viâ*) it, this is not the Astral Light, since the latter is not the container of *all* things but, at best, only the reflector of this *all*. Éliphas

Lévi very truly shows it "a force in Nature," by means of which "a single man who can master it ... might throw the world into confusion and transform its face"; for it is the "Great Arcanum of transcendent Magic." Quoting the words of the great Western Kabalist in their translated form, we may, perhaps, the better explain them by the occasional addition of a word or two, to show the difference between Western and Eastern explanations of the same subject. The author says of the great Magic Agent:

This ambient and all-penetrating fluid, this ray detached from the Sun's splendour ... fixed by the weight of the atmosphere and the power of central attraction ... the Astral Light, this electro-magnetic ether, this vital and luminous caloric, is represented on ancient monuments by the girdle of Isis, which twines round two poles ... and in ancient theogonies by the serpent devouring its own tail, emblem of prudence and of Saturn. It is the winged dragon of Medea, the double serpent of the caduceus, and the tempter of Genesis; but it is also the brazen snake of Moses encircling the Tau ... lastly, it is the devil of exoteric dogmatism, and is really the blind force, which souls must conquer, in order to detach themselves from the chains of Earth; for if they should not, they will be absorbed by the same power which first produced them, and will return to the central and eternal fire.

This great Archæus is now publicly discovered by, and *for*, only one man—J. W. Keely, of Philadelphia. For others, however, it *is* discovered, yet must remain almost useless. "So far shalt thou go...."

All the above is as practical as it is correct, save one error, which we have explained. Éliphas Lévi commits a great blunder in always identifying the Astral Light with what we call Âkâsha. What it really is will be expounded in Volume II.

Éliphas Lévi further writes:

The great Magic Agent is the fourth emanation of the life principle, of which the Sun is the third form ... for the day-star is only the reflection and material shadow of the Central Sun of truth, which illuminates the intellectual world of Spirit, and which itself is but a gleam borrowed from the Absolute.

So far he is right enough. But when the great authority of the Western Kabalists adds that, nevertheless, "it is not the immortal Spirit, as the Indian Hierophants have imagined"—we answer, that he slanders the said Hierophants, as they have said nothing of the kind; for even the Purânic exoteric writings flatly contradict the assertion. No Hindû has ever mistaken Prakriti—the Astral Light being only above the lowest plane of Prakriti, the Material Kosmos—for the "immortal Spirit." Prakriti is ever called Mâyâ, Illusion, and is doomed to disappear with the rest, the Gods included, at the hour of the Pralaya. As it is shown that Âkasha is not even the Ether, least of all then, we imagine, can it be the Astral Light. Those unable to penetrate beyond the dead letter of the *Purânas*, have occasionally confused Âkâsha with Prakriti, with Ether, and even with the visible Sky! It is true also that those who have invariably translated the term Âkâsha by "Ether"—Wilson, for instance—finding it called "the material cause of sound" possessing, moreover, this *one single property*, have ignorantly imagined it to be "material," in the physical sense. True, again, that if the characteristics are accepted literally, then, since nothing material or physical, and therefore conditioned and temporary, can be immortal—according to metaphysics and philosophy—it would follow that Âkâsha is neither infinite nor immortal. But all this is erroneous, since both the words Pradhâna, Primeval Matter, and Sound, as a property, have been misunderstood; the former term (Pradhâna) being certainly synonymous with Mûlaprakriti and Âkâsha, and the latter (Sound) with the Verbum, the Word or the Logos. This is easy to demonstrate; for it is shown in the following sentence from *Vishnu Purâna*. "There was neither day nor night, nor sky, nor earth, nor darkness, nor light, nor any other thing, save only One, unapprehensible by intellect, or that which is Brahman, and Pums, and Pradhâna ."

Now, what is Pradhâna, if it is not Mûlaprakriti, the Root of All, in another aspect? For though Pradhâna is said, further on, to merge into the Deity, as everything else does, in order to leave the One absolute during the Pralaya, yet is it held as infinite and immortal. The literal translation is given as: "One

Prâdhânika Brahma Spirit: THAT was"; and the Commentator interprets the compound term as a substantive, not as a derivative word used attributively, *i.e.*, like something "conjoined with Pradhâna." The student has to note, moreover, that the Purânic is a dualistic system, not evolutionary, and that, in this respect, far more will be found, from an Esoteric standpoint, in the Sânkhya, and even in the *Mânava-Dharma-Shâstra*, however much the latter differs from the former. Hence Pradhâna, even in the *Purânas*, is an aspect of Parabrahman, not an evolution, and must be the same as the Vedântic Mûlaprakriti. "Prakriti, in its *primary* state, is Âkâsha," says a Vedântin scholar. It is almost abstract Nature.

Âkâsha, then, is Pradhâna in another form, and as such cannot be Ether, the ever-invisible agent, courted even by Physical Science. Nor is it Astral Light. It is, as said, the *noumenon* of the seven-fold differentiated Prakriti—the ever immaculate "Mother" of the *fatherless* "Son," who becomes "Father" on the lower manifested plane. For Mahat is the first product of Pradhâna, or Âkâsha; and Mahat—Universal Intelligence, "whose *characteristic property* is Buddhi"—is no other than the Logos, for he is called Îshvara, Brahmâ, Bhâva, etc. He is, in short, the "Creator," or the Divine Mind in creative operation, "the Cause of all things." He is the "First-Born," of whom the *Purânas* tell us that "Earth and Mahat are the inner and outer boundaries of the Universe," or, in our language, the negative and the positive poles of dual Nature (abstract and concrete), for the *Purâna* adds:

In this manner—as were the *seven* forms of Prakriti reckoned from Mahat to Earth—so at the (time of elemental) dissolution (*pratyâhâra*), these seven successively reënter into each other. The Egg of Brahmâ (*Sarva-mandala*) is dissolved, with its seven zones (*dvîpa*), seven oceans, seven regions, etc.

These are the reasons why the Occultists refuse to give the name of Astral Light to Âkâsha, or to call it Ether. "In my Father's house are many mansions," may be contrasted with the Occult saying, "In our Mother's house are seven mansions," or planes, the lowest of which is above and around us—the Astral Light.

The Elements, whether simple or compound, could not have remained the same since the commencement of the evolution of our Chain. Everything in the Universe progresses steadily in the Great Cycle, while incessantly going up and down in the smaller Cycles. Nature is never stationary during Manvantara, as it is ever *becoming*, not simply *being*; and mineral, vegetable, and human life are always adapting their organisms to the then reigning Elements; and therefore *those* Elements were then fitted for them, as they are now for the life of present humanity. It will only be in the next, or Fifth, Round that the fifth Element, Ether—the gross body of Âkâsha, if it can be called even that—will, by becoming a familiar fact of Nature to all men, as Air is familiar to us now, cease to be, as at present, hypothetical and an "agent" for so many things. And only during that Round will those higher senses, the growth and development of which Âkâsha subserves, be susceptible of a complete expansion. As already indicated, a *partial* familiarity with the characteristic of matter—Permeability—which should be developed concurrently with the sixth sense, may be expected to develop at the proper period in this Round. But with the next Element added to our resources, in the next Round, Permeability will become so manifest a characteristic of matter, that the densest forms of this Round will seem to man's perceptions as obstructive to him as a thick fog, and no more.

Let us now return to the Life-Cycle. Without entering at length upon the description given of the Higher LIVES, we must direct our attention, at present, simply to the earthly Beings and the Earth itself. The latter, we are told, is built up for the *First* Round by the "Devourers," which disintegrate and differentiate the germs of other Lives in the Elements; pretty much, it must be supposed, as in the present stage of the world, the *ærobes* do, when, undermining and loosening the chemical structure in an organism, they transform animal matter, and generate substances that vary in their constitutions. Thus Occultism disposes of the so-called Azoic Age of Science, for it shows that there never was a time when the Earth was without life upon it. Wherever there is an atom of matter, a particle, or a molecule, even in its most gaseous condition, there is life in it, however latent and unconscious.

Whatsoever quits the Laya State, becomes active Life; it is drawn into the vortex of MOTION *; Spirit and Matter are the two States of the* ONE, *which is neither Spirit nor Matter, both being the Absolute Life, latent.... Spirit is the first differentiation of* SPACE; *and Matter the first differentiation of Spirit. That, which is neither Spirit nor Matter, That is IT—the Causeless* CAUSE *of Spirit and Matter, which are the Cause of Kosmos. And THAT we call the* ONE LIFE, *or the Intra-Cosmic Breath.*

Once more we say—*like must produce like*. Absolute Life cannot produce an inorganic atom, whether single or complex, and there is life even in Laya, just as a man in a profound cataleptic state—to all appearance a corpse—is still a living being.

When the "Devourers"—in whom the men of Science are invited to see, with some show of reason, atoms of the Fire-Mist, if they will, as the Occultist will offer no objection to this—when the "Devourers," we say, have differentiated the "Fire Atoms," by a peculiar process of segmentation, the latter become Life-Germs, which aggregate according to the laws of cohesion and affinity. Then the Life-Germs produce Lives of another kind, which work on the structure of our Globes.

Thus, in the First Round, the Globe, having been built by the primitive Fire-Lives—*i.e.*, formed into a sphere—had no solidity, no qualifications, save a cold brightness, no form, no colour; it is only towards the end of the First Round that it developed one Element, which, from its inorganic, so to say, or simple Essence, has become now, in our Round, the fire we know throughout the System. The Earth was in her first Rûpa, the essence of which is the Âkâshic Principle named ———, that which is now known as, and very erroneously termed, Astral Light, which Éliphas Lévi calls the "Imagination of Nature," probably to avoid giving it its correct name, as others do.

Speaking of it, in his Preface to the *Histoire de la Magie*, Éliphas Lévi says:

It is through this Force that all the nervous centres secretly communicate with each other; from it—that sympathy and antipathy are born; from it—that we have our dreams; and that the phenomena of second sight and extra-natural visions take place.... Astral Light ... destroys, coagulates, separates, breaks, gathers in all things.... God created it on that day when he said: *"Fiat Lux!"* ... It is directed by the Egregores, *i.e.*, the chiefs of the souls, who are the spirits of energy and action.

Éliphas Lévi ought to have added that the Astral Light, or Primordial Substance, if matter at all, is that which, called Light, *Lux* esoterically explained, *is the body of those Spirits themselves, and their very essence. Our physical light is the manifestation on our plane*, and the reflected radiance, of the Divine Light, emanating from the collective Body of those who are called the "Lights" and the "Flames." But no other Kabalist has ever had the talent of heaping up one contradiction on the other, of making one paradox chase another in the same sentence, and in such flowing language, as Éliphas Lévi. He leads his reader through the most lovely valleys, to strand him after all on a desert and barren rock.

Says the Commentary:

It is through and from the radiations of the seven Bodies of the seven Orders of Dhyânis, that the seven Discrete Quantities, whose Motion and harmonious Union produce the manifested Universe of Matter, are born.

The *Second* Round brings into manifestation the second Element—AIR; an element, the purity of which would ensure continuous life to him who would use it. In Europe there have been two Occultists only who have discovered and even partially applied it in practice, though its composition has always been known among the highest Eastern Initiates. The ozone of the modern Chemists is poison compared with the real Universal

Solvent, which could never be thought of unless it existed in Nature.

From the Second Round, Earth—hitherto a fœtus in the matrix of Space—began its real existence: it had developed individual sentient Life, its second Principle. The second corresponds to the sixth ; the second is Life continuous, the other, temporary.

The *Third* Round developed the third Principle—WATER; while the *Fourth* transformed the gaseous fluids and plastic form of our Globe into the hard, crusted, grossly material sphere we are living on. Bhûmi has reached her fourth Principle. To this it may be objected that the law of analogy, so much insisted upon, is broken. Not at all. Earth will reach her true ultimate form— her body shell—inversely in this to man, only toward the end of the Manvantara, after the Seventh Round. Eugenius Philalethes was right when he assured his readers, "on his word of honour," that no one had yet seen the "Earth," *i.e.*, Matter in its essential form. Our Globe is, so far, in its Kâmarûpic state—the Astral Body of Desires of Ahamkâra, dark Egotism, the progeny of Mahat, on the lower plane.

It is not molecularly constituted matter, least of all the human Body, Sthûla Sharîra, that is the grossest of all our "Principles," but verily the *middle* Principle, the real Animal Centre, whereas our Body is but its shell, the irresponsible factor and medium through which the beast in us acts all its life. Every intellectual Theosophist will understand my real meaning. Thus the idea that the human tabernacle is built by countless Lives, just in the same way as was the rocky crust of our Earth, has nothing repulsive in it for the true Mystic. Nor can Science oppose the Occult teaching, for it is not because the microscope will ever fail to detect the ultimate living atom or life, that it can reject the doctrine.

(*c*) Science teaches us that the living as well as the dead organisms of both man and animal are swarming with bacteria of a hundred various kinds; that from without we are threatened with the invasion of microbes with every breath we draw, and from within by leucomaines, ærobes, anærobes, and what not. But Science has never yet gone so far as to assert with the Occult doctrine, that our bodies, as well as those of animals, plants, and stones, are themselves altogether built up of such beings; which, with the exception of the larger species, no microscope can detect. So far as regards the purely animal and material portion of man, Science is on its way to discoveries that will go far towards corroborating this theory. Chemistry and Physiology are the two great magicians of the future, which are destined to open the eyes of mankind to great physical truths. With every day, the identity between the animal and physical man, between the plant and man, and even between the reptile and its nest, the rock, and man—is more and more clearly shown. The physical and chemical constituents of all being found to be identical, Chemical Science may well say that there is no difference between the matter which composes the ox, and that which forms man. But the Occult doctrine is far more explicit. It says: Not only the chemical compounds are the same, but the same infinitesimal *invisible* Lives compose the atoms of the bodies of the mountain and the daisy, of man and the ant, of the elephant and of the tree which shelters it from the sun. Each particle—whether you call it organic or inorganic—*is a* Life. Every atom and molecule in the Universe is both *life-giving* and *death-giving* to such forms, inasmuch as it builds by aggregation universes, and the ephemeral vehicles ready to receive the transmigrating soul, and as eternally destroys and changes the *forms*, and expels the souls from their temporary abodes. It creates and kills; it is self-generating and self-destroying; it brings into being, and annihilates, that mystery of mysteries, the *living body* of man, animal, or plant, every second in time and space; and it generates equally life and death, beauty and ugliness, good and bad, and even the agreeable and disagreeable, the beneficent and maleficent sensations. It is that mysterious LIFE, represented collectively by countless myriads of Lives, that follows in its own sporadic way the hitherto incomprehensible law of Atavism; that copies family resemblances, as well as those it finds impressed in the Aura of the generators of every future human being; a mystery, in short, that will receive fuller attention elsewhere. For the present, one

instance may be cited in illustration. Modern Science is
beginning to find out that ptomaine, the alkaloid poison
generated by decaying corpses and matter—a Life also,
extracted with the help of volatile ether, yields a smell as strong
as that of the freshest orange-blossoms; but that free from
oxygen, such alkaloids yield either a most sickening, disgusting
smell, or a most agreeable aroma, which recalls that of the most
delicately scented flowers; and it is suspected that such
blossoms owe their agreeable smell to the poisonous ptomaine.
The venomous essence of certain fungi, also, is nearly identical
with the venom of the cobra of India, the most deadly of
serpents. The French savants Arnaud, Gautier, and Villiers,
have found in the saliva of living men the same venomous
alkaloid as in that of the toad, the salamander, the cobra, and
the trigonocephalus of Portugal. It is proven that venom of the
deadliest kind, whether called ptomaine, or leucomaine, or
alkaloid, is generated by living men, animals and plants.
Gautier also discovered an alkaloid in the fresh carcase and
brains of an ox, and a venom which he calls xanthocreatinine,
similar to the substance extracted from the poisonous saliva of
reptiles. It is the muscular tissues, the most active organs in the
animal economy, that are suspected of being the generators or
factors of venoms, which have the same importance as carbonic
acid and urea in the functions of life, and are the ultimate
products of inner combustion. And though it is not yet fully
determined whether poisons can be generated by the animal
systems of living beings, without the participation and
interference of microbes, it is ascertained that the animal does
produce venomous substances in its physiological or living state.

Thus, having discovered the effects, Science has to find
their *primary* causes; and this it can never do without the help
of the old sciences, of Alchemy, Occult Botany and Physics. We
are taught that every physiological change, in addition to
pathological phenomena, diseases—nay, life itself, or rather the
objective phenomena of life, produced by certain conditions and
changes in the tissues of the body, which allow and force life to
act in that body—that all this is due to those
unseen "Creators" and "Destroyers," which are called, in such a

loose and general way, microbes. It might be supposed that these Fiery Lives and the microbes of Science are identical. This is not true. The Fiery Lives are the seventh and highest subdivision of the plane of matter, and correspond in the individual with the One Life of the Universe, though only on that plane of matter. The microbes of Science are the first and lowest subdivision on the second plane—that of material Prâna, or Life. The physical body of man undergoes a complete change of structure every seven years, and its destruction and preservation are due to the alternate functions of the Fiery Lives, as Destroyers and Builders. They are Builders by sacrificing themselves, in the form of vitality, to restrain the destructive influence of the microbes, and, by supplying the microbes with what is necessary, they compel them under that restraint to build up the material body and its cells. They are Destroyers also, when that restraint is removed, and the microbes, unsupplied with vital constructive energy, are left to run riot as destructive agents. Thus, during the first half of a man's life, the first *five* periods of seven years each, the Fiery Lives are indirectly engaged in the process of building up man's material body; Life is on the ascending scale, and the force is used in construction and increase. After this period is passed, the age of retrogression commences, and, the work of the Fiery Lives exhausting their strength, the work of destruction and decrease also commences.

An analogy between cosmic events in the descent of Spirit into Matter, for the first half of a Manvantara (planetary as well as human), and its ascent, at the expense of Matter, in the second half, may here be traced. These considerations have to do solely with the plane of matter, but the restraining influence of the Fiery Lives on the lowest sub-division of the second plane, the microbes, is confirmed by the fact mentioned in the theory of Pasteur above referred to, that the cells of the organs, when they do not find sufficient oxygen for themselves, adapt themselves to that condition and form *ferments*, which, by absorbing oxygen from substances which come in contact with them, produce their destruction. Thus the process is commenced by one cell robbing its neighbour of the source of its vitality, when the supply is insufficient; and the destruction so commenced steadily progresses.

Such experimenters as Pasteur are the best friends and helpers of the Destroyers, and the worst enemies of the Creators—if the latter were not at the same time Destroyers also. However it may be, one thing is certain in this: the knowledge of these primary causes, and of the ultimate essence of every Element, of its Lives, their functions, properties, and conditions of change—constitutes the basis of MAGIC. Paracelsus was, perhaps, the only Occultist in Europe, during the latter centuries of the Christian era, who was versed in this mystery. Had not a criminal hand put an end to his life years before the time allotted him by Nature, physiological Magic would have fewer secrets for the civilized world than it now has.

(*d*) But what has the Moon to do in all this, we may be asked. What have "Fish, Sin and Soma ," in the apocalyptic sentence of the Stanza, to do in company with the Life-microbes? With the latter nothing, except that they avail themselves of the tabernacle of clay prepared by them; with divine perfect Man everything, since "Fish, Sin and Moon" conjointly compose the three symbols of the immortal Being.

This is all that can be given. Nor does the writer pretend to know more of these strange symbols than may be inferred about them from exoteric religions—from the mystery, perhaps, which underlies the Matsya (Fish) Avatâra of Vishnu, the. Chaldean Oannes, the Man-Fish, recorded in the imperishable sign of the Zodiac, Pisces, and running throughout the two *Testaments* in the personages of Joshua "Son of Nun (the Fish)" and Jesus; from the allegorical "Sin," or Fall of Spirit into Matter; and from the Moon—in so far as it relates to the Lunar Ancestors, the Pitris.

For the present, it may be as well to remind the reader, that while the Moon-Goddesses were connected in every mythology, especially the Grecian, with child-birth, because of the influence of the Moon on women and conception, the Occult and actual connection of our satellite with fecundation is to this day unknown to Physiology, which regards every popular practice in this connection as gross superstition. As it is useless to discuss these in detail, we can only stop for the present to notice the lunar symbology casually, to show that the said superstition belongs to the most ancient beliefs, and even to Judaism—the basis of Christianity. With the Israelites, the chief function of Jehovah was child-giving, and the Esotericism of the *Bible*, interpreted kabalistically, shows undeniably that the Holy of Holies in the Temple was simply the symbol of the womb. This is now proven beyond doubt and cavil, by the *numerical* reading of the *Bible* in general, and of *Genesis* especially. This idea must certainly have been borrowed by the Jews from the Egyptians and Indians, whose Holy of Holies is symbolized by the King's Chamber in the Great Pyramid and the Yoni symbols of exoteric Hindûism. To make the matter clearer, and to show at the same time the enormous difference in the spirit of interpretation and the original meaning of the same symbols between the ancient Eastern Occultists and the Jewish Kabalists, we refer the reader to the Section on "The Holy of Holies," in the second Volume.

Phallic worship has developed only with the loss of the keys to the true meaning of the symbols. It was the last and most fatal turning from the highway of truth and divine knowledge into the side path of fiction, raised into dogma through human falsification and hierarchic ambition.

6. FROM THE FIRST-BORN, THE THREAD BETWEEN THE SILENT WATCHER AND HIS SHADOW BECOMES MORE STRONG AND RADIANT WITH EVERY CHANGE. THE MORNING SUN-LIGHT HAS CHANGED INTO NOON-DAY GLORY....

This sentence, "the Thread between the Silent Watcher and his Shadow becomes more strong with every Change," is another psychological mystery, that will find its explanation in Volume II. For the present, it will suffice to say that the "Watcher" and his "Shadows"—the latter numbering as many as there are reïncarnations for the Monad—are one. The Watcher, or the Divine Prototype, is at the upper rung of the Ladder of Being; the Shadow, at the lower. Withal, the Monad of every living being, unless his moral turpitude breaks the connection, and he runs loose and astray into the "Lunar Path"—to use the Occult expression—*is an individual Dhyân Chohan, distinct from others, with a kind of spiritual Individuality of its own*, during one special Manvantara. Its Primary, the Spirit (Âtman), is one, of course, with the One Universal Spirit (Paramâtmâ), but the Vehicle (Vâhan) it is enshrined in, the Buddhi, is part and parcel of that Dhyân-Chohanic Essence; and it is in this that lies the mystery of that *ubiquity*, which was discussed a few pages back. "My Father, that is in Heaven, and I—are one," says the Christian Scripture; and in this, at any rate, it is the faithful echo of the Esoteric tenet.

7. "This is thy present Wheel"—said the Flame to the Spark. "Thou art myself, my Image and my Shadow. I have clothed myself in thee, and thou art my Vâhan, to the Day 'Be With Us,' when thou shalt re-become myself and others, thyself and I" (*a*). Then the Builders, having donned their first Clothing, descend on radiant Earth, and reign over Men—who are themselves (*b*).

(*a*) The Day when the Spark will re-become the Flame, when Man will merge into his Dhyân Chohan, "myself and others, thyself and I," as the Stanza has it, means that in Paranirvâna—when Pralaya will have reduced not only material and psychical bodies, but even the spiritual Egos, to their original principle—the Past, Present, and even Future Humanities, like all things, will be one and the same. Everything will have reëntered the Great Breath. In other words, everything will be "merged in Brahman," or the Divine Unity.

Is this annihilation, as some think? Or *atheism*, as other critics—the worshippers of a *personal* deity, and believers in an unphilosophical paradise—are inclined to suppose? Neither. It is worse than useless to return to the question of implied atheism, in that which is *spirituality* of a most refined character. To see in Nirvâna annihilation, amounts to saying of a man plunged in a sound *dreamless* sleep—*one that leaves no impression on the physical memory and brain, because the sleeper's Higher Self is then in its original state of Absolute Consciousness*—that he, too, is annihilated. The latter simile answers to one side of the question only—the most material; since *reäbsorption* is by no means such a "dreamless sleep," but, on the contrary, *Absolute* Existence, an unconditioned unity, or a state, to describe which human language is absolutely and hopelessly inadequate. The only approach to anything like a comprehensive conception of it can be attempted solely in the panoramic visions of the Soul, through spiritual ideations of the divine Monad. Nor is the Individuality—*nor even the essence of the Personality*, if any be left behind—lost, because reäbsorbed. For, however limitless from a human standpoint, the paranirvânic state, yet it has a limit in Eternity. Once reached, the same Monad will *reëmerge* therefrom, as a still higher being, on a far higher plane, to recommence its cycle of perfected activity. The human mind, in its present stage of development, cannot transcend, scarcely can it reach this plane of thought. It totters here, on the brink of incomprehensible Absoluteness and Eternity.

(*b*) The "Watchers" reign over men during the whole period of Satya Yuga and the smaller subsequent Yugas, down to the beginning of the Third Root Race; after which it is the Patriarchs, Heroes, and the Manes, as in the Egyptian Dynasties enumerated by the priests to Solon, the incarnated Dhyânis of a lower order, up to King Menes and the human Kings of other nations. All were carefully recorded. In the views of symbologists this Mythopœic Age is of course regarded as only a fairy tale. But since traditions and even chronicles of such Dynasties of *Divine* Kings, of Gods reigning over men, followed by Dynasties of Heroes or Giants, exist in the annals of every nation, it is difficult to understand how all the peoples under the sun, some of whom are separated by vast oceans and belong to different hemispheres, such as the ancient Peruvians and Mexicans, as well as the Chaldeans, could have worked out the same "fairy tales" in the same order of events. However, as the Secret Doctrine teaches *history*—which, although esoteric and traditional, is, none the less, more reliable than profane history—we are entitled to our beliefs as much as anyone else, whether religionist or sceptic. And that Doctrine says that the

Dhyâni-Buddhas of the two higher Groups, namely, the Watchers or the Architects, furnished the many and various races with divine kings and leaders. It is the latter who taught humanity their arts and sciences, and the former who revealed to the incarnated Monads that had just shaken off their Vehicles of the lower Kingdoms, and who had, therefore, lost every recollection of their divine origin, the great spiritual truths of the transcendental Worlds.

Thus, as expressed in the Stanza, the Watchers "descend on radiant Earth and reign over men, *who are themselves*." The reigning Kings had finished their cycle on Earth and other Worlds, in the preceding Rounds. In the future Manvantaras they will have risen to higher Systems than our planetary World; and it is the Elect of our Humanity, the Pioneers on the hard and difficult path of Progress, who will take the places of their predecessors. The next great Manvantara will witness the men of our own Life-Cycle becoming the instructors and guides of a Mankind whose Monads may now be still imprisoned— semi-conscious—in the most intellectual of the animal kingdom, while their lower principles may be animating, perhaps, the highest specimens of the vegetable world.

Thus proceed the cycles of the septenary evolution, in Seven-fold Nature; the spiritual or divine; the psychic or semi-divine; the intellectual; the passional, the instinctual, or *cognitional*; the semi-corporeal; and the purely material or physical natures. All these evolve and progress cyclically, passing from one into another, in a double, centrifugal and centripetal, way, *one* in their ultimate essence, *seven* in their aspects. The lowest, of course, is that depending upon and subservient to our five physical senses, which are in truth *seven*, as shown later, on the authority of the oldest *Upanishads*. Thus far, for individual, human, sentient, animal and vegetable life, each the microcosm of its higher macrocosm. The same for the Universe, which manifests periodically, for purposes of the collective progress of the countless Lives, the outbreathings of the One Life; in order that, through the Ever-Becoming, every cosmic atom in this infinite Universe, passing from the formless and the intangible,

through the mixed natures of the semi-terrestrial, down to matter in full generation, and then back again, reäscending at each new period higher and nearer the final goal; that each atom, we say, may reach, *through individual merits and efforts*, that plane where it re-becomes the One Unconditioned ALL. But between the Alpha and the Omega there is the
weary "Road," hedged in by thorns, that goes down first, then—
Winds up hill all the way;
Yes, to the very end....

Starting upon the long journey immaculate, descending more and more into sinful matter, and having connected himself with every atom in manifested Space—the Pilgrim, having struggled through, and suffered in, every form of Life and Being, is only at the bottom of the valley of matter, and half through his cycle, when he has identified himself with collective Humanity. This, *he has made in his own image*. In order to progress upwards and homewards, the "God" has now to ascend the weary uphill path of the Golgotha of Life. It is the martyrdom of self-conscious existence. Like Vishvakarman, he has to sacrifice *himself to himself*, in order to redeem all creatures, to resurrect from the Many into the One Life. Then he ascends into Heaven indeed; where, plunged into the incomprehensible Absolute Being and Bliss of Paranirvâna, he reigns unconditionally, and whence he will re-descend again, at the next "Coming," which one portion of humanity expects in its dead-letter sense as the "Second Advent," and the other as the last "Kalkî Avatâra."

Summing Up.

The History of Creation and of this World, from its beginning up to the present time, is composed of *seven* chapters. The *seventh* chapter is not yet written.

T. SUBBA ROW.

The first of these "seven chapters" has been attempted and is now finished. However incomplete and feeble as an exposition, it is, at any rate, an approximation—using the word in a mathematical sense—to that which is the oldest basis for all subsequent cosmogonies. The attempt to render in a European tongue the grand panorama of the ever periodically recurring Law, impressed upon the plastic minds of the first Races endowed with Consciousness, by those who reflected the same from the Universal Mind, is daring; for no human language, save the Sanskrit—which is that *of the Gods*—can do so with any degree of adequacy. But the failures in this work must be forgiven for the sake of the motive.

As a whole, neither the foregoing nor what follows can be found in full anywhere. It is not taught in any of the six Indian schools of philosophy, for it pertains to their synthesis, the seventh, which is the Occult Doctrine. It is not traced on any crumbling papyrus of Egypt, nor is it any longer graven on Assyrian tile or granite wall. The Books of the Vedânta—the "last word of human knowledge"—give out but the metaphysical aspect of this world-cosmogony; and their priceless thesaurus, the *Upanishads*—*Upa-ni-shad* being a compound word, expressing the conquest of ignorance by the revelation of *secret*, *spiritual* knowledge—now requires the additional possession of a master-key, to enable the student to get at their full meaning. The reason for this I venture to state here as I learned it from a Master.

The name *Upanishad*, is usually translated "esoteric doctrine." These treatises form part of Shruti, or "revealed" Knowledge, Revelation in short, and are generally attached to the Brâhmana portion of the *Vedas*, as their third division.

the *Vedas* have a distinct dual meaning—one expressed by the literal sense of the words, the other indicated by the metre and the *svara* (intonation), which are as the life of the *Vedas*.... Learned pandits and philologists of course deny that *svara* has anything to do with philosophy or ancient esoteric doctrines; but the mysterious connection between *svara* and *light* is one of its most profound secrets.

There are over 150 *Upanishads* enumerated by Orientalists, who credit the oldest with being written *probably* about 600 years B.C.; but of *genuine* texts there does not exist a fifth of the number. The *Upanishads* are to the *Vedas* what the *Kabalah* is to the Jewish *Bible*. They treat of and expound the secret and mystic meaning of the Vedic texts. They speak of the origin of the Universe, the nature of Deity, and of Spirit and Soul, as also of the metaphysical connection of Mind and Matter. In a few words: *They* CONTAIN *the beginning and the end of all human knowledge, but they have ceased to* REVEAL *it*, since the days of Buddha. If it were otherwise, the *Upanishads* could not be called *esoteric*, since they are now openly attached to the Sacred Brâhmanical Books, which have, in our present age, become accessible even to the Mlechchhas (out-castes) and the European Orientalists. One thing in them—and this, in all the *Upanishads*—invariably and constantly points to their ancient origin, and proves (*a*) that they were written, in some of their portions, *before* the caste system became the tyrannical institution which it still is; and (*b*) that half of their contents have been eliminated, while some of them have been rewritten and abridged. "The great Teachers of the higher Knowledge and the Brâhmans are continually represented as going to Kshatriya kings to become their pupils." As Professor Cowell pertinently remarks, the *Upanishads* "breathe an entirely different spirit , a freedom of thought unknown in any earlier work, except in the *Rig Veda* hymns themselves." The second fact is explained by a tradition recorded in one of the MSS. on Buddha's life. It says that the *Upanishads* were originally attached to their *Brâhmanas* after the beginning of a reform, which led to the exclusiveness of the present caste system among the Brâhmans, a few centuries after the invasion of India by the "Twice-born." They were complete in those days, and were used for the instruction of the Chelâs who were preparing for Initiation.

This lasted so long as the *Vedas* and the *Brâhmanas* remained in the sole and exclusive keeping of the temple-Brâhmans— while no one else had the right to study or even read them outside of the *sacred* caste. Then came Gautama, the Prince of

Kapilavastu. After *learning* the whole of the Brâhmanical wisdom in the *Rahasya*, or the *Upanishads*, and finding that the teachings differed little, if at all, from those of the "Teachers of Life" inhabiting the snowy ranges of the Himâlayas, the disciple of the Brâhmans, feeling indignant because the Sacred Wisdom was thus withheld from all but Brâhmans, determined, by popularizing it, to save the whole world. Then it was that the Brâhmans, seeing that their Sacred Knowledge and Occult Wisdom was falling into the hands of the Mlechchhas, abridged the texts of the *Upanishads*, which originally contained thrice the matter of the *Vedas* and the *Brâhmanas* together, without altering, however, one word of the texts. They simply detached from the MSS. the most important portions, containing the last word of the Mystery of Being. The key to the Brâhmanical secret code remained henceforth with the Initiates alone, and the Brâhmans were thus in a position to publicly deny the correctness of Buddha's teaching by appealing to their *Upanishads*, silenced for ever on the chief questions. Such is the esoteric tradition beyond the Himâlayas.

Shrî Shankarâchârya, the greatest Initiate living in the historical ages, wrote many a Bhâshya (Commentary) on the *Upanishads*. But his original treatises, as there are reasons to suppose, have not yet fallen into the hands of the Philistines, for they are too jealously preserved in his monasteries (mathams). And there are still weightier reasons to believe that the priceless Bhâshyas on the Esoteric Doctrine of the Brâhmans, by their greatest expounder, will remain for ages still a dead letter to most of the Hindûs, except the Smârtava Brâhmans. This sect, founded by Shankarâchârya, which is still very powerful in Southern India, is now almost the only one to produce students who have preserved sufficient knowledge to comprehend the dead letter of the Bhâshyas. The reason for this, I am informed, is that they alone have occasionally real Initiates at their head in their mathams, as for instance, in the Shringa-giri, in the Western Ghâts of Mysore. On the other hand, there is no sect, in that desperately exclusive caste of the Brâhmans, more exclusive than is the Smârtava; and the reticence of its followers, to say what they may know of the Occult sciences and the Esoteric Doctrine, is only equalled by their pride and learning.

Therefore the writer of the present statement must be prepared beforehand to meet with great opposition, and even the denial of such statements as are brought forward in this work. Not that any claim to infallibility, or to perfect correctness in every detail of all which is herein written, has ever been put forward. Facts are there, and they can hardly be denied. But, owing to the intrinsic difficulties of the subjects treated of, and the almost insurmountable limitations of the English tongue, as of all other European languages, to express certain ideas, it is more than probable that the writer has failed to present the explanations in the best and the clearest form; yet all that could be done, under every adverse circumstance, has been done, and this is the utmost that can be expected of any writer.

Let us recapitulate and, by the vastness of the subjects expounded, show how difficult, if not impossible, it is to do them full justice.

(1) The Secret Doctrine is the accumulated Wisdom of the Ages, and its cosmogony alone is the most stupendous and elaborate of all systems, even as veiled in the exotericism of the *Purânas*. But such is the mysterious power of Occult symbolism, that the facts which have actually occupied countless generations of initiated seers and prophets to marshal, set down and explain, in the bewildering series of evolutionary progress, are all recorded on a few pages of geometrical signs and glyphs. The flashing gaze of those seers has penetrated into the very kernel of matter, and recorded the soul of things there, where an ordinary profane observer, however learned, would have perceived but the external work of form. But Modern Science believes not in the "soul of things," and hence will reject the whole system of ancient cosmogony. It is useless to say that the system in question is no fancy of one or several isolated individuals; that it is an uninterrupted record, covering thousands of generations of seers, whose respective experiences were made to test and verify the traditions, passed on orally by one early race to another, of the teachings of higher and exalted

Beings, who watched over the childhood of Humanity; that for long ages, the "Wise Men" of the Fifth Race, of the stock saved and rescued from the last cataclysm and the shifting of continents, passed their lives *in learning, not teaching*. How did they do so? It is answered: by checking, testing, and verifying, in every department of Nature, the traditions of old, by the independent visions of great Adepts; that is to say, men who have developed and perfected their physical, mental, psychic, and spiritual organizations, to the utmost possible degree. No vision of one Adept was accepted till it was checked and confirmed by the visions—so obtained as to stand as independent evidence—of other Adepts, and by centuries of experience.

(2) The fundamental law in that system, the central point from which all emerges, around and towards which all gravitates, and upon which is hung all its philosophy, is the One Homogeneous Divine SUBSTANCE-PRINCIPLE, the One Radical Cause.

... Some few, whose lamps shone brighter, have been led
From cause to cause to nature's secret head,
And found that one first Principle must be....

It is called "Substance-Principle," for it becomes "Substance" on the plane of the manifested Universe, an Illusion, while it remains a "Principle" in the beginningless and endless abstract, visible and invisible, SPACE. It is the omnipresent Reality; impersonal, because it contains all and everything.
Its *Impersonality* is the *fundamental conception* of the System. It is latent in every atom in the Universe, and is the Universe itself.

(3) The Universe is the periodical manifestation of this unknown Absolute Essence. To call it "Essence," however, is to sin against the very spirit of the philosophy. For though the noun may be derived in this case from the verb *esse*, "to be," yet IT cannot be identified with a "being" of any kind, that can be conceived by human intellect. IT is best described as neither Spirit nor Matter, but both. Parabrahman and Mûlaprakriti are One, in reality, yet TWO in the universal conception of the Manifested,

even in the conception of the One Logos, the first "Manifestation," to which, as the able lecturer shows, in the "Notes on the *Bhagavadgîtâ*," IT appears from the objective standpoint as Mûlaprakriti, and not as Parabrahman; as its Veil, and not the One Reality hidden behind, which is unconditioned and absolute.

(4) The Universe, with everything in it, is called Mâyâ, because all is temporary therein, from the ephemeral life of a fire-fly to that of the sun. Compared to the eternal immutability of the ONE, and the changelessness of that Principle, the Universe, with its evanescent ever-changing forms, must be necessarily, in the mind of a philosopher, no better than a will-o'-the-wisp. Yet, the Universe is real enough to the conscious beings in it, which are as unreal as it is itself.

(5) Everything in the Universe, throughout all its kingdoms, is *conscious*: *i.e.*, endowed with a consciousness of its own kind and on its own plane of perception. We men must remember that, simply because *we* do not perceive any signs of consciousness which we can recognize, say, in stones, we have no right to say that *no consciousness exists there*. There is no such thing as either "dead" or "blind" matter, as there is no "blind" or "unconscious" Law. These find no place among the conceptions of Occult Philosophy. The latter never stops at surface appearances, and for it the noumenal Essences have more reality than their objective counterparts; wherein it resembles the system of the mediæval Nominalists, for whom it was the universals that were the realities, and the particulars which existed only in name and human fancy.

(6) The Universe is worked and *guided*, from *within outwards*. As above so it is below, as in heaven so on earth; and man, the microcosm and miniature copy of the macrocosm, is the living witness to this Universal Law, and to the mode of its action. We see that every *external* motion, act, gesture, whether voluntary or mechanical, organic or mental, is produced and preceded by *internal* feeling or emotion, will or volition, and thought or mind. As no outward motion or change, when normal, in man's

external body, can take place unless provoked by an inward impulse, given through one of the three functions named, so with the external or manifested Universe. The whole Kosmos is guided, controlled, and animated by almost endless series of Hierarchies of sentient Beings, each having a mission to perform, and who—whether we give them one name or another, whether we call them Dhyân Chohans or Angels—are "Messengers," in the sense only that they are the agents of Karmic and Cosmic Laws. They vary infinitely in their respective degrees of consciousness and intelligence; and to call them all pure Spirits, without any of the earthly alloy "which time is wont to prey upon," is only to indulge in poetical fancy. For each of these Beings either *was*, or prepares to become, a man, if not in the present, then in a past or a coming Manvantara. They are *perfected*, when not *incipient*, men; and in their higher, less material, spheres differ morally from terrestrial human beings only in that they are devoid of the feeling of personality, and of the *human* emotional nature—two purely earthly characteristics. The former, or the "perfected," have become free from these feelings, because (*a*) they have no longer fleshly bodies—an ever-numbing weight on the Soul; and (*b*), the pure spiritual element being left untrammelled and more free, they are less influenced by Mâyâ than man can ever be, unless he is an Adept who keeps his two personalities—the spiritual and the physical—entirely separated. The incipient Monads, having never yet had terrestrial bodies, can have no sense of personality or *Ego*-ism. That which is meant by "personality" being a limitation and a relation, or, as defined by Coleridge, "individuality existing in itself but with a nature as a ground," the term cannot of course be applied to non-human Entities; but, as a fact insisted upon by generations of Seers, none of these Beings, high or low, have either individuality or personality as separate Entities, *i.e.*, they have no individuality in the sense in which a man says, "*I am myself* and no one else"; in other words, they are conscious of no such distinct separateness as men and things have on earth. Individuality is the characteristic of their respective Hierarchies, not of their units; and these characteristics vary only with the degree of the plane to which these Hierarchies belong: the nearer to the region of Homogeneity and the One Divine, the purer and the less accentuated is that individuality in the Hierarchy. They are finite in all respects, with the exception of their higher principles—the immortal Sparks reflecting the Universal Divine Flame, individualized and separated only on the spheres of Illusion, by a differentiation as illusive as the rest. They are "Living Ones," because they are the streams projected on the cosmic screen of Illusion from the Absolute Life; Beings in whom life cannot become extinct, before the fire of ignorance is extinct in those who sense these "Lives." Having sprung into being under the quickening influence of the uncreated Beam, the reflection of the great Central Sun that radiates on the shores of the River of Life, it is the Inner Principle in them which belongs to the Waters of Immortality, while its differentiated clothing is as perishable as man's body. Therefore Young was right in saying that Angels are men of a superior kind ... and no more. They are neither "ministering" nor "protecting" Angels, nor are they "Harbingers of the Most High"; still less the "Messengers of Wrath" of any God such as man's fancy has created. To appeal to their protection is as foolish as to believe that their sympathy may be secured by any kind of propitiation; for they are, as much as man himself is, the slaves and creatures of immutable Karmic and Cosmic Law. The reason for this is evident. Having no elements of personality in their essence, they can have no personal qualities, such as are attributed by men, in exoteric religions, to their anthropomorphic God—a jealous and exclusive God, who rejoices and feels wrathful, is pleased with sacrifice, and is more despotic in his vanity than any finite foolish man. Man, being a compound of the essences of all these celestial Hierarchies, may succeed in making himself, as such, superior, in one sense, to any Hierarchy or Class, or even combination of them. "Man can neither propitiate nor command the Devas," it is said. But, by paralyzing his lower personality, and arriving thereby at the full knowledge of the *non-separateness* of his Higher Self from the One Absolute SELF, man can, even during his terrestrial life, become as "one of us." Thus it is, by eating of the fruit of knowledge, which dispels ignorance, that man becomes like one of the Elohim, or the

Dhyânis; and once on *their* plane, the spirit of Solidarity and perfect Harmony, which reigns in every Hierarchy, must extend over him, and protect him in every particular.

The chief difficulty which prevents men of Science from believing in divine as well as in nature spirits is their Materialism. The main impediment before the Spiritualist which hinders him from believing in the same, while preserving a blind belief in the "Spirits" of the Departed, is the general ignorance of all—except some Occultists and Kabalists—about the true essence and nature of Matter. It is on the acceptance or rejection of the theory of the *Unity of all in Nature, in its ultimate Essence*, that mainly rests the belief or unbelief in the existence around us of other conscious Beings, besides the Spirits of the Dead. It is on the right comprehension of the primeval Evolution of Spirit-Matter, and its real Essence, that the student has to depend for the further elucidation in his mind of the Occult Cosmogony, and for the only sure clue which can guide his subsequent studies.

In sober truth, as just shown, every so-called "Spirit" is either a *disembodied or a future man*. As from the highest Archangel (Dhyân Chohan) down to the last conscious Builder (the inferior Class of Spiritual Entities), all such are *men*, having lived æons ago, in other Manvantaras, on this or other Spheres; so the inferior, semi-intelligent and non-intelligent Elementals are all *future* men. The fact alone, that a Spirit is endowed with intelligence, is a proof to the Occultist that such a Being must have been a *man*, and acquired his knowledge and intelligence throughout the human cycle. There is but one indivisible and absolute Omniscience and Intelligence in the Universe, and this thrills throughout every atom and infinitesimal point of the whole Kosmos, which has no bounds, and which people call Space, considered independently of anything contained in it. But the first differentiation of its *reflection* in the Manifested World is purely spiritual, and the Beings generated in it are not endowed with a consciousness that has any relation to the one we conceive of. They can have no human consciousness or intelligence before they have acquired such, personally and individually. This may be a mystery, yet it is a fact in Esoteric Philosophy, and a very apparent one too.

The whole order of Nature evinces a progressive march towards a higher life. There is design in the action of the seemingly blindest forces. The whole process of evolution, with its endless adaptations, is a proof of this. The immutable laws that weed out the weak and feeble species, to make room for the strong, and which ensure the "survival of the fittest," though so cruel in their immediate action, all are working toward the grand end. The very *fact* that adaptations *do* occur, that the fittest *do* survive in the struggle for existence, shows that what is called "unconscious Nature" is in reality an aggregate of forces, manipulated by semi-intelligent beings (Elementals), guided by High Planetary Spirits (Dhyân Chohans), whose collective aggregate forms the Manifested Verbum of the Unmanifested Logos, and constitutes one and the same time the Mind of the Universe and its immutable Law.

For Nature, taken in its abstract sense, *cannot* be "unconscious," as it is the emanation from, and thus an aspect on the manifested plane of, the Absolute Consciousness. Where is that daring man who would presume to deny to vegetation and even to minerals *a consciousness of their own*? All he can say is, that this consciousness is beyond his comprehension.

Three distinct representations of the Universe, in its three distinct aspects, are impressed upon our thoughts by the Esoteric Philosophy: the *Pre-existing*, evolved from the *Ever-existing*, and the *Phenomenal*—the world of illusion, the reflection, and shadow thereof. During the great mystery and drama of life, known as the Manvantara, real Kosmos is like the objects placed behind the white screen upon which shadows are thrown. The actual figures and things remain invisible, while the wires of evolution are pulled by unseen hands. Men and things are thus but the reflections, *on* the white field, of the realities *behind* the snares of Mahâmâyâ, or the Great Illusion. This was taught in every philosophy, in every religion, ante- as well as post-diluvian, in India and Chaldea, by the Chinese as by the Grecian Sages. In the former countries these three Universes were allegorized, in exoteric teachings, by the three Trinities, emanating from the central eternal Germ, and forming with it a Supreme Unity: the *initial*, the *manifested*, and the *creative* Triad, or the Three in One. The last is but the symbol, in its concrete expression, of the first *ideal* two. Hence Esoteric Philosophy passes over the necessarianism of this purely metaphysical conception, and calls the first one, only, the Ever-Existing. This is the view of every one of the six great schools of Indian philosophy—the six principles of that unit body of Wisdom of which the Gnôsis, the *hidden* Knowledge, is the seventh.

The writer hopes that, however superficially the comments on the Seven Stanzas may have been handled, enough has been given, in this cosmogonic portion of the work, to show the archaic teachings to be on their very face more *scientific* (in the modern sense of the word) than any other ancient Scriptures left to be judged on their exoteric aspect. Since, however, as before confessed, this work *withholds far more than it gives out*, the student is invited to use his own intuitions. Our chief care is to elucidate that which has already been given out, and, to our regret, very incorrectly at times; to supplement the knowledge hinted at—whenever and wherever possible—by additional matter; and to bulwark our doctrines against the too strong attacks of modern Sectarianism, and more especially against those of our latter-day Materialism, very often miscalled Science, whereas, in reality, the
words "Scientists" and "Sciolists" ought alone to bear the responsibility for the many illogical theories offered to the world. In its great ignorance, the public, while blindly accepting everything that emanates from "authorities," and feeling it to be its duty to regard every *dictum* coming from a man of Science as a proven fact—the public, we say, is taught to scoff at anything brought forward from "heathen" sources. Therefore, as materialistic Scientists can be fought solely with their own weapons—those of controversy and argument—an Addendum is added to each Volume contrasting the respective views, and

showing how even great authorities may often err. We believe that this can be done effectually, by showing the weak points of our opponents, and by proving their too frequent sophisms, which are made to pass for scientific *dicta*, to be incorrect. We hold to Hermes and his "Wisdom," in its universal character; they—to Aristotle, as against intuition and the experience of the Ages, fancying that Truth is the exclusive property of the Western world. Hence the disagreement. As Hermes says: "Knowledge differs much from sense; for sense is of things that surmount it, but Knowledge is the end of sense"—*i.e.*, of the illusion of our physical brain and its intellect; thus emphasizing the contrast between the laboriously acquired knowledge of the senses and Mind (Manas), and the intuitive omniscience of the Spiritual Divine Soul (Buddhi).

Whatever may be the destiny of these actual writings in a remote future, we hope to have so far proven the following facts:

(1) The Secret Doctrine teaches no Atheism, except in the sense underlying the Sanskrit word Nâstika, a rejection of idols, including every anthropomorphic God. In this sense every Occultist is a Nâstika.

(2) It admits a Logos, or a Collective "Creator" of the Universe; a Demiurge, in the sense implied when one speaks of an "Architect" as the "Creator" of an edifice, whereas that Architect has never touched one stone of it, but, furnishing the plan, has left all the manual labour to the masons; in our case the plan was furnished by the Ideation of the Universe, and the constructive labour was left to the Hosts of intelligent Powers and Forces. But that Demiurge is no *personal* deity—*i.e.*, an imperfect *extra-cosmic God*, but only the aggregate of the Dhyân Chohans and the other Forces.

(3) The Dhyân Chohans are dual in their character; being composed of (*a*) the irrational *brute Energy*, inherent in Matter, and (*b*) the intelligent Soul, or cosmic Consciousness, which directs and guides that Energy, and which is the *Dhyân Chohanic Thought, reflecting the Ideation of the Universal Mind*. This results in a perpetual series of physical manifestations

and *moral effects* on Earth, during manvantaric periods, the whole being subservient to Karma. As that process is not always perfect; and since, however many proofs it may exhibit of a guiding Intelligence behind the veil, it still shows gaps and flaws, and even very often results in evident failures—therefore, neither the collective Host (Demiurge), nor any of the working Powers individually, are proper subjects for divine honours or worship. All are entitled to the grateful reverence of humanity, however, and man ought to be ever striving to help the divine evolution of *Ideas*, by becoming, to the best of his ability, a *co-worker with Nature*, in the cyclic task. The ever unknowable and incognizable Kârana alone, the Causeless Cause of all causes, should have its shrine and altar on the holy and ever untrodden ground of our heart—invisible, intangible, unmentioned, save through the "still small voice" of our spiritual consciousness. Those who worship before it, ought to do so in the silence and the sanctified solitude of their Souls; making their Spirit the sole mediator between them and the Universal Spirit, their good actions the only priests, and their sinful intentions the only visible and objective sacrificial victims to the *Presence*.

"When thou prayest, thou shalt not be as the hypocrites are ... but enter into *thine inner chamber, and having shut thy door, pray to thy Father which is in secret.*" Our Father is *within us* "in secret," our Seventh Principle in the "inner chamber" of our soul-perception. "The Kingdom of God" and of Heaven is *within* us, says Jesus, not *outside*. Why are Christians so absolutely blind to the self-evident meaning of the words of wisdom they delight in mechanically repeating?

(4) Matter is Eternal. It is the Upâdhi, or Physical Basis, for the One Infinite Universal Mind to build thereon its ideations. Therefore, the Esotericists maintain that there is no inorganic or "dead" matter in Nature, the distinction between the two made by Science being as unfounded as it is arbitrary and devoid of reason. Whatever Science may think, however—and *exact* Science is a fickle dame, as we all know by experience—Occultism knows and teaches differently, as it has

done from time immemorial, from Manu and Hermes down to Paracelsus and his successors.

Thus, Hermes, the Thrice Great, says:

Oh, my son, matter *becomes*; formerly it *was*; for matter is the vehicle of becoming. Becoming is the mode of activity of the uncreate and foreseeing God. Having been endowed with the germ of becoming, matter is brought into birth, for the creative force fashions it *according to the ideal forms*. Matter not yet engendered had no form; it becomes, when it is put into operation.

To this the late Dr. Anna Kingsford, the able translator and compiler of the Hermetic Fragments, remarks in a footnote:

Dr. Ménard observes that in Greek the same word signifies *to be born* and *to become*. The idea here is, that the material of the world is in its essence eternal, but that before creation or "becoming" it is in a passive and motionless condition. Thus it "was" before being put into operation; now it "becomes," that is, it is mobile and progressive.

And she adds the purely Vedântic doctrine of the Hermetic philosophy that:

Creation is thus the period of activity of God, who, according to Hermetic thought, has two modes—Activity or Existence, God evolved (Deus explicitus); and Passivity of Being, God involved (Deus implicitus). Both modes are perfect and complete, as are the waking and sleeping states of man. Fichte, the German philosopher, distinguished Being (Seyn) as One, which we know only through existence (Daseyn) as the Manifold. This view is thoroughly Hermetic. The "Ideal Forms" ... are the archetypal or formative ideas of the Neo-Platonists; the eternal and subjective concepts of things subsisting in the Divine Mind, prior to "creation" or becoming.

Or, as in the philosophy of Paracelsus:

Everything is the product of one universal creative effort.... There is nothing *dead* in Nature. *Everything is organic and living*, and therefore the whole world appears to be a living organism.

(5) The Universe was evolved out of its ideal plan, upheld through Eternity in the Unconsciousness of that which the Vedântins call Parabrahman. This is practically identical with the conclusions of the highest Western philosophy, "the innate, eternal, and self-existing Ideas" of Plato, now reflected by Von Hartmann. The "Unknowable" of Herbert Spencer bears but a faint resemblance to that transcendental Reality believed in by Occultists, often appearing merely a personification of a "force behind phenomena"—an infinite and eternal Energy, from which all things proceed, whereas the author of the *Philosophy of the Unconscious* has come (in this respect only) as near to a solution of the great Mystery as mortal man can. Few have been those, whether in ancient or mediæval philosophy, who have dared to approach the subject or even hint at it. Paracelsus mentions it inferentially, and his ideas are admirably synthesized by Dr. F. Hartmann, F.T.S., in his *Paracelsus*, from which we have just quoted.

All the Christian Kabalists understood well the Eastern root idea. The active Power, the "Perpetual Motion of the great Breath," only awakens Cosmos at the dawn of every new Period, setting it into motion by means of the two contrary Forces, the centripetal and the centrifugal Forces, which are male and female, positive and negative, physical and spiritual, the two being the one *Primordial* Force, and thus causing it to become objective on the plane of Illusion. In other words, that dual motion transfers Cosmos from the plane of the Eternal Ideal into that of finite manifestation, or from the *noumenal* to the *phenomenal* plane. Everything that *is*, *was*, and *will be*, eternally IS, even the countless Forms, which are finite and perishable only in their objective, but not in their *ideal* form. They existed as Ideas, in the Eternity, and, when they pass away, will exist as reflections. Occultism teaches that no form can be given to anything, either by Nature or by man, whose ideal type does not already exist on the subjective plane: more than this; that no form or shape can possibly enter man's consciousness, or evolve in his imagination, which does not exist in prototype, at least as an approximation. Neither the form of man, nor that of any animal, plant or stone, has ever

been "created"; and it is only on this plane of ours that it commenced "becoming," that is to say, objectivizing into its present materiality, or expanding *from within outwards*, from the most sublimated and supersensuous essence into its grossest appearance. Therefore *our* human forms have existed in the Eternity as astral or ethereal prototypes; according to which models, the Spiritual Beings, or Gods, whose duty it was to bring them into objective being and terrestrial life, evolved the protoplasmic forms of the future Egos from *their own* essence. After which, when this human Upâdhi, or basic mould, was ready, the natural terrestrial Forces began to work on these supersensuous moulds, *which contained, besides their own, the elements of all the past vegetable and future animal forms of this Globe*. Therefore, man's *outward* shell passed through every vegetable and animal body, before it assumed the human shape. But as this will be fully described in Volume II, in the Commentaries, there is no need to say more of it here.
According to the Hermetico-Kabalistic philosophy of Paracelsus, it is Yliaster—the ancestor of the just-born Protyle, introduced by Mr. Crookes into Chemistry—or primordial Protomateria, that evolved out of itself the Cosmos.

When creation took place, the Yliaster divided itself; it, so to say, melted and dissolved, developed out of itself the Ideos or Chaos (Mysterium Magnum, Iliados, Limbus Major, or Primordial Matter). This Primordial Essence is of a monistic nature, and manifests itself not only as vital activity, a spiritual force, an invisible, incomprehensible, and indescribable power, but also as vital matter of which the substance of living beings consists. In this Limbus or Ideos of primordial matter, ... the only matrix of all created things, the substance of all things is contained. It is described by the ancients as the Chaos ... out of which the Macrocosmos, and afterwards, by division and evolution in Mysteria Specialia, each separate being came into existence. All things and all elementary substances were contained in it *in potentiâ* but not *in actu*.

This makes the translator, Dr. F. Hartmann, justly observe that "it seems that Paracelsus anticipated the modern discovery of the 'potency of matter' three hundred years ago."

The Magnus Limbus, then, or Yliaster, of Paracelsus is simply our old friend "Father-Mother," *within*, before it appeared in Space. It is the Universal Matrix of Kosmos, personified in the dual character of Macrocosm and Microcosm, or the Universe and our Globe, by Aditi-Prakriti, spiritual and physical Nature. For we find it explained in Paracelsus that:

The Magnus Limbus is the nursery out of which all creatures have grown, in the same sense as a tree may grow out of a small seed; with the difference, however, that the great Limbus takes its origin from the Word of God, while the Limbus minor (the terrestrial seed or sperm) takes it from the earth. The great Limbus is the seed out of which all beings have come, and the little Limbus is each ultimate being that reproduces its form, and that has itself been produced by the great. The little Limbus possesses all the qualifications of the great one, in the same sense as a son has an organization similar to that of his father.... As ... Yliaster dissolved, Ares, the dividing, differentiating, and individualizing power ... began to act. All production took place in consequence of separation. There were produced out of the Ideos the elements of Fire, Water, Air and Earth, whose birth, however, did not take place in a material mode, or by simple separation, but spiritually and dynamically, just as fire may come out of a pebble, or a tree out of a seed, although there is originally no fire in the pebble, nor a tree in the seed. "Spirit is living, and Life is Spirit, and Life and Spirit produce all things, but they are essentially one and not two." ... The elements, too, have each one its own Yliaster, because all the activity of matter in every form is only an effluvium of the same fountain. But as from the seed grow the roots with their fibres, afterwards the stalk with its branches and leaves, and lastly the flowers and seeds; likewise all beings were born from the elements, and consist of elementary substances out of which other forms may come into existence, bearing the characteristics of their parents. The elements as the mothers of all creatures *are of an invisible, spiritual nature, and have souls*. They all spring from the Mysterium Magnum.

Compare this with *Vishnu Purâna*.
From Pradhâna presided over by Kshetrajna proceeds the unequal development of those qualities.... From the great principle (Mahat) Intellect ... is produced the origin of the subtle elements and of the organs of sense. ...

Thus it may be shown that all the fundamental truths of Nature were universal in antiquity, and that the basic ideas upon Spirit, Matter and the Universe, or upon God, Substance and Man, were identical. Taking the two most ancient religious philosophies on the globe, Hindûism and Hermeticism, from the Scriptures of India and Egypt, the identity of the two is easily recognizable.

This becomes apparent to one who reads the latest translation and rendering of the "Hermetic Fragments" just mentioned, by our late lamented friend, Dr. Anna Kingsford. Disfigured and tortured as these have been in their passage through sectarian Greek and Christian hands, the translator has most ably and intuitively seized the weak points and tried to remedy them by means of explanations and footnotes. She says:

The creation of the visible world by the "working gods" or Titans, as agents of the Supreme God, is a thoroughly Hermetic idea, recognizable *in all religious systems*, and in accordance with modern scientific research , which shows us everywhere the Divine Power operating through natural Forces.

To quote from the translation:

That Universal Being, that contains all, and which is all, puts into motion the soul and the world, all that nature comprises. In the manifold unity of universal life, the innumerable individualities distinguished by their variations are, nevertheless, united in such a manner that the whole is one, and that everything proceeds from Unity.

And again from another translation:

God is not a mind, but the cause that the Mind is; *not a spirit*, but the cause that the Spirit is; not light, but the cause that the Light is.

The above shows plainly that the "Divine Pymander," however much distorted in some passages by Christian "smoothing," was nevertheless written by a philosopher, while most of the so-called "Hermetic Fragments" are the production of sectarian pagans with a tendency towards an anthropomorphic Supreme Being. Yet both are the echo of the Esoteric Philosophy and the Hindû *Purânas*.

Compare two invocations, one to the Hermetic "Supreme All," the other to the "Supreme All" of the later Âryans. Says a Hermetic Fragment cited by Suidas:

I adjure thee, Heaven, holy work of the great God; I adjure thee, Voice of the Father, uttered in the beginning when the universal world was framed; I adjure thee by the Word, only Son of the Father Who upholds all things; be favourable, be favourable.

This is preceded by the following:

Thus the Ideal Light was before the Ideal Light, and the luminous Intelligence of Intelligence was always, *and its unity was nothing else than the Spirit enveloping the Universe. Out of Whom is neither God nor Angels, nor any other essentials,* for He is the Lord of all things and the Power and the Light; and all depends on Him and is in Him.

A passage contradicted by the very same Trismegistus, who is made to say:

To speak of God is impossible. For the corporeal cannot express the incorporeal.... That which has not any body nor appearance, nor form, nor matter, cannot be apprehended by sense. I understand, Tatios, I understand, that which it is impossible to define—that is God.

The contradiction between the two passages is evident; and this shows (*a*) that Hermes was a generic *nom de plume* used by a series of generations of Mystics of every shade, and (*b*) that great discernment has to be used before accepting a Fragment as esoteric teaching only because it is undeniably ancient. Let us now compare the above with a like invocation in the Hindû Scriptures—undoubtedly as old, if not far older. Here it is. Parâshara, the Âryan "Hermes," instructs Maitreya, the Indian Asclepios, and calls upon Vishnu in his triple hypostasis:

Glory to the unchangeable, holy, eternal, supreme Vishnu, of one universal nature, the mighty over all; to him who is Hiranyagarbha, Hari, and Shankara, the creator, the preserver, and destroyer of the world; to Vâsudeva, the liberator (of his worshippers); to him whose essence is both single and manifold; who is both subtle and corporeal, indiscrete and discrete; to Vishnu, the cause of final emancipation. Glory to the supreme Vishnu, the cause of the creation, existence, the end of this world; *who is the root of the world*, and who *consists of the world*.

This is a grand invocation, with a deep philosophical meaning underlying it; but, for the profane masses, as suggestive as is the Hermetic prayer of an anthropomorphic Being. We must respect the feeling that dictated both; but we cannot help finding it in full disharmony with its inner meaning, even with that which is found in the same Hermetic treatise where it is said:

Trismegistus: Reality is not upon the earth, my son, and it cannot be thereon.... Nothing on earth is real, there are only appearances.... He is not real, my son, as man. The real consists solely in itself and remains what it is.... Man is transient, therefore he is not real, he is but appearance, and appearance is the supreme illusion.
Tatios: Then the celestial bodies themselves are not real, my father, since they also vary?
Trismegistus: That which is subject to birth and to change is not real ... there is in them a certain falsity, seeing that they too are variable....
Tatios: And what then is the primordial Reality, O my Father?
Trismegistus: He Who is one and alone, O Tatios; He Who is not made of matter, nor in any body. Who has neither colour nor form, Who changes not nor is transmitted, but Who always Is.

This is quite consistent with the Vedântic teaching. The leading thought is Occult; and many are the passages in the Hermetic Fragments that belong bodily to the Secret Doctrine.

This Doctrine teaches that the whole Universe is ruled by intelligent and semi-intelligent Forces and Powers, as stated from the very beginning. Christian Theology admits and even *enforces* belief in such, but makes an arbitrary division and refers to them as "Angels" and "Devils." Science denies the existence of both, and ridicules the very idea. Spiritualists believe in the "Spirits of the Dead," and outside these deny entirely any other kind or class of invisible beings. The Occultists and Kabalists are thus the only rational expounders of the ancient traditions, which have now culminated in dogmatic faith on the one hand, and dogmatic denial on the other. For both belief and unbelief each embrace but one small corner of the infinite horizons of spiritual and physical manifestations: and thus both are right from their respective standpoints, yet both are wrong in believing that they can circumscribe the whole within their own special and narrow barriers, for—they can never do so. In this respect, Science, Theology, and even Spiritualism show little more wisdom than the ostrich, when it hides its head in the sand at its feet, feeling sure that there can be thus nothing beyond its own point of observation and the limited area occupied by its foolish head.

As the only works now extant upon the subject under consideration, within reach of the profane of the Western "civilized" races, are the above-mentioned Hermetic Books, or rather Hermetic Fragments, we may contrast them in the present case with the teachings of Esoteric Philosophy. To quote for this purpose from any other would be useless, since the public knows nothing of the Chaldean works, which are translated into Arabic and preserved by some Sufi Initiates. Therefore the "Definitions of Asclepios," as lately compiled and glossed by Dr. Anna Kingsford, F.T.S., some of which sayings are in remarkable agreement with the Eastern Esoteric Doctrine, have to be resorted to for comparison. Though not a few passages bear a strong impression of some later Christian hand, yet on the whole the characteristics of the Genii and Gods are those of Eastern teachings, although concerning other things there are passages which differ widely in our doctrines.

As to the Genii, the Hermetic philosophers called Theoi (Gods), Genii and Daimones, those Entities whom we call Devas (Gods), Dhyân Chohans, Chitkala (the Kwan-Yin, of the Buddhists), and various other names. The Daimones are—in the Socratic sense, and even in the Oriental and Latin theological sense—the guardian spirits of the human race; "those who dwell in the neighbourhood of the immortals, and thence watch over human affairs," as Hermes has it. In Esoteric parlance, they are called Chitkala, some of which are those who have furnished man with his fourth and fifth Principles from their own essence, and others the so-called Pitris. This will be explained when we come to the production of the *complete man*. The root of the name is Chit, "that by which the consequences of acts and species of knowledge are selected for the use of the soul," or conscience, the *inner voice* in man. With the Yogins, Chit is a synonym of Mahat, the first and divine Intellect; but in Esoteric Philosophy Mahat is the root of Chit, its germ; and Chit is a quality of Manas in conjunction with Buddhi, a quality that attracts to itself by spiritual affinity a Chitkala, when it develops sufficiently in man. This is why it is said that Chit is a voice acquiring mystic life and becoming Kwan-Yin.

Extracts From An Eastern Private Commentary, Hitherto Secret.

xvii. *The Initial Existence, in the first Twilight of the Mahâmanvantara , is a* CONSCIOUS SPIRITUAL QUALITY. *In the Manifested Worlds , it is, in its Objective Subjectivity, like the film from a Divine Breath to the gaze of the entranced seer. It spreads as it issues from Laya throughout Infinity as a colourless spiritual fluid. It is on the Seventh Plane, and in its Seventh State, in our Planetary World.*
xviii. *It is Substance to* OUR *spiritual sight. It cannot be called so by men in their Waking State; therefore they have named it in their ignorance "God-Spirit."*

xix. *It exists everywhere and forms the first Upâdhi on which our World is built. Outside the latter, it is to be found in its pristine purity only between the Stars of the Universe, the Worlds already formed or forming; those in Laya resting meanwhile in its bosom. As its substance is of a different kind from that known on Earth, the inhabitants of the latter, seeing* THROUGH IT, *believe in their illusion and ignorance that it is empty space. There is not one finger's breadth of void Space in the whole Boundless ....*

xx. *Matter or Substance is septenary within our World, as it is so beyond it. Moreover, each of its states or principles is graduated into seven degrees of density. Sûrya , in its visible reflection, exhibits the first or lowest state of the seventh, the highest state of the Universal* PRESENCE, *the pure of the pure, the first manifested Breath of the Ever-Unmanifested Sat . All the central physical or objective Suns are in their substance the lowest state of the first principle of the Breath. Nor are any of these any more than the Reflections of their Primaries, which are concealed from the gaze of all but the Dhyân Chohans, whose corporeal substance belongs to the fifth division of the seventh principle of the Mother-Substance, and is, therefore, four degrees higher than the solar reflected substance. As there are seven Dhâtu, so there are seven Forces in Man and in all Nature.*

xxi. *The real substance of the Concealed is nucleus of Mother-Substance. It is the Heart and Matrix of all the living and existing Forces in our Solar Universe. It is the Kernel from which proceed to spread on their cyclic journeys all the Powers that set in action the Atoms, in their functional duties, and the Focus within which they again meet in their Seventh Essence every eleventh year. He who tells thee he has seen the Sun, laugh at him, as if he had said that the Sun moves really onward in his diurnal path....*

xxiii. *It is on account of his septenary nature, that the Sun is spoken of by the ancients as one who is driven by seven horses equal to the metres of the Vedas; or, again, that, though he is identified with the seven Gana in his orb, he is distinct from them, as he is, indeed; as also that he has Seven Rays, as indeed he has....*

xxv. *The Seven Beings in the Sun are the Seven Holy Ones, self-born from the inherent power in the Matrix of Mother-Substance. It is they who send the seven principal Forces, called Rays, which at the beginning of Pralaya will centre into seven new Suns for the next Manvantara. The energy, from which they spring into conscious existence in every Sun, is what some people call Vishnu, which is the Breath of the* ABSOLUTENESS.

We call it the One Manifested life—itself a reflection of the Absolute....

xxvii. *The latter must never be mentioned in words or speech,* LEST IT SHOULD TAKE AWAY SOME OF OUR SPIRITUAL ENERGIES *that aspire towards* ITS *state, gravitating ever toward unto* IT *spiritually, as the whole physical universe gravitates towards* ITS *manifested centre—cosmically.*

xxviii. *The former—the Initial Existence—which may be called, while in this state of being, the* ONE LIFE, *is, as explained, a Film for creative or formative purposes. It manifests in seven states, which, with their septenary sub-divisions, are the Forty-nine Fires mentioned in sacred books....*

xxix. *The first is the ... "Mother". Separating itself into its primary seven states, it proceeds down cyclically; when having consolidated itself in its* LAST *principle, as* GROSS MATTER, *it revolves around itself and informs, with the seventh emanation of the last, the first and the lowest element . In a Hierarchy, or Order of Being, the seventh emanation of her last principle is:*

(a) In the Mineral, the Spark that lies latent in it, and is called to its evanescent being by the Positive awakening the Negative ....

(b) In the Plant, it is that vital and intelligent Force which informs the seed and develops it into the blade of grass, or the root and sapling. It is the germ which becomes the Upâdhi of the seven principles of the thing it resides in, shooting them out as the latter grows and develops.

(c) In every Animal, it does the same. It is its Life-Principle and vital power; its instinct and qualities; its characteristics and special idiosyncrasies....

(d) To Man, it gives all that it bestows on all the rest of the manifested units in Nature; but develops, furthermore, the reflection of all its "Forty-nine Fires" in him. Each of his seven principles is an heir in full to, and a partaker of, the seven principles of the "Great Mother." The breath of her first principle is his Spirit . Her second principle is Buddhi . We call it, erroneously, the seventh. The third furnishes him with the Brain Stuff on the physical plane, and with the Mind that moves it —according to his organic capacities.

(e) It is the guiding Force in the cosmic and terrestrial Elements. It resides in the Fire provoked out of its latent into active being; for the whole of the seven sub-divisions of the ... principle reside in the terrestrial Fire. It whirls in the breeze, blows with the hurricane, and sets the air in motion, which element participates in one of its principles also. Proceeding cyclically, it regulates the motion of the water, attracts and repels the waves,according to fixed laws, of which its seventh principle is the informing soul.

(f) Its four higher principles contain the Germ that develops into the Cosmic Gods; its three lower ones breed the Lives of the Elements .

(g) In our Solar World, the One Existence is Heaven and Earth, the Root and the Flower, the Action and the Thought. It is in the Sun, and is as present in the glow-worm. Not an atom can escape it. Therefore, the ancient Sages have wisely called it the manifested God in Nature....

It may be interesting, in this connection, to remind the reader of what T. Subba Row said of the Forces—mystically defined.

Kanyâ means a virgin, and represents Shakti or Mahâmâyâ. The sign in question is the sixth Râshi or division, and indicates that there are six primary forces in Nature ....

These Shaktis stand as follows:

(1) *Parâshakti.*—Literally the great or supreme force or power. It means and includes *the powers of light and heat.*

(2) *Jñânashakti.*—Literally the power of intellect, of real wisdom or knowledge. It has two aspects:

I. The following are *some* of its manifestations *when placed under the influence or control of material conditions.* (*a*) The power of the mind in interpreting our sensations. (*b*) Its power in recalling past ideas (memory) and raising future expectation. (*c*) Its power as exhibited in what are called by modern psychologists "the laws of association," which enables it to form *persisting* connections between various groups of sensations and possibilities of sensations, and thus generate the notion or idea of an external object. (*d*) Its power in connecting our ideas together by the mysterious link of memory, and thus generating the notion of self or individuality.

II. The following are *some* of its manifestations *when liberated from the bonds of matter*:

(*a*) Clairvoyance. (*b*) Psychometry.
(3) *Ichchhâshakti.*—Literally *the power of the will.* Its *most ordinary manifestation* is the generation of certain nerve currents, which set in motion such muscles as are required for the accomplishment of the desired object.

(4) *Kriyâshakti.*—The mysterious power of thought which enables it to produce external, perceptible, phenomenal results by its own inherent energy. The ancients held that *any idea will manifest itself externally if one's attention is deeply concentrated upon it.* Similarly *an intense volition will be followed by the desired result.*

A Yogi generally performs his wonders by means of Ichchhâshakti and Kriyâshakti.

(5) *Kundalinî Shakti.*—The power or force which moves in a serpentine or curved path. It is the universal life-principle which everywhere manifests in Nature. This force includes the two great forces of attraction and repulsion. Electricity and magnetism are but manifestations of it. This is the power which brings about that "continuous adjustment of *internal relations to external relations,*" which is the essence of life according to Herbert Spencer, and that "continuous adjustment of *external relations to internal relations,*" which is the basis of transmigration of souls, Punarjanman (Re-birth), in the doctrines of the ancient Hindû philosophers.

A Yogi must thoroughly subjugate this power or force, before he can attain Moksha....

(6) *Mantrikâshakti.*—Literally the force or power of letters, speech or music. The whole of the ancient *Mantra Shâstra* has this force or power in all its manifestations for its subject matter.... The influence of its music is one of its ordinary manifestations. The power of the mirific ineffable name is the crown of this Shakti.

Modern Science has but partly investigated the first, second and fifth of the forces or powers above named, but is altogether in the dark as regards the remaining powers.... The six forces are in their unity represented by the Astral Light.

The above is quoted to show the real Hindû ideas on the subject. It is all esoteric, though not covering the tenth part of *what might be said.* For one thing, the six names of the six Forces mentioned are those of the six Hierarchies of Dhyân Chohans, synthesized by their Primary, the seventh—who personify the Fifth Principle of Cosmic Nature, or of the "Mother" in its mystical sense. The enumeration alone of the Yoga Powers would require ten volumes. Each of these Forces has a living *Conscious Entity* at its head, of which Entity it is an emanation.

But let us compare with the Commentary above cited the words of Hermes, the Thrice Great:

The creation of life by the sun is as continuous as his light; nothing arrests or limits it. Around him, like an army of satellites, are innumerable *choirs of Genii*. These dwell in the neighbourhood of the Immortals, and thence watch over human things. They fulfil the will of the Gods by means of *storms, tempests, transitions of fire and earthquakes*; likewise by famines and wars, for the punishment of impiety. ...

It is the sun who preserves and nourishes all creatures; and, even as the Ideal World, which environs the sensible world, fills this last with the plenitude and universal variety of forms, so also the sun, enfolding all in his light, accomplishes everywhere the birth and development of creatures.... "*Under his orders is the choir of the Genii, or rather the choirs, for there are many and diverse, and their number corresponds to that of the stars. Every star has its Genii, good and evil by nature, or rather by their operation, for operation is the essence of the Genii....*All these Genii *preside over mundane affairs*, they shake and overthrow the constitution of states and of individuals; they *imprint their likeness on our souls*, they are present in our nerves, our marrow, our veins, our arteries, and *our very brain-substance*.... At the moment when each of us receives life and being, he is taken in charge by the Genii who preside over births, and who are classed beneath the astral powers . Perpetually they change, not always identically, but revolving in circles. They permeate by the body two parts of the soul, that it may receive from each the impress of his own energy. But the reasonable part of the soul is not subject to the Genii; it is designed for the reception of God, who enlightens it with a sunny ray. Those who are thus illumined are few in number, and from them the Genii abstain: for neither Genii nor Gods have any power in the presence of a single ray of God.But all other men, both soul and body, are directed by Genii, to whom they cleave, and whose operations they affect.... The Genii have then the control of mundane things and our bodies serve them as instruments."

The above, save a few sectarian points, represents that which was a universal belief, common to all nations, till about a century or so back. It is still as orthodox in its broad outlines and features among Pagans and Christians alike, if one excepts a handful of Materialists and men of Science.

For whether one calls the Genii of Hermes and his "Gods," "Powers of Darkness" and "Angels," as in the Greek and Latin Churches; or "Spirits of the Dead," as in Spiritualism; or, again, Bhûts and Devas, Shaitan or Djin, as they are still called in India and Mussulman countries—*they are all one and the same thing*—ILLUSION. Let not this, however, be misunderstood in the sense into which the great philosophical doctrine of the Vedântists has been lately perverted by Western schools.

All that which *is*, emanates from the ABSOLUTE, which, by reason of this qualification alone, stands as the One and Only Reality—hence, everything extraneous to this Absolute, the generative and causative Element, *must* be an Illusion, most undeniably. But this is only so from the purely metaphysical view. A man who regards himself as mentally sane, and is so regarded by his neighbours, calls the visions of an *insane* brother—hallucinations which make the victim either *happy or supremely wretched*, as the case may be—likewise illusions and fancies. But, where is that madman for whom the hideous shadows in his deranged mind, his *illusions*, are not, for the time being, as actual and as real as the things which his physician or keeper may see? Everything is relative in this Universe, everything is an Illusion. But the experience of any plane is an actuality for the percipient being, whose consciousness is on that plane, though the said experience, regarded from the purely metaphysical standpoint, may be conceived to have no objective reality. But it is not against Metaphysicians, but against Physicists and Materialists that Esoteric teaching has to fight; and for these latter Vital Force, Light, Sound, Electricity, even to the objectively drawing force of Magnetism, have no objective being, and are said to exist merely as "modes of motion," "sensations and *affections* of matter."

Neither the Occultists generally, nor the Theosophists, reject, as erroneously believed by some, the views and theories of the Modern Scientists only because these views are opposed to Theosophy. The first rule of our Society is to render unto Cæsar what is Cæsar's. Theosophists, therefore, are the first to recognize the intrinsic value of Science. But when its high priests resolve consciousness into a secretion from the grey matter of the brain, and everything else in Nature into a mode of motion, we protest against the doctrine as being unphilosophical, self-contradictory, and simply absurd, from a *scientific* point of view, as much and even more than from the Occult aspect of the Esoteric Knowledge.

For truly the Astral Light of the derided Kabalists has strange and weird secrets for him who can see in it; and the mysteries concealed within its incessantly disturbed waves *are there*, the whole body of Materialists and scoffers notwithstanding.

The Astral Light of the Kabalists is by some very incorrectly translated "Ether," the latter is confused with the hypothetical Ether of Science, and both are referred to by some Theosophists as synonymous with Âkâsha. This is a great mistake.

The author of *A Rational Refutation* writes, thus unconsciously helping Occultism:

A characterization of Âkâsha will serve to show how inadequately it is represented by "ether." In dimension it is ... infinite; it is not made up of parts; and colour, taste, smell, and tangibility do not appertain to it. So far forth it corresponds exactly to time, space, Îshvara and soul. Its speciality, as compared therewith, consists in its being the *material cause of sound*. Except for its being so, one might take it to be one with vacuity.

It is *vacuity*, no doubt, especially for Rationalists. At any rate Âkâsha is sure to produce vacuity in the brain of a Materialist. Nevertheless, though Âkâsha is certainly not the Ether of Science—not even the Ether of the Occultist who defines the latter as one of the principles of Âkâsha only—it is as certainly, together with its primary, the cause of sound, a psychical and spiritual, not a material cause by any means. The relations of Ether to Âkâsha may be defined by applying to both Âkâsha and Ether the words used of the God in the *Vedas*, "So himself was indeed (his own) son," one being the progeny of the other and yet itself. This may be a difficult riddle to the profane, but very easy to understand for any Hindû—even though not a Mystic.

These secrets of the Astral Light, along with many other mysteries, will remain non-existent to the Materialists of our age, in the same way as America was a non-existent myth for Europeans during the early part of the mediæval ages, whereas Scandinavians and Norwegians had actually reached and settled in that very old "New World" several centuries before. But, as a Columbus was born to re-discover, and to force the Old World to believe in antipodal countries, so will there be born Scientists who will discover the marvels now claimed by Occultists to exist in the regions of Ether, with their varied and multiform denizens and conscious Entities. Then, *nolens volens*, Science will have to accept the old "superstition," as it has several others. And having been once forced to accept it, its learned professors in all probability—judging from past experience, as in the case of Mesmerism and Magnetism, now re-baptized Hypnotism—will father the thing and reject the name. The choice of the new appellation will, in its turn, depend on the "modes of motion"—the new name for the older "automatic physical processes among the nerve fibrils of the brain" of Moleschott—and also, most likely, upon the last meal of the namer, since, according to the founder of the new Hylo-Idealistic Scheme, "cerebration is generically the same as chylification." Thus, were one to believe this preposterous proposition, the new name of the archaic truth would have to take its chance on the inspiration of the namer's liver, and then only would these truths have a chance of becoming scientific!

But, TRUTH, however distasteful to the generally blind majority, has always had her champions ready to die for her, and it is not the Occultists who will protest against its adoption by Science under whatever new name. But until absolutely forced on the notice and acceptance of Scientists, many an Occult truth will be tabooed, as the phenomena of the Spiritualists and other psychic manifestations were, to be finally appropriated by its ex-traducers without the least acknowledgment or thanks. Nitrogen has added considerably to chemical knowledge, but its discoverer, Paracelsus, is to this day called a "quack." How profoundly true are the words of H. T. Buckle, in his admirable *History of Civilization*, when he says:

Owing to circumstances still unknown there appear from time to time great thinkers, who, devoting their lives to a single purpose, are able to anticipate the progress of mankind, and to produce a religion or a philosophy by which important effects are eventually brought about. But if we look into history we shall clearly see that, although the origin of a new opinion may be thus due to a single man, the result which the new opinion produces will depend on the condition of the people among whom it is propagated. If either a religion or a philosophy is too much in advance of a nation, it can do no present service, but must bide its time until the minds of men are ripe for its reception.... Every science, every creed has had its martyrs. *According to the ordinary course of affairs, a few generations pass away, and then there comes a period when these very truths are looked upon as commonplace facts, and a little later there comes another period in which they are declared to be necessary, and even the dullest intellect wonders how they could ever have been denied.*

It is barely possible that the minds of the present generations are not quite ripe for the reception of Occult truths. Such perchance will be the retrospect furnished to the advanced thinkers of the Sixth Root-Race of the history of the acceptance of Esoteric Philosophy—fully and unconditionally. Meanwhile the generations of our Fifth Race will continue to be led away by prejudice and preconceptions. Occult Sciences will have the finger of scorn pointed at them from every street-corner, and everyone will seek to ridicule and crush them in the name, and for the greater glory, of Materialism and its so-called Science. The present Volumes, however, show, in an anticipatory answer to several of the forthcoming Scientific objections, the true and mutual positions of the defendant and plaintiff. The Theosophists and Occultists stand arraigned by public opinion, which still holds high the banner of the inductive Sciences. The latter have, then, to be examined; and it must be shown how far their achievements and discoveries in the realm of natural law are opposed, not so much to our claims, as to facts in nature. The hour has now struck to ascertain whether the walls of the modern Jericho are so impregnable, that no blast of the Occult trumpet is ever likely to make them crumble.

The so-called "Forces," with Light and Electricity heading them, and the constitution of the Solar orb must be carefully examined; as also Gravitation and the Nebular theories. The natures of Ether and of other Elements must be discussed; thus contrasting Scientific with Occult teachings, while revealing some of the hitherto secret tenets of the latter.

Some fifteen years ago, the writer was the first to repeat, after the Kabalists, the wise Commandments in the Esoteric Catechism.

Close thy mouth, lest thou shouldst speak of *this* , and thy heart, lest thou shouldst think aloud; and if thy heart has escaped thee, bring it back to its place, for such is the object of our alliance.

And again, from the *Rules of Initiation*.

This is a secret which gives death: close thy mouth lest thou shouldst reveal it to the vulgar; compress thy brain lest something should escape from it and fall outside.
A few years later, a corner of the Veil of Isis had to be lifted; and now another and a larger rent is made.

But old and time-honoured errors—such as become with every day more glaring and self-evident—stand arrayed in battle-order now, as they did then. Marshalled by blind conservatism, conceit and prejudice, they are constantly on the watch, ready to strangle every truth, which, awakening from its age-long sleep, happens to knock for admission. Such has been the case ever since man became an animal. That this proves in every case *moral death* to the revealers who bring to light any of these old, old truths, is as certain as that it
gives *life* and *regeneration* to those who are fit to profit even by the little that is now revealed to them.

www.ingramcontent.com/pod-product-compliance
Lightning Source LLC
LaVergne TN
LVHW061344060426
835512LV00012B/2560